Quest for Excellence

The Arthur A. Dugoni Story

◊

Martin Brown

I hope you enjoy my "Quest."

Arthur A. Dugoni

Foreword

Just about the time I began asking, "Who would write the story of Art Dugoni," Ron Redmond, our exceptional University of the Pacific alumnus and regent, stepped forward to lead the effort. No surprise that the one person more than any other who partnered with Art to make the dream of a Dugoni School a reality also understood the importance of telling the Dugoni story. We all will be grateful for Ron's gift of this biography, a portion of his and Margaret Redmond's exceptional generosity to the school over the years, along with the Pacific Dugoni Foundation for their support as well. I knew the creation of this biography was important because Art Dugoni had become, for me, the most remarkable educator I had ever met. I will try to explain…

In the year 2000, as provost of the University of the Pacific, I asked Art to walk his fellow school deans attending our annual retreat at the Feather River Inn, Pacific's charming, rustic summer camp nestled in the northern Sierra, through the history of his deanship. I was hoping he would reveal how he spun his magic. He wowed us all with his detailed memory of how he, with his team, created one of the world's best dental schools, one carefully planned step at a time.

I think it was then that I realized without qualification that Art Dugoni was the most remarkable educator I had ever known. I had served large schools and small, been active locally and nationally in higher education, read widely on leadership and reflected often on the dynamics of education at all levels. Yes, Art Dugoni was remarkable. That is one important thing this biography is about. How is it that one man could serve his school, dental education, and the profession of dentistry, and transform them all?

Martin Brown's biography provides some fascinating answers to the mystique of Art, with little-known stories of his colorful family and childhood days in San

Francisco's predominantly Italian neighborhood of North Beach, his passion for oratory, his forfeiture of a high school scholarship, his falling hopelessly in love with Kaye during the uncertain days of World War II, his chance decision to complete his dental degree at the College of Physicians and Surgeons back home in San Francisco, and much more. Readers who think they know Art will be delightfully surprised at what they discover here.

Amid all these wonderful stories, I see three key values shining through. First in nearly everyone's mind is Art's *care for people*, his wholesale devotion to the dignity, self-worth and welfare of each individual in his life. This became the heart of the "humanistic model" of teaching and learning at the Arthur A. Dugoni School of Dentistry, pioneered by his predecessor Dean Dale Redig. The school's culture really came about because Art Dugoni *embodied* the humanistic values that underpin the success of the school. Art's care for people goes beyond friendliness, respect, and compassionate listening. It comes from his conviction that he can enable every person to become more fully human, a more fully caring individual, through his warm, uplifting interaction. So many former students speak of his inspiration. The word "inspire" literally means, "Breathing life into another." That is Art Dugoni.

Second is Art's aim to *be the best*. His daily goal was to "knock your socks off," from the start. He wanted to be the best that he could be, yes—like many of us. But more: Art expected to be *the best, period*. This relentless drive for excellence came from his heart and soul, not from his head. He did not calculate the cost, nor did he measure his achievements by medals and citations. He measured them by the response of his communities, from the school to the global profession. Failure was never an option, even though he was always acutely aware of his mistakes along the way. Yes, he loved the best of everything in life —knock your socks off quality, as Art has always said, from his Lexus to the P&S Ball. But he was never defined by these things. His motivators were not power or wealth. Perhaps prestige — deserved recognition certainly — but far more than any of these human motivators was Art's *internal* drive to do his best, to be the best, and with his cosmic capacity and energy, that "best" turned out to be a universe of achievement.

Beyond these two core values—his passion for touching people's lives with loving care and his striving to be the best—lies a powerful *immigrant ethos* that so defined the "greatest generation" of Americans who served on the gigantic stage of World War II. That immigrant experience lies deep in Art's DNA. A good dose of that ethos is a relentless work ethic that does not assume you deserve anything, and certainly nothing handed to you without personal effort. But another measure of that ethos is a faith tradition rich in heart and power. As an Italian Catholic, Art grew up knowing truths others could not tap into. His good friend and successor, Dean Pat Ferrillo, who grew up in the same tradition, said Art "actually practiced his faith more than any dean I know." What finally drove Art forward was not his own self-development, but his profound sense of responsibility to be a child of God in service to humanity, as he was called to do. Art is more mission-driven than anyone I know. His faith—especially his faith in humanity—was active and apparent in everything he did.

Without these core values, Art Dugoni could not have become the giant that he is as a leader in education. A great teacher engages and sparks learners. We usually think of that happening around a classroom, as Ron Redmond recounts in his introduction. But what makes Art so remarkable is that he *sparks learners everywhere he goes.* His graciousness—never affected, always genuine—is a hand outstretched to students eager to learn. His human touch of kind persistence always carries with it an implicit exhortation for us to risk more, to stretch further, and to give more generously. He lights the candle of aspiration in nearly every student through his personal attention.

He understood that by setting the highest expectations for himself, he could be *a model for others.* And because he knew that so many students and colleagues looked up to him as an inspiring leader and exemplar of the best in the profession, Art worked all the harder to meet and exceed their expectations, ever striving to be the best. The more successful he became, the more important to him was his serving as a living model of what a human being might become. And one essential part of that model was not to outgrow being a student himself.

He knew that a great educator had concentric rings of influence that extended from individual student to classes, out to the school that included all faculty, staff and alumni, but even much further. More than a model, he was *mentor to all*—to deans and presidents, coach and cheerleader to his professional colleagues at the local, state and national levels of dentistry—indeed across the world. I strongly suspect that no other dental educator has had the impact of Art Dugoni on the entire field of dental education and the positive upswing of pride in the profession and practice of dentistry. He was driven by achievement to accomplish extraordinary goals because he tapped into the power of the team, the synergy of people working in common purpose, from his brown bag lunches with students to his leadership of the American Dental Association. Thus Art was the consummate educator at all levels, a reconciler who built communities.

Third, and most importantly, Art understood that a consummate educator does not simply enable apprentices to become practicing professionals. A great educator is really a *developer of people*, bringing out of each student—and I am one of those students—whole capacities unknown to that student until Dugoni somehow tapped them. "We build people, and along the way they become doctors," as Art always said about his school. This pronouncement epitomizes the holistic view of education Art perfected, and through the example of his school, transformed all of dental education.

It could be said Art created a persona, an image, a brand, a model of himself as an ideal, then proceeded to devote his life to becoming that ideal model. What is so astonishing is that he virtually achieved what he set out to do. Who of us has shaped our lives to such a disciplined degree that we seem to approach the ideal of ourselves? Of course, Art wisely pitched his tent on a few very important things—he never raced his cars or set his eyes on Pebble Beach, never wavered in his focus on dental education and the dental profession. He remained faithful to one remarkable woman and their extraordinary family. But within that world, he redefined for an entire profession what human excellence could mean by setting new standards of human achievement in dentistry. All of us touched by his life find ourselves raising our own sights and aims because of his example.

Distilled even further, we could say that Art's persona was his school, his self-identity was a *community of people passionate about excellence and service*. As one of his colleagues observed, everything he did was school-related. There was no such thing as "letting his hair down" and "escaping it all," except, perhaps, sometimes with Kaye and the family. He never golfed just for fun. In many respects, this community passionate about excellence and service that we call the Arthur A. Dugoni School of Dentistry *was* Art Dugoni. This is why his passion for the school and the profession never ended, right into his most senior years. He simply could not extricate himself from the school because the school and he were in many ways one and the same. To say that the school "could not survive without him" (his DNA will be there forever) is to say that Art could not survive without the school.

He could not have achieved all that he did without the strength and character of his spouse Kaye, who in many ways is a traditional family-bound wife with their flock of seven children, fifteen grandchildren, and four great grandchildren. Family was a rock-solid part of who he was, but the family could not limit his ambitious goals of global proportions. Kaye would never permit the children to censure their father for his absence, nor would she let her husband step over the boundary of life decisions that she set down when another door of opportunity opened. One of those was the call to become president of University of the Pacific: she would not move from the South Bay for any reason, and Art respected that fully. A mark of his devotion to Kaye, his life partner of more than sixty-five years, we witness in his diligent care-giving and attention as she confronts a variety of health needs.

Martin Brown's biography is bright testimony to what one person can accomplish, and for legions of us, Art Dugoni is the most remarkable educator we have ever met. Every dean at University of Pacific knew that Art was Pacific's most transformative dean—likely of all time. We surrounded Art that day at the Feather River Inn, admiring a person who had redefined excellence in every aspect of being a dean and an educator. Art is a great man, in the grand way that the poet Stephen Spender observes, "I think continually of those who were truly great...[who] left the vivid air signed with their honour."

Phil Gilbertson
Provost Emeritus
University of the Pacific

Introduction

Throughout his personal and professional life, Art Dugoni has believed passionately in the transformative nature of education. He has spent most of his life engaged in the business of selling ideas: as an educator, a dean, a leader and spokesperson for an entire profession, and as a private businessman. You might call him, "The Great Persuader."

I should know. My professional life is largely due to the influence of this great persuader.

In the fall of 1965, when I was beginning my final year of study for my Doctorate in Dental Surgery from the College of Physicians & Surgeons, which had recently been renamed the School of Dentistry, University of the Pacific, I was taking a course in undergraduate orthodontics taught by Dr. Dugoni.

One day, as I was leaving his classroom, he tapped me on the shoulder and asked what I planned to do after graduation. I told him that I was going to open a "crown and bridge" practice in Palo Alto. He thought that was fine. But after a pause, he asked me if I had considered a career in orthodontics. I had not, but that planted a seed. When I discussed the idea later that night with my new bride, Margaret, without hesitation she gave it her blessing.

It seems simple now, but when I look back over the many decades that have passed since that conversation, Art, taking the extra time to talk to me about my career options, greatly changed the future direction of my life.

That seed of an idea did not just grow into a tree; it started a grove of trees that provided a bountiful life, not just for Margaret and me, but for our children, grandchildren, and future generations.

I have no idea how many times in his sixty-five years as an educator that Art Dugoni changed the course of an individual's life, but I'm certain it has happened countless times. Part of the magic of Art Dugoni is that he consistently challenged all his students to be the very best they could be. And he inspired us to do so much more with our lives and our careers than we might have ever thought possible.

Art is the son of Italian immigrants. Born in San Francisco, he started school with only a smattering of English. Learning the language of his parents adopted country was his first great challenge. But Art quickly proved himself to be a diligent student. He became the first in his family to complete high school, get a college degree, a doctorate, and over the years, complete a long list of other academic achievements. His remarkable mother, Lina, instilled in him an abiding belief that education was life's game changer. Here in America, pedigree did not define you near so much as competency.

As dean of the School of Dentistry, Art had the opportunity, over a period of three decades, to shape the future of dentistry and education. He took a model of humanistic education began by his predecessor, Dr. Dale Redig, and perfected it. He instilled in his faculty that future practitioners were best served by having educators who motivated and inspired, rather than bully and demean.

He had no doubt that each and every teacher could make an incalculable difference in the lives of their students. He took the motto of Dr. Harry True, one of his beloved mentors and chair of the Department of Restorative Dentistry when he was a student at P&S, and turned it into a mantra: "It's not good enough unless it's the best you can do!" Art instilled in everyone that philosophy. He led, not by edict, but by inspiration. He knew a leader's vision never becomes a reality until it reaches the level of being a *shared* vision.

Art did unheard-of things as dean. He shared the school's budget with everyone: from students, to staff, to faculty, to alumni and supporters. The greater success of the school was the work of everyone who walked through its doors.

He brought in communication and presentation consultants to improve the faculty's presentation skills, always believing that you can't teach those that you can't reach. He encouraged his team leaders, as well as faculty and staff, to continue their own educational growth by pursuing graduate degrees in education and management.

At the same time, Art, a man of seemingly limitless energy, instilled in all the belief that you needed to leave your own distinct mark on your profession by helping to shape its future.

To that end, he served as president of the California Dental Association, the American Dental Association, the American Board of Orthodontists, the American Association of Dental Schools, and the American Dental Association Foundation.

"How can you truly be a part of your profession," he often asked, "if you don't have a seat at the table when its future is being shaped by legislators and others?"

This is the biography of one individual who shaped the future of his profession like no other before him. It begins with the arrival of his parents and his grandparents to America, and documents a life of extraordinary accomplishment.

Dr. Dugoni's speeches, correspondence, DVDs of his program on dentistry on Lifetime Medical Television, and what his colleagues have written about him leave future generations a record of his professional life. What has not existed until now is an effort to document the total span of his personal and professional life and to put into perspective the internal and external forces that shaped this extraordinary individual.

In the not-too-distant past, Art was a little boy growing up on Russian Hill, high above San Francisco's North Beach neighborhood. There, on a cramped side street called Glover, he was surrounded by dozens of relatives, including both his maternal grandparents and maternal great grandmother living in homes just a few feet apart. On Jackson Street between Larkin and Hyde, you can still walk past Spring Valley Elementary School where Art, age five in 1930, stood crying inside the gate, asking his mother not to leave him alone in the company of strangers.

Art is the young man who, several years later, got a scholarship to an elite private high school in San Francisco, but felt out of place among an affluent student body while he had just one shirt and one pair of pants to wear to school every day.

Art is the young man who worked part-time in a butcher shop, to help pay for the cost of his high school education, and later managed a youth center on evenings and Saturdays while he pursued his Doctorate in Dental Surgery. Always studious and serious-minded, Art had a flare for the dramatic and loved debate and public speaking. That, combined with his work in the butcher shop, earned him the nickname, "The Ham" at St. James High School.

Art delivered the valedictory address in June 1943 at St. James, and again in July 1948 at Physicians & Surgeons when, at the age of twenty-three, he posed this question to his fellow graduates: "Why should men dream when they have the power to control their wills, to develop their minds, to demand reality in its fullest? 'I am going to be a success' will always be the master of, 'If I could only be a success.'"

Art's many talents and powerful presence created the illusion that it was all rather easy for him. But in truth, it of course was not. If you begin reading this book to learn more about a legend, along the way you'll find a human being.

In his life, Art has been a son, student, suitor, husband, father, grandfather, great grandfather, doctor, dean, educator, philanthropist, businessman, administrator, writer, public speaker, inventor, and humanist. In each one of these roles, he never settled for doing less than his very best.

Today, at his age, Art has been blessed and challenged by a life of four full seasons. In each of those seasons he has pursued his goals with vigor and determination. At his side, throughout nearly all of those years, has been his extraordinary wife, Kaye, a woman whom he fell madly in love with in 1943 when he was just eighteen years old.

The quest for excellence has been a guiding star in all his endeavors. That quest motivates him to this day, eighty-nine years after his life adventure began.

Dr. Ron Redmond, Regent
University of the Pacific

L'Importanza Della Famiglia
(The Importance of Family)

Art Dugoni is the child of Italian immigrants. To understand his life, it is essential that you know this. The man who grew to master the subtleties of the English language came to school at age five speaking mostly a mixture of Italian and Piedmontese, a unique dialect spoken by people of Northern Italy living near the French border.

For the first nine years of his life, Art lived on a small street located high above San Francisco's North Beach neighborhood. As Art recalls, on Glover Street, everyone spoke Italian, and most of the residents were Art's maternal relatives. In his words, "Up until the time I entered grade school, I thought everyone in the world was Italian!"

Three Generations of Mothers: Art, at twenty months, with his mother, Lina Bianco Dugoni; great grandmother, Orsola Sciondino; and grandmother, Rosa Sciondino Bianco.

Chapter One

A Lamp Lifted Beside a Golden Door

On a pleasant evening in early May 2008, as the sun slowly dissolved into the far western edge of New York harbor, Art Dugoni boarded a private boat for the short ride from lower Manhattan to Ellis Island. He was one of a select group chosen that year to receive the Ellis Island Medal of Honor.

The medal honors the contributions made by immigrants, their children and grandchildren, to the greater success of their chosen nation. The list of past honorees has included presidents, Bill Clinton and George H.W. Bush; secretaries of state, Hillary Clinton and Henry Kissinger; entertainers, Bob Hope and Frank Sinatra; athletes, Joe DiMaggio and Muhammad Ali, Nobel Laureates, and top business and community leaders. The award serves as a stark reminder that America is a nation of immigrants immeasurably enriched by the contributions of citizens who came to these shores from distant places to raise a family and build a better future. Now, two families from Northern Italy, the Biancos and the Dugonis, would have their first born child in America added to this distinguished list.

When Art and his fellow honorees arrived at the island, a red carpet and an honor guard made up of all branches of the United States Armed Forces waited to greet them.

In black tie, looking a good deal younger than his eighty-two years, Art came down the gangplank and was overwhelmed by a sense of history. Here was the place where his maternal grandparents, Rosa and Benedetto Bianco, arrived on October 15, 1910 aboard the *SS LaLorraine*, accompanied by their six-year-old daughter Orsolina and her one-year-old brother, Michele. Thirty months later, on April 15, 1913, Vittorio Dugoni and his youngest son, sixteen year-old Arturo, sailing from Genoa, arrived here aboard the *SS America*. Both families gave their city of origin as Torino, better known to Americans as "Turin."

Could his grandparents and parents who came to this place nearly a century before, imagine a moment like this? What was their journey to this new world like? How do people summon up the courage to leave all they know in life for an uncertain future in an unknown land? Art looked around and wondered about this generation of pioneers and his place in their story. He and his fellow honorees were ushered into the building as a marine band trumpeted their arrival. A century of family history had been etched into his heart. And this was the place where his story began.

* * * * *

For the Biancos and the Dugonis, Ellis Island and the great city that lay at its doorstep, marked only the first half of their journey. The second half would be the long train trip across the American continent. The Biancos had family bringing them to California, but for Art's grandfather, Vittorio Dugoni, San Francisco was the final destination for a very different reason.

Vittorio, a married man with three children, was following a married woman to America. Her name was Mrs. Ferrero, a surname commonly found in the Piedmont Region of Italy. There is little known about Vittorio's lover other than a few lines of oral history passed down from Arturo's older sister, Maria, to her daughter, Art's cousin, Yolanda. Mrs. Ferrero's husband, a man much older than herself, was apparently willing to ignore his wife's indiscretions in exchange for her companionship. Maria was quite certain that Mrs. Ferrero was one of many relationships that Vittorio enjoyed.

Maria claimed her father's relations with other women were no great secret. Certainly he saw himself as a "ladies man," Yolanda explained. She describes her grandfather as a dapper man who took great pride in his appearance. "He regularly wore a stickpin in his necktie that was shaped like a love knot and a gold ring on the small finger of his right hand with two overlapping hearts."

Vittorio Angelo Dugoni was born in Turin in 1862. It's not known with certainty what year Angela Villa, Art's paternal grandmother, was born, but she is listed as age twenty-six when she married Vittorio in 1891. The likely year of her birth was 1865.

Vittorio, a strikingly handsome man with thick wavy black hair, worked in a fine leather shop located on the Villa Roma in the heart of Turin. He was a skilled craftsman, an expert machinist, and a highly intelligent man. But Vittorio had a dark side. He was known to his contemporaries as a man with a bad temper, and a heavy drinker. These two traits seem to have haunted Vittorio his entire life.

Angela's two brothers advised her not to marry the handsome and passionate Vittorio, cautioning that he was a *uomo malvagio* (a bad man). But Angela feared that, at age twenty-six, she may never find a man to marry her if she turned down Vittorio's proposal. So she agreed. Three months after their wedding day, Vittorio struck Angela for the first time.

Vittorio's temper was legendary, and it was not only directed at Angela, as he proved one day in the glove shop when in an argument with his boss he shouted: "Tu sei un asino rivestita in oro," (You are an ass covered in gold.) Vittorio was fired on the spot, and a short time later he and Angela moved to the outskirts of Turin where he took a job in an umbrella factory. Once again, because of his skilled hands as a craftsman, Vittorio was greatly valued by his employer. Yolanda's mother, Maria, was born in 1892, followed by Alberto in 1894 and then their last child, Art's dad, Arturo Carlo Natale Dugoni, born in 1897.

For several years, Vittorio's work in the umbrella factory went well. Again, his highly skilled hands and quick intelligence served him well. He designed a machine that allowed multiple layers of silk, used to create a fine umbrella, to lay on top of each other while they were being cut to fit the umbrella's spokes. This was a significant time saving device. The owners of the shop patented the process, suggesting that they would share a portion of their profits with Vittorio. For whatever reason, that profit share never happened, and when Vittorio complained that he was being cheated, he lost yet another job.

Vittorio decided it was now time to begin his own business. Why he chose the business of olive oil is unknown, but that business also ended unhappily. It led to an estrangement between Vittorio and his son Alberto, who he accused of stealing from him the money collected from one of Vittorio's customers. What bitter feelings that may have created in the volatile Dugoni home is uncertain. But it was at this point that Vittorio decided to leave Italy, leave Angela, and leave two of his three children behind.

It is safe to assume that Art's father, Arturo, at age sixteen, had a difficult time with this rupture in his family, and what must have been an abrupt end to the only life he had known. In any event, he soon found himself living in San Francisco, out of school, but quite certainly not idle. As Yolanda explains, for all his faults, Vittorio was a man who always worked hard, and during this time of transition for the immigrant father and son, she believes her Uncle Arturo was undoubtedly working hard as well.

There are no surviving oral histories of Arturo's turbulent upbringing. Art's sister Evelyn, his only surviving sibling, is also uncertain about this period of her father's life. But she does recall Arturo, who was known as Red for his full head of red hair, saying he slept in the back of his dad's shop, and was "adopted" by older women in their neighborhood of North Beach, who would bring him soups and pastas, constantly telling him that he was too thin.

As a child, Yolanda recalls seeing for herself how gifted Vittorio was with his hands, "My grandfather could fix almost anything, especially small things like purse latches, locks, and frames."

But prior to starting his own business, Vittorio went to work for a manufacturer in San Francisco that specialized in making and repairing leather harnesses for workhorses. In 1917, he opened his first retail location on Columbus Avenue and moved that business to nearby Stockton Street in 1919.

It's not known when his affair with Mrs. Ferrero ended. But in 1914, Vittorio sent money home for Angela and his two remaining children, to come to America. Over the past year, money had come intermittently to the family. But with this invitation, Vittorio attached a stern warning, "I'll send no more money if you don't come now to America."

Angela, long unhappy with her unfaithful husband, nevertheless felt it was her place to do as Vittorio instructed.

Arturo's sister, Maria, apparently not anxious to see her father again, was tempted to stay in Italy where she was considering a job making gloves and other fine handmade leather products for an exclusive shop in Florence. Soon after Vittorio wrote insisting the family come to America, the Italian army upon the outbreak of World War I drafted Alberto.

Maria thought long and hard about whether to make the journey to San Francisco. Ultimately, she decided her place was with her mother, so they traveled together to England and sailed from Southampton aboard a British ship to Boston. Germany, now at war with Italy, England, and France, had U-Boats on the prowl. Several times during their journey to America, their ship's engines were shut down to avoid unwanted and potentially lethal attention. Months after Angela and Maria's crossing, another British passenger ship, the *RMS Lusitania*, was attacked by a German U-Boat resulting in 1,198 deaths. Maria had no doubt that if this had happened prior to their journey, her mother would have never crossed the Atlantic.

After a few very cold days in Boston, mother and daughter pushed on to California. Arriving by train in Oakland, they boarded a ferry for the final leg of their journey. As their boat approached San Francisco's ferry building, Maria sighted her father Vittorio standing on the pier. Years later, she confessed to Yolanda, "That's the only time I can ever remember being happy to see my father."

In 1928, fourteen years after their arrival, and nine years after the conclusion of World War I, Alberto found his way to San Francisco. Art's uncle, was an unwelcome sight. When he worked, he proved himself to be a valued and gifted craftsman. But ultimately, Alberto's drinking proved to be his undoing and he never had success holding down a steady job or supporting himself. As his niece Evelyn recalled decades later, "He was a very nice man with a very bad drinking problem."

* * * * *

Not much is known about how Arturo Dugoni and Orsolina Bianco met.

It's possible that it was an arranged meeting, given the fact that their families came from the same corner of Northern Italy, a short distance from the French border. But another possibility, suggested by Art's sister, Evelyn, is the two met one day when Lina walked into Vittorio's North Beach shop and Red was working behind the counter.

The details are unknown, but family history indicates that Red enthusiastically courted Lina. Arturo Dugoni was a handsome young man who served in the American army during World War I. He was short—about five-foot-six—rail thin, with a fair complexion and a full head of closely cropped red hair. Lina was a petite, spritely teenager, with a megawatt smile that beamed from her five-foot frame. She had a quality, one that was evident her entire life, that drew people to her. It's likely that Arturo was just one of her admirers.

How ever their paths crossed, they were apparently made for each other. Red pursued his sweetheart passionately. On Saturday evenings after work, he would head out from his dad's shop on Stockton Street, carrying flowers and candy in one of the leather suitcases sold in Vittorio's shop. As Red explained years later, he was more than a little embarrassed to walk up the hills and climb the steep steps up to the top of Russian Hill, where Lina lived, carrying a box of candy and a bouquet of flowers. So Red would reach the front steps of 45 Glover, Rosa and Benedetto's home, remove the gifts he had brought his Lina, and tuck the bag into a small alley space from where he would retrieve it for his journey back to North Beach.

The young lovers were married on June 3, 1923. Red was twenty-six, Lina just nineteen. Two years later, on June 29, 1925, Arturo and Orsolina Dugoni's first child was born at the Lane Hospital of Stanford University Medical Center in San Francisco. The happy couple named their baby for his father and his father's brother. But rather than Arturo Alberto, the child was christened Arthur Albert Dugoni. A new chapter in the family's American journey had begun!

Angela Villa as a young woman in Turin, Italy.

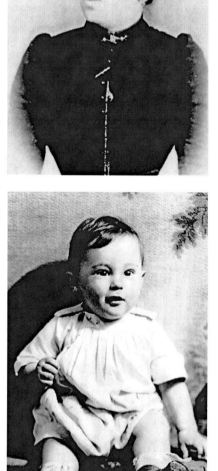

Vittorio in his Italian Army uniform, 1885.

The first American born child:
Arthur Albert Dugoni, 1925

New Arrivals to America: Art's maternal grandparents, Benedetto and Rosa Bianco, with their children Lina and Leo.

Arturo in 1918 in his American army uniform.

Reunited in America: Angela and Vittorio with two of their three children, Arturo and Maria. The vase behind them is for Alberto, off fighting for Italy.

Chapter Two

The Loving Embrace of Glover Street

You have to be a San Francisco resident with a thirst for discovery or a lost tourist to find yourself standing on Glover Street. In fact, very few San Franciscans would know how to locate this steep and narrow one-block path tucked between the cross streets of Jones and Leavenworth.

Glover is mostly unknown, because it sits high above the Broadway tunnel, a busy artery that carries nearly all the traffic heading east or west between the Embarcadero, Chinatown, North Beach, and Pacific Heights, Presidio Heights and the inner and outer Richmond districts, spanning the distance between San Francisco and the Pacific Ocean.

Lina and Red settled into one half of a duplex on Glover Street, just two doors uphill from Rosa and Benedetto's home. Here, on this snug little street, Art Dugoni spent the first nine years of his life. In addition to his parents and maternal grandparents, numerous members of the Bianco, Ricca, Sciondino, and other related families settled on Glover Street during the first two decades of the twentieth century.

Art was an only child for slightly over five years. As such, he was the darling of not only his parents and grandparents, but aunts, uncles, cousins and one great-grandmother as well. Surrounded by family, Glover Street was an open air cradle that nurtured Red and Lina's first child. Art was surrounded by loving, welcoming arms everywhere he turned.

Ultimately, Red and Lina would have a total of three children. Considered by some in their era to be a *small* family, the tradition of their region of Northern Italy leaned toward smaller families, as opposed to the stereotyped larger families of Southern Italy.

From the start of Art's life, his maternal grandparents took the lead in his upbringing and, with over half of Glover Street related to the Biancos and the Dugonis, it's almost unimaginable that Art lacked for affection or attention during these early years. Art has few recollections of grandpa Vittorio, but easily recalls time spent with Benedetto. Art's memories of "Grandpa Ben" run long and deep.

Vittorio and Angela settled a short distance away in North Beach. In 1928, Angela died of complications from type 2 diabetes, when her grandson Art was only three. A new treatment for the disease, purified insulin injections, had been developed just five years earlier. According to oral history, Art's aunt Maria claimed that Vittorio was told of that treatment option, but he saw no reason to bear the expense; after all, Angela, who was now past sixty, had, in his words, "lived a full life."

The final years of Vittorio's life were equally disturbing. After Angela's death, he moved onto Glover Street and he opened a new leather goods business on Stockton Street, which he ran until his death. He continued to be a gifted and hardworking tradesman, but he was also uncompromising with customers. As Yolanda explained, "He did not have an ingratiating personality. Even in his shop, he was surly to his would-be customers. Heaven help the woman who tried to bargain him down on the price of a leather handbag. He would snatch the purse out of her hands and say, 'Today, I have already eaten.'" Apparently, the key to his survival as a merchant had little to do with his personal charm and a lot to do with the high quality of his merchandise.

As Vittorio's vitality began to diminish, his life began to spiral downward. Art's mother, Orsolina, kept her father-in-law at a distance, but apparently honored his role as her husband's father. Clearly, however, she sought to limit her children's exposure to him, which was one reason Art all but ignored Vittorio's existence. Evelyn had clearer memories of Vittorio, who she says was always disrespectful to her mother. But, like Art, she doesn't recall ever once stepping foot into his shop on Stockton Street, even though it was a relatively short distance from their house.

Vittorio's time on Glover Street was relatively brief. He rented an apartment on the corner of Powell and Vallejo, close to the heart of North Beach and a short walking distance to his Stockton Street shop. He became a founding member of the *Loggia Vita Nova* — the New Life Lodge—a business organization for Italian merchants. His business kept going, but the Great Depression took a heavy toll in sales.

On the evening of Columbus Day, 1941, Vittorio placed a revolver to his head and pulled the trigger. He was nearly eighty years old.

As Yolanda explained, "Poverty humiliated my grandfather." For many years, Vittorio had maintained a savings account. In the last year of his life, he steadily drew down the funds in that account. The last five dollars was withdrawn days before his suicide. Out of cash, out of hope, and unable to receive government assistance, he apparently gave up.

The night of his suicide, Sunday, October 12, 1941, a rift in the family opened a wound that took more than seventy years to fully heal. Both Evelyn and Yolanda have clear memories of that night. Art's aunt and uncle, Yolanda's parents, Maria and Michele Cavallo, lived in a home on White Street, a small side alley off Vallejo Street between Hyde and Larkin, a short walk downhill from Glover. Evelyn recalls Vittorio having dinner with the family the afternoon of his death. (Both families had agreed to have Vittorio come to their home for a meal at least once a week.) Several hours after Vittorio had left that evening, a call came and Red answered the phone.

"I can remember, to this day, how upset my dad was," Evelyn says. "A short while later, mom and dad left the house and were gone for several hours."

Art's cousin Yolanda picks up the story from there. "My parents and Art's parents had a terrible fight that Sunday night." Yolanda, who was fifteen at the time, was sent to her room. Now, at age eighty-seven, she can close her eyes and still hear her parents and her aunt and uncle shouting at each other. "I was still a child. I knew my grandfather had died, but I did not know what the adults were arguing about, other than blaming each other for what had just happened."

Whatever happened that night, after a private service for Vittorio and a burial at the Italian Cemetery in Colma, beside the plot of his late wife, Angela, neither Red, Maria, nor their spouses ever saw each other again. The church provided no comfort—refusing to hold a service that would acknowledge the victim of suicide.

Yolanda and Art met as adults for the first time in February 2013, nearly seventy-two years after the night of their grandfather's death. They had exchanged notes in 1991, speculating about the number of Dugonis they had located in both Italy and America. And they wondered if Vittorio had children other than the three he had fathered with Angela.

Vittorio, the brilliant, handsome, gifted, hardworking, and tragically flawed man lived on in both his son, Arturo and his grandson, Arthur. Both worked tirelessly at their crafts—Red as a master pastry chef at San Francisco's Golden Pheasant Restaurant and the St. Francis Hotel, and Art, as an orthodontist, educator and leader in his profession. Art inherited none of Vittorio's demons, but clearly was blessed with his talented hands, his quick mind, and the ability to tirelessly work long hours.

* * * * *

The first trait that both Art and his kid brother, William, inherited from grandpa Benedetto was his physical size. Both boys grew to be well over six-feet. But in those traits harder to see, Benedetto could also be seen in the warmth of their personalities, and most apparently in Art's humanistic touch and powerful presence.

There's something of a mystery about how the Biancos came to settle in San Francisco. They resided in San Francisco when the 1920 US census was taken, ten years after their 1910 arrival at Ellis Island.

What is known is that Rosa and Benedetto opened a restaurant in downtown Los Angeles. It's possible they came to San Francisco and then moved to Los Angeles, but it appears more likely they headed to Los Angeles after their arrival at Ellis Island. Family lore has it that the restaurant failed because the authentic Italian cuisine it served was not accepted by the patrons of that era. Another equally important reason could have been their location—reportedly on Broadway, close to the site of the old *Los Angeles Times* building, which had been destroyed by a bomb just days before the Bianco family arrived in America. The October 1, 1910 attack by a group of "union terrorists" killed twenty members of the *Times* staff. Not long after the tragedy, *The Times* built a new building on the same site. If this indeed was near the Biancos' ill-fated eatery, the adverse impact on the entire area, and on establishments owned by immigrants during that time, was well documented.

Whatever caused the restaurant's failure, it's unimaginable that it had anything to do with the quality of the food being served. By all accounts, Benedetto was an outstanding chef. Long after his death in 1956, a number of well-respected Italian restaurants in San Francisco served dishes that Benedetto created. But, unfortunately, the failure of their venture in Los Angeles embittered Benedetto to life in the food service industry. Instead, he made his living working in a mattress factory adjacent to the old Del Monte Cannery, which today is part of the Fisherman's Wharf tourist area of San Francisco.

The family's oral history suggests Rosa and Benedetto's financial ruin was so complete that various family members in Northern California sent them five dollars to help pay for their passage up to San Francisco. Most likely, the family's path to starting over in California brought them to Glover Street where their cousins, aunts and uncles had already established a homestead. And with immigrant determination, they had secured a home of their own sometime before 1920.

In the family, Art was known as "Chich"—a name he got from Benedetto who called him *Cici* ("dear one") in their Northwestern Italian dialect of "Piedmontese."

This was actually the first language that Art learned. Still spoken today by over two million people, the use of the language is now discouraged by the central Italian government, but it continues to thrive and is taught in many schools in Turin and throughout the region.

* * * * *

The one common thread that runs through all the oral histories of Glover Street is the fact that Rosa and Benedetto's home was the center of the family's socialization. Sundays were very special, and of particular importance were special religious holidays when a family feast would start before noon and go well into the night.

Everyone alive today still remembers those gatherings. All agree Grandpa Benedetto was in charge of the cooking, and the other men were all part of his Sunday staff. And the ravioli was clearly the house specialty. No one who ate at Benedetto's table fails to mention his ravioli. They also remember Benedetto's homemade wine operation that began prior to prohibition and long outlasted America's "dry days" with the calamitous Volstead Act. The vast majority of Americans believed that prohibition was aimed at stopping the sale of hard liquor. To their surprise, the Volstead Act, passed in 1919 over the veto of President Woodrow Wilson, led to a ban of beer and alcohol sales as well, a prohibition that millions of Americans ignored and laid the seeds for the act's eventual repeal in December 1933.

Benedetto converted the basement coal bin of his home at 45 Glover into a fermentation vat for grapes that he would have brought up his steep hill by truck and rolled down through his coal chute. Apparently, in making a choice between coal storage for heat during the relatively mild winters of Northern California and grape storage, the production of red wine won out.

Several times a year, Benedetto, his son, Lina's brother, Michael (always called Leo by the family), Art's dad, Red, and other men in the family, would take off their shoes and socks, roll-up their pant legs, and jump into the vat and stomp the grapes. This is an ancient process that produces the "must," crushed whole grapes, which further ferment as the carbon dioxide it contains is released into the air. Leo's son, Robert Bianco, a retired attorney who today lives on his own small winery in St. Helena, in California's Napa Valley, can remember as a young boy sleeping in the bedroom above the basement of his grandfather's house and getting high on the fumes of that fermenting must.

Art's dad produced his own wine as well. "As a ten-year-old boy," Art recalls, "I thought my dad was a chemist, because he was always testing his wine.

He would get on his back under one of the storage cask's spigots, slowly turn it on and let a few drops of wine hit his tongue. He took a lot of pride in his homemade brew."

After dinner at each of their huge family gatherings, the women were left with the job of cleaning up. And, at any of these family gatherings, that was no small task.

No event was complete without a family entertainment hour. When Art was a young boy, radio broadcasting was in its infancy, and television was a distant dream. Benedetto took it upon himself to organize the afternoon and evening's entertainment. A lover of opera, Benedetto assigned various parts of classic operas to different members of his family, handing out sheet music to all the participants.

Opera was an Italian creation of the early seventeenth century and it rose to worldwide popularity because of the genius of its greatest composers during the nineteenth and early twentieth centuries. Before he was age ten, Art earned the equivalent of an advanced degree in the masterworks of Rossini, Donetti, Verdi, and the work of Benedetto's contemporary, Giacomo Puccini, who gave the world such lasting classics as *La Boheme*, *Tosca*, and *Madama Butterfly*.

Grandpa Ben loved them all. But at the very top of the list of great Italian composers was Giuseppe Verdi, whose death in 1901 led to an unprecedented outpouring of grief throughout Italy. His two best known operas, *Rigoletto* and *La traviata*, premiered just two years apart in 1851 and 1853.

"Everyone got to play a part, even me, and over time, the other grandkids as well," Art recalls. Who in the family took on such challenging roles as Rigoletto, his daughter Gilda, or the philandering Duke of Mantua, no one surviving to this day recalls. But one can imagine that between the eating, the drinking, and the singing it must have been quite a memorable scene. Those Sunday dinners are still legendary. Art's parents are remembered as well by the still-surviving participants. "Red was always pleasant, but quiet," Robert Bianco explains, whereas Art's mom, Lina, was happy at any point to take center stage. As Robert says, "The force of her personality could suck all the air out of the room."

Looking back, Evelyn explains, "Art is a blend of both Mom and Dad. A quiet thoughtful man and a showman."

* * * * *

Just as family feast days provided a lasting rhythm to the family's annual routine, Sunday morning church services provided a respite from an otherwise busy workweek. Art's dad was particularly quiet about matters of faith, and he kept his distance from the neighborhood church. Our Lady of Guadalupe, still there today, but no longer open, is located at the corner of Broadway and Mason, just steps away from one of San Francisco's iconic cable car lines.

Red often insisted that if he entered a church it would certainly "catch on fire." Apparently, because of his irregular attendance, Red was convinced his presence would be frowned upon by the parish priest. So, his solution was simply to not attend.

Lina, on the other hand, was a devout Catholic for most of her very long life. It must have been difficult for her when she was not able to attend Art's first Holy Communion in May 1932. By that time, she had two more children who needed her attention: Evelyn, who was nearly two, and a five-month old baby boy, Art's youngest sibling, William.

Lina made sure, however, that Art was dressed properly, with clean pants and a white shirt and tie she had taken from her dad and retailored to fit her son for this special occasion. Lina also took from her purse three dimes and a nickel, no small amount at the height of the Great Depression, which she gave to Art for the church's collection plate. Finally, she handed him an umbrella that was nearly as big as him in case it began to rain before he returned home. With that, she sent her son on his way down the steep grade of Broadway to Our Lady of Guadalupe, a short distance away.

Nearing the end of the service, while the other children fidgeted nervously, Art dug deep into his pockets, looking for the three dimes and a nickel he had been given just an hour before. But, after several tries, he became convinced that, somehow, he had lost the money. Upon leaving the church, Art approached one of the nuns and tearfully explained how he could not find the money that his mother had given him for the collection plate. He was told to go back inside and pray before the statue of St. Jude, the patron saint of all lost causes. So, Art knelt before St. Jude insistent that, if ever there was a lost soul in need of a miracle, it was he at this very moment.

Art left the church, wondering how he would explain the missing money to his mother. As he reluctantly made the long climb back up Broadway, the dark clouds that had been threatening all morning finally let loose, and Art struggled to open the umbrella his mother insisted he take. As he finally accomplished the task and the aging black umbrella with the worn wooden handle pushed open, three dimes and a nickel rained down upon him. Breathlessly, Art scrambled to pick up the money before it rolled down Broadway in four separate directions. With the money finally tucked safely in his pocket, Art looked skyward through the raindrops and thanked St. Jude. Moments later, Art did as he promised and delivered his coins to the church; he then rushed home to tell his mother about his very first miracle.

* * * * *

As Art recalls, his mother was a constant presence in his early life. Lina is remembered by him as very bright and very determined to see her oldest son succeed in their adopted country. No one in her family, or her husband's family, had completed high school. Lina was determined that Art would be a good student, complete high school, go onto college, and hopefully, one day, become "a professional man, perhaps even a doctor."

After all, this was America, where anything was possible. Your family caste did not determine your future. The deciding factor was your ambition. Social connections and social standing could certainly be helpful, but it was not essential to your passage "up the ladder of success." Education, however, was essential. Study and application was the great equalizer. Lina was certain that Art could go as far as his imagination, ambition, and her encouragement would take him. If he should falter, Lina would be there to challenge him to meet and exceed their shared expectations for his future.

It didn't take long for Art to begin to show that he was not only a gifted student, but an ambitious one as well. Art stood out in every school he attended, and from an early age, the arc of his life story began to show the promise that Lina had hoped and prayed that it would.

* * * * *

Art's introduction to education came at Spring Valley Elementary School, which stands to this day near the intersection of Hyde and Jackson, straddling San Francisco's Russian Hill and Nob Hill neighborhoods. Founded in 1852, Spring Valley is the oldest continuously operating public school in California. It was one of the seven schools established in the boom years following the gold rush, when San Francisco was quickly transformed from an encampment on the eastern edge of the Pacific to a booming metropolis. Spring Valley is the only one of these original schools still welcoming students more than 160 years after opening its doors. The original school was destroyed in the 1906 earthquake and fire, but it was rebuilt and reopened after several years of holding classes in a series of temporary shelters.

This historic institution was just two blocks west and three blocks south of Art's home on Glover Street. And, since the family lived near one of the city's highest points, Art's young legs got a good workout heading down those five blocks early every morning that school was in session and then back up every afternoon.

Today, Art has no recollection of his first years at Spring Valley, save one that could be shared with countless others who started school at a time when there was no preschool preparation. More than eighty years after entering Spring Valley, Art can still remember his mother dropping him off that first week of school and crying as she left him there for her walk back home. He remembers as well, the great relief he felt when he left school to find his mother smiling proudly and standing by the gate waiting for him, just as she had promised.

Speaking the language of America was not really an issue in the Dugoni home until Art began elementary school. At that point, Lina and Red, as so many immigrant parents had done before them, decided to limit the use of Piedmontese in the home and speak, almost exclusively, English. This was their testament to the idea that they were leaving behind one world and embracing another. It was in this new world, after all, that their children, and one day their grandchildren, would build their future lives.

Evelyn, born July 21, 1930, arrived just two months before Art began school. Red and Lina, typical of many Northern Italian families, planned on having a small family. But eight months after Evelyn's arrival, Lina became pregnant again, this time with an unplanned child. On December 25, 1931, Lina gave birth to William, whom she called "her Christmas angel." The family was very close, as you can see in photos from the 1930s and 1940s. And, typical of other families, the three children had their own distinct personalities. Evelyn, affectionately called "Evie" by her surviving brother, Art, was her father's sweetheart. William, always Bill, and older brother, Art, were every inch Lina's boys. And Lina was determined that these two young men would both be successful. In time, they accomplished all and more than she could have ever hoped they would. But, Lina's boys were two very different personalities. Art was quieter, shier and far more studious. Bill was the prankster, seeing the humor in all situations with a special love of teasing his beloved mother and his grandmother, Rosa.

Bill famously called Rosa one day, imitating one of the popular radio game show hosts of the time. "Mrs. Bianco?" he asked, trying hard not to laugh. When she confirmed that this was indeed Rosa Bianco of San Francisco, Bill informed her that she had won the show's grand prize if she could perform one simple trick. She had to put the phone receiver down, step back several feet, and tweet like a bird loud enough for the studio audience and all the listeners at home to hear her. Hoping for a big cash prize, Rosa played along and tweeted just as loudly as she could. When she walked back to the phone she asked if that was good enough, and Bill confirmed that, indeed, it was. She had won that day's grand prize, a case of Hartz Mountain bird seed, courtesy of the show's sponsor.

The difference between the three Dugoni siblings became more apparent with each passing year. As one cousin explained, "Evie and Bill were always ready to go out on a Saturday to Playland and Ocean Beach, while Art was determined to stay home and study."

* * * * *

Growing up on Glover Street led to many of Art's most cherished memories, but the family's time there was relatively short-lived. In 1935, before Art reached his tenth birthday, Red and Lina relocated to a home that better fit the needs of a growing family and freed them from what perhaps was too close of a loving family's embrace.

At 449 Pennsylvania Avenue in San Francisco's Potrero Hill neighborhood, Lina found a home she and her husband could afford to purchase that provided them with two bedrooms and a dining room that could be converted at night into a bedroom for Art. Best of all, there was a Catholic school just steps away from their front door.

Art remembers nothing about the move away from Russian Hill. But what he does remember is how much time he spent on streetcars and cable cars riding back up those steep hills to Glover Street, where he had forever left a part of his heart.

Arturo and Arthur in 1931.

Lina and Art at the Russian River.

Art at age twelve with
Lina, Rosa, Evelyn and William.

Art's confirmation day;
Evelyn's first holy communion.

Vittorio, ever ambitious but not always successful, in front of one of his North Beach retail stores.

Chapter Three

The Winds of Fortune

While St. Teresa of Avila Catholic Church at Missouri and 19th Street still welcomes parishioners to this day, the original elementary school, which held classes for students from grades one through eight, is long gone. From the time he entered St. Teresa's fifth grade to when he left Gonzaga University, Art attended five different schools, all of which were affiliated with the Catholic Church. Art never gave that fact much thought as a young man. The Catholic faith was an integral part of his life. Like the Italian culture that enveloped his childhood, devotion to the church and to his faith was simply a given.

From a very early age, Art believed that in life you were all in or all out. Therefore, it's easy to understand why, as a pre-teen, he seriously considered the priesthood as his life's calling. Although he has remained dedicated to his faith throughout a long life, he recognized that the priesthood was not right for him. He could not see himself going "all in," as he explained, so he placed his focus elsewhere.

Art's father was a chef, Grandpa Ben was a chef turned mattress maker and Grandpa Vittorio was a retail merchant—none were future professions Lina wanted for either of her boys. By the force of her character, Lina was a natural-born impresario and Art, Evelyn, and William were her three prized productions. She never missed an opportunity to open doors for Art, who was certainly the shyer and quieter of her three children. One door she opened was encouraging the family's dentist Jean P. Cantou to speak to her thirteen-year-old son about a career in dentistry.

Cantou was the son of French immigrants, a 1932 graduate of P&S, an abbreviation for the school's full name, the College of Physicians and Surgeons. It was founded in 1896 and affiliated more than sixty-five years later with the University of the Pacific. In January 1962 the school was re-named the University of the Pacific School of Dentistry.

Cantou took seriously the informal charge of his peers to bring "young men of merit" into the profession of dentistry. His dental office, located at 1515 19th Street in San Francisco's Potrero Hill neighborhood, was a short walk from the Dugoni home on Pennsylvania Avenue.

Like many of his fellow graduates, in addition to his practice, Cantou was an instructor at P&S, and he invited the young Dugoni to come and visit the school and meet several of the students, who were in different stages of what was then a four-year program to receive their Doctorate in Dental Surgery.

Nearly seventy-five years later, Art remembers very little of that visit to P&S. But what he does remember clearly is a boyhood love of science and feeling great admiration for, as he recalled, "those who used science to heal." To the modern era, the healing arts of the 1930s might seem primitive. But, to those alive at the time, this was the age of discovery. From astronomy to physics, from design and technology to medicine, this was a time of new ideas; it was an age that would not be slowed even by the harsh realities of a global depression.

It was during Art's early years at St. Teresa's that he clearly began to blossom as a student. His two passions, science and language arts, took shape at this time. His third passion, athletics—principally track and field and basketball—emerged as well.

Red cultivated Art's initial love of sports by running with him around their Potrero Hill neighborhood. Between the demands of his job as pastry chef at the St. Francis Hotel and his work at home helping to raise a growing family, Red had few opportunities to spend time with his oldest son. Running was one of those rare times the two could be together, and Art treasured every moment. Art quickly ran faster and further than Red ever expected. Red, with a small frame, a barrel chest, and powerful legs was built for speed. As a young man, Red won a gold medal in a San Francisco marathon event. That medal was one of only a few prized possessions that Red passed down to Art. Tragically, many years later, the medal was stolen from Art's home in Atherton during a burglary. So much of Red faded away over the decades that the loss of this memento was a particularly bitter disappointment to Art.

* * * * *

Art was only four when the stock market crashed in October 1929. And, while Art was sheltered in the long and loving arms of a large family, the next ten years brought the longest and hardest depression any generation of Americans has ever experienced. By Art's eighth birthday in 1933, the nation's unemployment rate, which in 1925 was just 3%, hit a staggering high of 25%. Meanwhile, deflation had lowered the value of goods by over 22%. With prices plummeting, American farmers began to fail, which triggered the largest number of bank failures in the nation's history. This was an unprecedented disaster that many thought would lead to the collapse of the nation's financial system and the unraveling of society.

Food lines, a common sight in cities across the nation, ran for several blocks in San Francisco. For every one hundred jobs for apricot pickers in Contra Costa County, there were 142 applicants hoping to make the standard wage of twenty-five cents per hour.

In 1933, conditions were so bad in the Bay Area job market that men lined up every morning on the Marin side of the massive new construction site for the Golden Gate Bridge, anxious to replace any workers injured on the job that day.

But, at the lowest point of the depression, in early March 1933, with banks closed from coast to coast to prevent further runs of the nation's rapidly dwindling cash reserve, Franklin Roosevelt took the oath of office and began an aggressive one hundred day plan to reverse the nation's tailspin.

Reminiscent of Charles Dickens opening lines for *A Tale of Two Cities*, "It was the best of times, it was the worst of times," the 1930s also brought stunning change to San Francisco. In October 1936, Pan American Airways' Clipper Service began connecting San Francisco Bay to Hong Kong with a one way fare of $950, approximately $15,000 in today's dollars. Just three weeks after the Clipper's first historic flight, the Bay Bridge opened, connecting Oakland and San Francisco. That was followed six months later, in May 1937, by the opening of the Golden Gate Bridge, connecting the agricultural North Bay counties of Marin, Napa, and Sonoma with their largest regional market, San Francisco. No one at the time knew that this new bridge was destined to become an icon beckoning travelers to the Bay Area from around the globe. In a few short years, the city that had been crippled by a devastating depression was emerging with renewed faith in the future.

The Golden Gate International Exposition opened in the middle of San Francisco Bay on Treasure Island in 1939. Created on an artificial island, it was lit nightly to symbolize the Bay Area's determination to exit the era of the Great Depression with a renewed sense of purpose and economic vitality.

During this time of national and local turmoil, Art was busy growing and learning. In a photo of the family taken on the newly opened Golden Gate Bridge, twelve-year-old Art is dwarfed by other family members. But four years later, as a high school sophomore, Art is the tallest member of his family, head and shoulders over both his mom and dad.

At St. Teresa's, his academic performance was so outstanding that he earned a scholarship to the prestigious St. Ignatius High School in San Francisco's Outer Sunset district. But, while he did well there academically, he missed his neighborhood and the kids he had gone to school with at St Teresa's, most of whom had graduated to St. James High School in the heart of the sunnier and warmer Mission district.

But it was more than just warmer weather beckoning Art closer to home. The boys of SI were mostly second and third generation Americans. A relative few were the children of immigrants. And while Lina made certain that he had a clean shirt and a clean pair of pants each school day, it was always the same shirt and the same pants. And while many of his classmates arrived by car, Art took two streetcars, spending an hour or more each day getting to and from school. Finally, in a city still beaten down by the Great Depression, Art didn't like the idea of needing a scholarship, which, to him, in the culture of the time, amounted to receiving a handout.

So, Art told Red and Lina that he wanted to transfer to St. James High School. They were supportive, but concerned about the annual cost of $250. Art took a job after school and on weekends at a neighborhood butcher shop to help pay his own tuition and entered St. James in September of 1940 for the start of his sophomore year.

It was here, at St. James, that Art encountered the first great mentor of his long life in education — Brother John McCluskey, the principal of St. James. In looking back at St. James school newspapers of 1942 and 1943, it becomes apparent that many of the characteristics and talents that people came to recognize as unique to Art Dugoni in his adult years began to flourish during this period of his life.

His drive to achieve becomes apparent as he tackles academics, athletics, and extra-curricular activities with boundless energy. A photo of Art at sixteen in his track uniform reveals a young man with movie star quality features and broad shoulders. He had a relaxed and confident smile. His love of public speaking emerged as well at this time. Although he was still shy and still bookish, given a stage and a theme, Art flourished.

In the 1930s and '40s, during the age of Churchill and Roosevelt, debate and public oratory were popular forms of competition in San Francisco and around the nation. Words carefully chosen and well spoken had the power to lift people out of their uncertainty over the present and invest their faith on a brighter future. Whether it was FDR's Great Depression suggestion that, "We have nothing to fear, but fear itself," or Churchill reminding his fellow Britons just two days after the fall of France, "Let us therefore brace ourselves to our duties, and so bear ourselves, that if the British Empire and its Commonwealth last for a thousand years, men will still say, this was their finest hour." The power of public speaking had taken center stage.

At St. James, Art's lifelong love affair with the written and spoken word began to flourish. Encouraging the development of this passion was Brother McCluskey, who, like others in his order of Marianists, had a faithful devotion to the advancement of Catholic youth.

Seventy years after delivering a speech on the life of Patrick Henry, Art could still remember his opening line: "Out of the thick, murky, desolate patch of darkness must come light and so a day is born." Those national competitions challenged Art's ability to present his beliefs in a language he hardly used before the age of five, and also expanded his sense of self confidence, both as a writer and public speaker. It provided an early promise of a bright future in the heart of a kid whose mother reminded him regularly that, in America, ambition was the key to unlocking unimaginable success.

This love for the craft of language is one of the most common threads found in charismatic leaders. It served Art well throughout his long career. Growing up in an age when families gathered around the radio to hear FDR's Fireside Chats, it's easy to see where Art might have drawn his inspiration.

The one event that impacted Art's life most significantly occurred on December 7, 1941 when the Empire of Japan attacked Pearl Harbor. San Francisco became the focal point for America's preparation for a long war in the Pacific. Remnants of that era are evident to this day in and around San Francisco. From Fort Mason, where millions of tons of equipment were loaded onto countless cargo ships to support the war effort in the Pacific, to Battery Townsend in the Marin Headlands, where huge guns were encased in concrete bunkers with adjacent underground troop barracks in preparation for a Japanese assault on the west coast of the United States.

Like so many of his contemporaries, commonly known today as the "Greatest Generation," this epic national struggle changed Art's life forever.

The months following Pearl Harbor revealed to Americans just how long this new war would be. Hitler was in control of nearly the entire European continent, and in the Pacific, the Japanese were rapidly capturing key strategic islands, all of which would have to be retaken by an American Navy still reeling from the devastation of Pearl Harbor.

As this somber reality set in during those early dark days of 1942, with astounding swiftness, America underwent a rapid and dramatic metamorphosis from a nation at peace to a nation at war. In April 1942, by executive order, President Roosevelt created the War Manpower Commission. Later that year, the nation's Selective Service System was placed under the direction of the WMC that was tasked with the enormous responsibility of allocating America's human resources to three vital areas: agriculture, industrial and, most importantly, its armed services.

To military planners, faced now with the harsh realities of fighting a war that had consumed most of Europe, most of Asia, and the Pacific, it became obvious that the draft age of twenty would never meet the needs of both the Army and the Navy.

On October 12, 1942, one year after Vittorio's death, President Roosevelt addressed the nation to announce he was calling on the Selective Service to lower the age of induction for men into the armed services to eighteen. From the Dugoni home on Potrero Hill—where Art would celebrate his eighteenth birthday in eight months' time—to homes across the nation, a chill went through the hearts of parents everywhere. It was becoming clearer with each passing day that this world war would, in time, touch the lives of every American.

Two months later, shortly before Christmas 1942, Principal McCluskey called Art and two of his classmates, Bill Murphy and Jim Munill, into his office. That meeting was such a memorable turning point for Art, the intervening seven decades vanished as he recollected that day...

"Brother John told the three of us that our grades were good enough to go directly into the University of San Francisco and skip the spring semester of our senior year of high school. We would be able to graduate with our class that coming June, and even participate in several class events that final term, but by entering college before we were draft-eligible that coming June, we might be selected for a spot in an officer training program. In order to qualify for one of those programs, however, all three of us needed at least some time in college.

"Of course, there was no certainty that being an officer as opposed to an enlisted man would assure our surviving the war. McCluskey was simply doing what he had always done for his boys: looking out for them. All three of us discussed the idea with our dads that night. My dad had served in World War I and, as awful as that conflict was, he could imagine that this war raging now around the globe could go on for much longer.

"Murphy's dad and mine were immigrants. Neither of them had the benefit of a high school education, and they both told us to follow the advice of "an educated man." Jim Munill's dad was a college professor, and he told Jim to make up his own mind. So Jim, who was a terrific athlete and a gifted public speaker, decided to stay for the remainder of his senior year. It was the decision Bill and I would have made given the same chance by our dads. We were both looking forward to the spring term of our senior year, but these were extraordinary times, so we both enrolled in classes at USF in January 1943."

As Art goes on to explain, "All three of us entered the military on or before our eighteenth birthday, but only Jim was drafted straight out of high school and served in combat. My two classmates are gone now, but thankfully, they both survived a war that killed hundreds of thousands of young Americans, not to mention tens of millions of individuals around the world."

Art's time at USF lasted only that spring term of 1943. He returned to St. James every chance he got, competing in intramural track events and oratory competitions. At the same time, he also competed in track at USF.

Now over six feet, weighing only 150 pounds, Art was running the one hundred-yard dash in eleven seconds. His signature event was the 880-yard run, a race he never lost. His time of two minutes, one second was one of the fastest times set at high schools throughout San Francisco.

Photos of Art during this time reveal why he was called "String" by his friends and classmates. It was a name that would stay with Art for many years. His ability in the 880-yard dash and high jump competitions reappeared decades later in two of his grandchildren, Joseph and Mary Katherine, both of whom excelled in high jump.

But to the boys of St. James, Art would be remembered as "Ham," a name he earned for two reasons. One, his love of public speaking, and two, his job as a butcher's assistant, the part time job he took three years earlier to pay for his high school education.

In the St. James graduation supplement, Art is pictured in a suit addressing the "St. James Tenth Annual Reunion Class of 1943." Their tongue-in-check tribute to him reads:

"His calling is toward the butcher trade,

But he hopes, a physician, he will be made.

Physician or butcher, the difference is nil

He'll practice both on whoever is ill."

Prior to those final high school days, enjoying the camaraderie of the twenty-two boys in his St. James senior class, while also a student at USF, Art enlisted in the Navy. In March, he took an exam in hopes of qualifying for the Navy's V-12 officer training program. His first request was that he be sent to a pre-med or pre-dent program, and he hoped that the school would be Stanford. In April, he learned that he had been accepted. Colleges throughout the nation participated in the V-12 program. In truth, Art could have been assigned to any one of those schools. Strictly by chance, Gonzaga University was selected as Art's destination, and he was placed in pre-dent. It was a fortuitous choice. Just six blocks away from the campus, on East Mission Avenue in Spokane, lived a girl fourteen months Art's junior, Katherine Groo.

Opposite page: Art and a fellow music student after an accordion lesson on Potrero Hill.
Opposite page: "String," a perfect name for Art at age eighteen.

Art and family gather to celebrate his graduation from high school.

The young men of St. James High School on the brink of an uncertain future.

Chapter Four

Love and War

In late June 1943, just one day before Art turned eighteen, he prepared to leave San Francisco for Spokane. Other than returning home for leave, he would not again be a resident of his native city for three years. Starting at Gonzaga, followed by several months at the US Naval Training Center in Farragut, Idaho, and then eighteen months in Kansas City, where he completed the first two years of his doctorate work in dental sciences, Art would grow from adolescent to adult. Equally significant in determining his future, his life would be overtaken by a passionate love affair.

The trip to Spokane marked the first time Art would be away from his parents for an extended period of time. Lina wept long enough and hard enough while accompanying the young recruit to his departure point that Art's younger brother, Bill, then age twelve, said, "Mom, when it's my time to leave, you're not going with me to the train station."

Art was not immediately going off to war, but Lina was more than justified in her concern. While the hope was that he'd be able to ride out the balance of the war while pursuing his education in dentistry, everyone knew there was no guarantee. In June 1943, with America struggling to gain a toehold in Europe, and the war with Japan for control of the Pacific looking like a battle that would go island to island in a seemingly endless progression to Japan and liberation of the Chinese mainland, the entire nation was a blend of stoic optimism and tense concern. After his months of officer training, Art might be assigned to continue his education at a dental school, or be placed as an ensign on a naval ship. Like millions of other Americans, the Dugonis had no sense of certainty as to what tomorrow might bring.

Prior to his departure, Lina, determined as ever to make connections for her oldest son, introduced Art to another young man from San Francisco's Italian American community who was also headed to Gonzaga. Angelo Sangiacomo, one year Art's senior, came over to the Dugoni home in the days before their departure, met Art, and promised Lina that he would look after her son. That was the beginning of a lifelong friendship between the two men, both of whom would go on to experience the blessings of happy families, incredible careers, and long lives.

Gonzaga, a Jesuit university founded in 1887, was glad to host the Navy. Between the lingering effects of the depression and the departure of students and faculty to join the war effort, the institution was under great financial strain. The presence of the US Navy helped to secure what was then a struggling institution.

In March 1943, Gonzaga was approved for the Navy's V-12 collegiate program. On the first day of July, 300 V-12 cadets arrived on campus. Their curriculum consisted of lectures in English, mathematics, physics, history, and chemistry. Naval officers lived on campus to instruct recruits in naval etiquette, physical fitness training, and to drill and enforce Navy discipline. The Jesuit faculty, however, taught a majority of the academic courses.

In mid-August, six weeks after Art's arrival at Gonzaga, the school organized a reception to introduce the Spokane community to the new cadets. A number of Spokane's eligible young ladies were in attendance, including Katherine, Mary and Joann Groo, three of the four Groo sisters. That night, Art met Katherine for the very first time, and his heart skipped a beat.

"So many memories have faded over the years, but not the memory of when I first saw Kaye," Art explained. "That has always stayed with me. She was soft-spoken and so gentle in her manner...unassuming, and without pretense. I was certain that I had never seen such a beautiful girl." As young as Art was when they met, eighteen, Kaye, born on August 12, 1926, had just celebrated her seventeenth birthday.

Art remembers himself as being quite shy at eighteen. "Most times, I avoided girls," Art said. "At St. James, I studied and did athletics. When I wasn't doing that, I was working at the butcher shop. It took all my courage to give her my phone number that night and suggest that she call and leave a message for me at my dormitory if she ever got the chance."

A week after their first encounter, Kaye's best friend, Winona, called Art, pretending to be Kaye. In truth, Kaye was as shy as Art. To Winona Ellerton, however, shyness was just a stumbling block on the road to romance. So, she sat next to Kaye on the living room couch of the Groo home as she dialed Art's dorm and got him to come to the phone. Their high school's first big dance of the senior year was coming up in two weeks and "Kathie," the name Kaye went by as a youth, wanted to know if Art would accompany her to the event. Art was thrilled and decided this was the time to be bold, so he suggested that they first go out on a date together. "Dinner and a movie that Saturday night?" Winona repeated as she placed her hand over the phone and shook her head in agreement with a smiling Kaye.

The date was set, but Art quickly realized he had a problem: no money! So, he approached his new friend, Angelo Sangiacomo, and asked for a loan of five dollars to take his date to dinner and a movie. Angelo was happy to help, but he only had a ten dollar bill in his wallet. Reluctantly, he handed over the money and said he would get his change when he saw Art at church on Sunday.

The date was the wonderful night Art had dreamed of having. When he awoke Sunday morning, he found Angelo standing at the foot of his bunk asking for his change. "I told him I spent the whole ten dollars the night before. We had to take a streetcar, have a meal, and pay for the movies." Sangiacomo, who in later life would become one of San Francisco's biggest property owners, stared at Art in amazement and said, "How could you possibly spend ten dollars on one date?"

That "extravagant" Saturday date, followed by the Stardust Ball at Kaye's high school that next week, was really all it took for Art and Kaye to become inseparable. On the night of the ball, it was easy to tell that these two had found each other. Kaye's dance card has just one name filled in from top to bottom, "Art." The photograph taken that night of Kaye dressed in an off the shoulder black gown and Art in his sailor's uniform, looks like a publicity still for two young

Hollywood stars from a 1940s black and white love story. Until Art's time at Gonzaga and then at nearby Farragut Naval Base ended, these two young lovers would spend every moment they could find in each other's company.

The first five years of their relationship would have mostly been lost to the fog of time, if not for a collection of letters kept over seventy years by Kaye.

The first two "letters" are actually postcards that begin in January of 1944. At first, these notes are addressed by Art to "Dear Kathie," but soon become declarations of love written to "My Dearest Darling." Kaye's letters to Art were burned by him shortly before he left for Kansas City, for fear they would be found by "prying eyes." Frequently, however, you can tell much of what Kaye wrote to Art by the response that he sends. At first, many of the letters are just days apart, but after Art has left the Spokane area and has been reassigned to Kansas City, they begin to diminish in frequency and intensity. And, not unlike countless other stories of young love, the relationship falls victim to a separation of nearly two years in which Kaye declares that she has "found another boy." Remarkably, however, even at this time of separation, these two young lovers maintain a considerate, respectful, if no longer intimate tone.

* * * * *

The war brought its own form of commotion to Art's life. He was not able to complete the spring term of his senior year at St. James. The Jesuit institution, University of San Francisco, was almost a blur passing quickly through his life in the spring of 1943. And his first assignment in the Navy's V-12 program to Gonzaga was relatively short-lived as well. Art spent approximately fifteen months at Gonzaga before being transferred to Farragut.

Farragut Naval Training Center was one of those miracles of America during the war years. The whole complex, on the southern tip of Lake Pend Oreille, which hugs the Washington-Idaho border, sprung up virtually overnight. It was assembled with incredible speed in 1942 and decommissioned in 1946. Approximately 300,000 sailors came through this version of Navy boot camp, and Art was one of them.

When he began his time at Farragut, Art got the mandatory buzz cut and sent a clump of brown hair pinned to a letter to Kaye. Fortunately for Art, Farragut was only fifty-five miles from Kaye's home. On weekend leave, when possible, Art would board a train and rush back to Kaye.

It's quite clear that, during the combined eighteen months that Art spent in Spokane and Farragut, the Groo house was his home away from home. Art could not have found himself in a better place. Russell and Kitty Groo, Kaye's parents, were, by all accounts, the personification of Norman Rockwell's America. Russ and Kitty both were the products of multi-generational American families. Of course, their real history was not as simple and neat as a Rockwell cover for the *Saturday Evening Post* magazine.

Isaac Groo, Russell's grandfather, came from a town called Neversink, New York. It was there that Isaac became active in the Mormon movement. In 1854, when Russell's father, Orson, was just two years old, Isaac joined a wagon train of Mormon pioneers heading west to Utah where Brigham Young had established the epicenter of the Church of Latter Day Saints. Halfway into their journey, the wagon train's members were stricken with cholera. Many perished, including Isaac's father-in-law. But Isaac, his wife Elizabeth, and their son Orson survived. Once in Utah, Isaac quickly gained the respect of church elders and became a leader in the Mormon movement. In time, he took five additional wives and fathered a total of twenty-eight children. But, after his father's death and the birth of his own three sons, of which Russell was the youngest, Orson left the church and relocated to Idaho.

It was in Montpelier, Idaho, near Bear Lake, where Russell met and fell in love with a local girl named Catherine. Known in the family as Kitty, her father, John Brennan, was a devout Irish Catholic and when Kitty agreed to marry Russell, she had only one condition: the children must be raised Catholic. The couple stayed in Montpelier until their firstborn, Kaye's older brother, John, was nearly eight.

Kitty, who was devout in her faith, feared greatly that her children would never get a proper Catholic education unless they lived in a bigger community. Spokane, 650 miles to the Northwest of Montpelier had, as Kitty exclaimed, a church on every corner! And, of equal importance, it had the Catholic schools she wanted her children to attend.

In 1928, the couple bought their dream house at 813 E. Mission Avenue in Spokane. There, they raised their five children, of whom Kaye was the fourth.

By all accounts, Kitty and Russell created a loving and happy home. John, the couples' oldest, left for the Pacific in 1942, and Art never met him until after the war. But Art was surrounded by the Groo girls, Mary and Joann, who were older than Kaye, and Patricia, two years younger than Kaye, whom Art affectionately called "the kid."

Mary and Patricia are gone now, but Joann, who became a nun in the order of the Sisters of the Holy Names in Marylhurst, Oregon, remembers Art and Kaye as teenage lovers.

"They were just the sweetest couple you can imagine," she said. "When I was home from nursing school on the weekends, I'd accompany them down to Mission Park and sing love songs as they sat on an old stone bridge over a peaceful pond. One of their favorites was Gershwin's 'Embraceable You.' We all loved just about everything Sinatra did and, of course, Bing Crosby, who grew up in Spokane and attended Gonzaga, was a favorite of ours as well."

Art took every opportunity to see Kaye, some visits within Navy rules and some visits by bending the rules. "I often had trouble studying in the evenings at my noisy dorm," Art explained. "So, an instructor of mine, Father James Linden, showed me an upstairs office in Goller Hall where I could work undisturbed.

"In the office, there was a life-sized statute of St. Joseph that came in handy on Saturday nights. I dragged that statue down two flights of steps and placed it in my bunk with my sailor's cap over its head and tucking the covers up around it. It did the trick; by eight, I was with Kaye, and I'd sneak back into the dorm close to midnight. I got my exercise moving St. Joseph back and forth, but being with Kaye was well worth it."

"The Groo house was always a happy place," Sister Joann, now ninety, recalls happily. "Art was a frequent visitor on weekends, coming often to visit Kaye and often invited by my parents to stay for dinner. Mom played the piano and read her poetry. Kids always had fun at my parent's house. The house had beautiful wood inlaid ceilings, built-in bookcases and built-in China cabinets. In 1928, when my parents bought the place, it was a new house from a builder who created it for his family, but decided later to live in another part of the city. It's probably small and modest by today's standards, but back then, it was considered to be a spacious and very comfortable home.

"I was well acquainted with Art," Sister Joann continued. "He was wonderfully warm and outgoing. My parents were very fond of him."

One Saturday in mid-October Art and Kaye headed out for a long bike ride on what appeared to be a perfect autumn afternoon. But ten miles from the Groo home, the weather suddenly turned from mild to cold. The two turned around but the wind got increasingly bitter as they pedaled the ten miles back to Mission Avenue. By the time they arrived, Kaye's mom was dismayed to see her daughter and her boyfriend both shivering without stop. Art remembers Kitty quickly heating bricks, and putting them both in the same bed. She put a quilt over the bricks and placed them side by side, covered with blankets. She then put a board between them in anticipation that the two young lovers might quickly thaw.

Of course, these blissful months at the Groo home were always tempered by the fact that John, who was just twenty-three at the time, was in the Pacific. It wasn't until after the war that the family realized just how perilous those years had been for John. His nearest brush with death came in the jungles of New Guinea. Fighting there and in some of the surrounding islands began in January 1942. Combat continued until the conclusion of the war in August 1945. In 1943, the Japanese surrounded his platoon at a time when several of the men, including John, were bedridden with acute cases of malaria. They could not be moved and would have almost certainly perished if captured by the Japanese. Fortunately, native New Guineas hid them in their huts until the Japanese had left the area. Much of John's story was unknown until his return home. The full pain and horror of his story, however, he refused to share with anyone until a full twenty years after the war's conclusion.

Kaye's father, Russell was loved by everyone, including Art. His business was run out of a small factory where he would build and repair both car and truck batteries. He repaired the city's service vehicles as well, from buses to utility trucks.

In spite of a thriving business, Russell Groo kept things simple. When one of his customers came to retrieve their cars, he would say, for example, "That will be eight dollars." If a customer proffered a ten-dollar bill, Russell told them to go over to the cigar box on his desk, deposit the bill and take their change. Spokane in 1943 was just that kind of town.

* * * * *

Time passed quickly at Gonzaga, and when Art was transferred to Farragut, it was still uncertain what his next assignment would be.

"I remember being scared as hell," Art recalls. "Most of the people in the barracks were seasoned naval personnel, and I was only nineteen." At times, it seemed to Art like the entire world passed through Farragut, which was the largest naval training base anywhere in the world.

In December 1944, with a bitter cold gripping Farragut, the days were short and the nights were long and lonely. One of those nights, Art wrote to Kaye confessing how happy he was to have her in his life. Speculating on how dreary life at Farragut would be if not for knowing she was close by he wrote:

"I thought of you last night before I fell asleep. I keep thinking about your green-blue eyes and your happy smile. Until I met you, I never thought I could love anyone as much as I do you. My whole life has become entangled with you. You're in every phase of my thoughts, of my day dreams, of my planning."

Art spent that Christmas away from home and completed Farragut in mid-January 1945.

After a brief leave to go home to San Francisco, he left on the first day of February for the University of Missouri, Kansas City, where he would begin work on his Doctorate in Dental Surgery.

Art's first letter to Kaye on the day of his arrival in Kansas City recounts a grueling, sleepless journey across much of the country only to be disappointed in the dental school that had been selected for him by the Navy.

"Dearest Darling,

Events of the day have not been conducive to optimism," he writes of a long bus ride across Kansas City on a bitterly cold Sunday morning. Finally, I found a building right in the middle of a ramshackle area with a shingle reading, 'Kansas City Western Dental College.' Hold your breath! It's exactly one-half block long and one-quarter of a block wide. It must have been built in the days of Jesse James."

Art asks Kaye's forgiveness, knowing full well that his letter is, "just one continual gripe!!!" He explains that he can barely keep his eyes open, having spent two nights in "a railroad car from 1887!" He shares with Kaye that, during those nights, he listened to a sailor who had spent twenty-six months fighting in the Philippines. "The things I heard," Art writes, "have made me, by far, the wiser." He quotes the sailor as saying, "I was born a Catholic, but now I have no religion. If there's justice, if there's a God, he wouldn't let such awfulness exist."

As for the others on the train, Art describes them, particularly some of the women, as being of "questionable character." Then he adds, "As long as I have any say about it, you'll never travel on a train alone."

Art closes by writing, "If I could only be with you, I'd give up almost anything. I've got it so bad that I don't care who knows it. As each second ticks away, I love you more. Even in this day of bleak confession, you are my guiding star."

A week after his arrival, Art writes that he went over to the Kansas side of Kansas City to be fitted for his naval officers' uniform. For the first time since his introduction to Gonzaga, it was time to take off the bell-bottom sailor's uniform and exchange it for that of a midshipman. When told that his new uniform should arrive in three weeks, he wrote to Kaye, "I doubt if the pants I have on could last three more weeks — they certainly are worn thin."

The flow of letters from Kansas City reveals that Art was unhappy there, at least during those early weeks. Being out of his old uniform and into his new one seems to be the extent of Art's happiness during that time. He writes, "I don't like the college very well, nor the professors either. It's taken the drive out of me." He continues to speak of how desperately he is missing Kaye, who he calls his "Dearest darling angel," and asks her to write often.

Art opens his letter on 24 March 1945 by writing, "Here's another Saturday night almost gone and the sixty-third day since we were together." Art recalls the last day they were together when he saw the tears in her eyes and he writes, "We were so close, so afraid of being separated. I can still hear the beating of your heart and the warmth of your nearness—it makes me shake all over." He closes by reminding her of the lyric to one of their favorite Sinatra recordings of a Cole Porter love song: "I won't be content until I can make love to you, night and day, day and night."

Away from Kaye, Art frequently writes on a Saturday night and always references that he'll say prayers for her and her family when at mass the following morning. In fact, Art never writes on a Saturday night without mentioning that he will be in church come Sunday morning.

Less than three weeks after Art's letter in late March, on April 12, word came from Warm Springs, Georgia that President Roosevelt had died. Four days after the president's death, the final Battle of Berlin began. On May 2nd, the twelve year reign of terror instigated by the rise of Hitler and his Third Reich came to an end.

An obscure Missouri senator chosen as FDR's running mate just eight months earlier was suddenly the nation's commander in chief. Harry Truman's home in the small town of Independence was a short drive from the University of Missouri, Kansas City campus. Art no longer felt lost in what seemed like such a remote part of America as the world turned its eyes to the humble hometown of the nation's thirty-third president.

Art's determination to succeed in dental school began to show as the weeks and months flew past. As he did throughout his youth, he took comfort in athletics. He joined the basketball team because it offered some comfort from the pain of being so far away from Kaye. As a center and team captain, he became a starter and the leading scorer on the Navy team. Art was twice selected to the all-star team. He played regularly until he left Kansas City in June 1946. Participating in a competitive sport lifted him past his early frustrations at school and diminished the pain of being so far from his beloved Kaye. Along the way, he became almost a straight-A student.

In August 1945, the war in the Pacific came to an end with the unconditional surrender of the Japanese Empire. The V-12 program continued in operation for several months and was ended in 1946. On January 29, 1946, Art was given an honorable discharge from the Navy. Wanting to complete the spring term at Kansas City Western, he was left at a crossroads. Not only had the Navy paid for Art's tuition, it paid him a living stipend as well. Now, he would have to pay tuition to UMKC and cobble together part-time work to make his living expenses. He got a part-time job selling cotton candy and sodas at Swope Park in Kansas City. Fortunately, the Navy gave him a separation payment of $245, a handsome sum at that time, but he still had to live frugally to make it through the end of the spring term.

Meanwhile, the letters between Art and Kaye had grown further apart, as one might expect of two very young lovers separated for eighteen months and a distance of 1,600 miles. Still, there was a relationship, but it was tempered at times by passing attractions to others.

When Art boarded a train for the long journey back home, he was determined to close this chapter in his life, reestablish his connection with Kaye, and complete the last two years of dental school at the University of California, San Francisco (UCSF). As had often been the case in his life, little would go according to plan.

Winona Ellerton, who called Art pretending to be Kaye, still giving Kaye advice.

The Groo family: Kitty and Russell, with Kaye, Patricia, Mary and Joann. John, not pictured, is off serving in the Pacific.

Art, straight off the bus at Gonzaga.

When Art met Kaye his
heart skipped a beat.

Art recalls, "On the night of the Stardust
Ball we both had stars in our eyes."

Chapter Five

"Termites Holding Hands"

In various retellings of Art Dugoni's story, a misconception has developed that he was somehow destined to attend the College of Physicians & Surgeons because of his introduction to the school and to the profession of dentistry by his family's dentist, Dr. Jean Cantou. That was never the case. Like many other things that have happened in Art's life, his path to P&S was the result of random circumstances.

When Art arrived back home, he applied first to UCSF because it was a state school, and he knew it would be his most affordable option. "My family's income was very modest. I knew I could take odd jobs, but tuition would still be a mountain to climb," Art explained.

But, as fate would have it, Art's reception at UCSF wasn't what he expected. "I was told that I would have to take an examination in each of the courses I had completed at UMKC, and that there was no assurance that I'd be able to start as a third year student, but there was a good chance that I'd be required to repeat my second year." When Art made his case that Kansas City Western Dental was a good school and his grades were consistently above average, his rebuttal was greeted with obvious skepticism, and the suggestion that UCSF was a far superior school.

It is interesting to note that, ten years later, in 1956, Art was speaking at the UCSF School of Dentistry on advances in high-speed instrumentation. Attending the lecture was Dean Willard C. Fleming, who had been dean since 1939. Fleming came up to Art at the conclusion of the lecture and said, "How did we miss a bright young man like you at UCSF?" Art recalls that he smiled and thought: "You really don't want to know!"

After his admissions interview, Art left UCSF greatly discouraged. He knew there was a private school of dentistry down in the city's Mission District, but he also knew that the cost of attending that school would be a lot more. On the other hand, he had to weigh the possible loss of income in delaying the start of his practice by as much as a year or more if, indeed, UCSF required him to repeat his entire second year. So, Art took a streetcar down to the Mission, hoping to find a better option.

Art mistakenly walked into the Armory at the intersection of 14th and Mission (a building still there to this day) thinking that it was P&S. Someone pointed down the block and across the street. Art had a vague memory of having been there once before as a youngster with Cantou, but he had no clear memory of the building or its exact location.

"I was taken aback," Art explained, "by the building's condition." Its physical condition quickly brought back memories of Kansas City Western Dental. Art would soon learn why P&S students and faculty believed the only thing keeping the old dental school building from falling down around them was a determined gathering of "termites all holding hands."

"I walked into the building and the school secretary, Mrs. Houghton, led me in to meet Dean Ernie Sloman, who was smoking a small cigar and had one foot up on the desk."

Sloman was a stout man. He stuck out his hand and greeted Art warmly. It must have been an interesting moment—one of the dental profession's most influential figures of the first half of the twentieth century was meeting a young man who would become one of the profession's most influential figures of the second half of the twentieth century. In a variety of ways, Sloman would have a profound effect on Art's future, and that effect began the very first day they met.

Art took an almost instant liking to the man students affectionately referred to as "Uncle Ernie." Sloman told Art that he was impressed with his transcripts, but at the moment, he was not sure how this would work out. Art's heart skipped a beat as the dean took a few moments to think about the situation.

"We won't start the next term until September," Sloman said after a long pause. In 1946, P&S was back on a four-year degree program, after graduating a three-year class in 1944 in response to an urgent wartime need to meet a shortage of practicing dentists, both at the front line and at home.

Sloman suggested Art go see Dr. Elmer McEvoy, who ran the school's clinic. "Go get a white coat, and we'll start assigning you patients," he said. "We'll have enough time to figure out if you're successful, and if it all works out, you can start in September as a third year student, or you can return to Kansas City."

Art found himself inspired by Sloman, who was worthy of imitation. The stories of Sloman run long and deep in the history of the school that had been founded in 1896. In the months following his death, Sloman was the subject of many tributes, none more moving than the one given to a P&S alumni association meeting by Dr. George M. Hollenbeck, a legendary dentist who, in his storied career in Los Angeles, had a long list of Hollywood legends as patients, including Katherine Hepburn, Clark Gable, Howard Hughes, Olivia de Havilland, and William Powell. Hollenbeck, a poor self-made man born in Kansas in 1886, became a philanthropist in his later life. In 1952, he presented a bust of Sloman to the school, saying that he had never been more impressed by any single colleague:

"Throughout his entire career, he manifested a total indifference to the accumulation of wealth for himself. He was a very human fellow, the friend of everyone, the foe of no one. Civic leader, scientist, author, administrator, teacher, anatomist, surgeon, dental statesman, and respected advisor, not only to our profession, but also to that of medicine. He stands without peer in the ranks of our profession."

Hollenbeck, who graduated from the UMKC program in 1907 was awed by the quality of the program Arthur McDowell, Sloman's predecessor, and Sloman himself, had built. "The equal of any dental educational institution in America, from the standpoint of faculty, instruction, and the general high attainment of its graduates. This record is all the more remarkable when consideration is given to the fact that this institution is not well-equipped physically and has no monetary endowment. But it does have an endowment which money cannot buy, the unswerving loyalty of its faculty, student body, and alumni, and last but not least, the respect with which the institution is held in educational circles and by the entire dental profession."

Hollenbeck concluded on a personal note that, in "everything which he undertook, whether it was a card or golf game, or the most intricate phase of a technical dental problem, Ernie Sloman did it with ease and in a masterly manner."

If you're thinking that this seems a rather grand tribute to a man who ran a school held together by "an army of termites," consider this remarkable fact: Two days before the end of 1951, Harry Truman appointed Ernie Sloman, who was then the president-elect of the American Association of Dental Schools, to the newly formed President's Commission on the Health Needs of the Nation. The entire commission was made up of only fifteen members from around the nation, and Sloman was selected as the dental profession's lone representative.

Over forty years later, during the first Clinton Administration, Art was the only dentist appointed to a commission headed by Hillary Clinton to initiate national healthcare reform. This is another interesting parallel connecting Dean Dugoni and one of his most important mentors, Dean Sloman.

* * * *

It was a struggle to take on the tuition of a private school, which, at the time, was approximately $200 per quarter, but Art was determined to make it work. He went back to his old part-time job at the butcher shop that had made it possible for him to pay his way through St. James, and he took on a new job as an athletic coach at the Columbia Park's Boys Club down in the Mission.

After meeting Sloman and many of the students and faculty, Art was convinced that he had found an excellent home to complete the two years remaining to earn his degree. Today, with the benefit of history, we know it was the start of a lifetime love affair with this one very special institution. But, in the summer of 1946, having just celebrated his twenty-first birthday, his thoughts turned back to Kaye.

Surely, as he had written, they were destined to share their futures together. But Art was soon to learn that Kaye was not nearly so certain.

Left: Art, in Kansas City, gets his first naval officer's uniform just in time.
Right: Lina happy to have her son back in San Francisco.

Kaye, seated front row right, in college studying for her degree in medical technology.

The dental clinic at P&S the year Art graduated, 1948.

Ernest Sloman, the P&S dean who decided to give Art a chance.

Chapter Six

"If God Has Kept Together Our Hearts"

Kitty Groo and Lina Dugoni were of like minds, at least when it came to one topic: Kaye and Arthur would make a wonderful life together. Now, if they could only get their children to recognize that fact.

Clearly, by the summer of 1946, the passion of their earlier relationship was reduced to the lingering embers of a fire that burned brightly two years before. Letters to and from Kansas City during 1945 grew further and further apart. With Art back home in San Francisco, Lina and Kitty knew it was time to give those embers a chance to reignite. Lina suggested that Art invite Kaye for a two-week visit that would include a trip to Yosemite. Kitty encouraged the idea of a trip and, along with Russell, invested in a roundtrip ticket for Kaye to fly down to San Francisco.

What actually happened during the visit is somewhat unclear. Interviewed in 2012, Kaye's sister Joann recalls Kaye telling her that Art was "not the same boy she fell in love with." During their long absence, Art had matured in ways she found off-putting. His look had certainly changed as seen in his 1946-47 *P&S Chips Yearbook* photo. Art now sported a pencil-thin mustache, which, at the time, he felt added some badly needed maturity to his very young face.

Art's letter, written on September 16, 1946, makes it clear that Lina and Kitty's plan to give the couple a little push ended badly. Kaye's "Dear Art" letter arrived on a Thursday, and Art waited until the following Monday to respond. He writes that Kaye had been ill for most of her visit to San Francisco, including their car trip to Yosemite.

Apparently, Kaye had met a boy in Spokane named Tommy, and that new attraction added to her very uncertain feelings about Art. Art writes that, at the airport when she was leaving to return home, "I didn't even get a goodbye kiss, your thoughts seemed to be in another world."

In response to Kaye's letter regarding Tom, Art wrote, "I had planned so much, had built so many dreams, and I had only one thought—to recapture a very beautiful love, even if I had lost it to another."

But Art writes of many missed opportunities. He talks of telling her these things,

"….in a letter or when I see you again. (Don't laugh!)" He asks her to consider if she really loves Tom, and if she doesn't, Art suggests, "…don't see any more of him."

Art urges Kaye not to live day-to-day, but to think of her happiness over the span of a lifetime. He suggests that Tom is a passing interest, but that their connection is much deeper and more meaningful. Then Art adds, "Please tell me to shut up if you think that this is none of my business."

In this long letter, Art never becomes angry with Kaye; rather he criticizes himself saying, "I guess I'm a prized ass…the love I knew then was so great that what I feel now is inadequate by comparison. Perhaps I lived too much in my dreams."

With a remarkable sense of grace for a man of twenty-one years, Art concludes, "I pray that Jesus will show you the path that leads to lasting happiness, and has mercy on me for being so thoughtless and so stupid."

In a brief postscript, Art writes, "Regards to Tom—don't tell him what I wrote as it is only for you."

Noting that it was "near midnight" when he was finishing this letter and that he was "very tired," it's a safe guess that Art went to sleep that night with a broken heart. It's unknown just how long he stayed that way. What is known is the correspondence between Kaye and Art fell silent for a period of sixteen months. The only letter Kaye held onto during that long silence was one she received from her sister Joann who was now a nun in the order of the Novitiate of the Sisters of the Holy Names in Marylhurst, Oregon. In her letter, she cautions Kaye to think long and hard about the choice between Art and Tom.

Sister Joann suggests that Kaye "take her time," regarding Tommy. In this letter, written one month after Art's letter of September 1946, she writes, "I am sure he must be a fine person, or you would never have told Art that you and he are finished. You know how much we all think of Art, and I am especially fond of him — but I would like anyone that my sis singled out."

Then, in a passage indicative of the strong Catholic home they both grew up in, Joann writes, "I am willing to accept all the things you have said about Tommy…but the fact that he is not a Catholic is a <u>big</u> drawback." Adding, "Mixed marriages never bring the unity that is so essential. Children need the example of both parents and the help of family prayers and devotions, attending the sacraments with mother and dad, and being understood as far as religion goes by both parents."

Joann then quickly added, "Is that a little strong?" She admits, "My advice has really turned into a sermon, but please forgive me, for I am writing from the bottom of my heart." In the end, however, she encourages Kaye to stay with Tom if she "feels that strongly about building a future with him."

It's difficult to say with any certainty what led to the end of Kaye's romance with Tom, but it's clear that Lina and Kitty remained steadfast in their hope that Kaye and Art would find each other once more.

The letters between Art and Kaye begin again in January 1948. All of Kaye's letters to Art, just like those of earlier years, no longer exist. But you can tell a lot from what Art writes in response.

Art opens with, "I still find it hard to believe that you wrote me. I've wanted to write many times, but I felt that my letters weren't wanted or perhaps that they might hurt…Many of my letters to you have ended in the scrap pile around my desk."

Revealing as to what was going on during his final year at P&S, Art writes, "I'm well into my senior year…it's rough, and many times it gets me down, but I'm still hoping to make it. I plan to enter medical school after I graduate, as medicine is still my love."

As for his home life, he writes, "Things here at home are wonderful. For some reason, the folks love me and treat me like a king…Dad is working very hard and the years are beginning to tell. Mom thinks of you often—it seems you captured her heart."

There is one other letter written in the spring of 1948. Art is kind and engaging, but the passionate tone of the winter of 1945 is still clearly absent. This letter, with the simple salutation of "Dear Kathie," wanders through a variety of topics, one of which was relating the surprise visit of Kaye's parents. "Mom didn't tell me that your folks had phoned and said they were coming over, so when our doorbell rang, I answered it and almost passed out. It was wonderful to see your mom and dad—they are just as I remembered them, two of the nicest people I have ever known. Seeing them brought back wonderful memories of days I wish were here again. I guess those were some of the happiest days I have ever known."

Sister Joann believes that it was during this visit that Kitty and Lina hatched another plan to push Kaye and Art a little closer. A present arrived for Art the week after his late July graduation…a gift that Art assumed was from Kaye, but Joann was quite sure was her mother's doing.

Art was amazed that Kaye had thought of him at all, convinced that, while they had become friends…that this was all they would ever be. If the graduation gift was the result of Lina and Kitty's plotting, it was apparently a late in the game Hail Mary pass that actually worked.

In one remarkable eight-page letter written on August 30, 1948, five weeks after his graduation from P&S, Art gave up all pretenses and poured his heart out. It is a letter that not only shows his mastery of language, but more importantly, the depth of his passion:

"Dearest Kathy,

I hope that this letter may express completely what I feel and have wanted to tell you for almost two years. I have just completed two years filled with nothing—no memories, no happiness, no plan for living. I only hope, as this letter unfolds, I can make you understand what I have wanted to write for so long…

"In order to make this letter understandable, I guess I'd better start at the beginning…when you came to see me in San Francisco (that year that I'd like to cut out of my life)…

"I don't know if you understand what happened, but I don't. I only realize that

I was to blame, but I can't understand my actions, my stupidity…What always stands out in my mind is that night at the airport when you left—it was a cold goodbye. I wanted to take you in my arms and tell you how I felt and never let you leave. Instead, I let you go—so many times I've cried thinking if I could only live those two weeks over again.

"About two months after you left, I wanted to write you, but I couldn't—call it pride—call it stupidity; I don't know! I have a long letter at home in one of my textbooks that I wrote back then to your mother, because I felt that maybe she could help and advise me. I wanted to write you, but I felt in my clumsy way I'd hurt you deeply, and that by writing I would only cause you more pain and that you would be happier if I left you alone. I can't understand why I didn't send that letter.

"…For two years my whole life has been incomplete. I've wondered what you were doing—I wanted to come and see you, but I was afraid I'd be unwanted… or that you were married or had found happiness with someone new, and I didn't want to spoil it.

"I have a confession, Kaye. I have loved you since I was eighteen—I have really never stopped loving you—I guess I'll always love you. I don't know if this means anything to you or not, but somehow I feel that it might.

"We had so much together, and I know we can find it again. My folks know how I feel, and they have urged me to write for a long time, for they think a great deal of you and have learned to love you. Mom mentions you all the time—many times she blames herself for what happened between us.

"…I'm sorry this letter is so poorly written. I only hope you can understand a little of what I've tried to write. Somehow, I just can't seem to write all that I feel—all the things you mean to me, that no one else ever could. I have lived two years of bitter unhappiness because I could never forget you. You have been a part of everything I have accomplished. I've worked hard only to try to forget that I didn't have you—that you had slipped away from me."

In this remarkable letter's final pages, Art goes on to tell Kaye of his future plans. He concludes by saying, "If, somehow, God has kept together our hearts without us knowing it, I promise you'll never get away from me again."

Kaye with Tommy in 1947.

Art, dating again, but still thinking of Kaye.

Art on the prowl, 1947 on
the beach at Lake Tahoe.

Kaye on the top step, next to
two of her three sisters: the
singing nun, Joann, and Patricia.

Chapter Seven

Giving It the Best in Us

During that two-year long winter in a relationship that has now spanned seventy years, Art immersed himself in a different kind of passion. He put his attention, and seemingly endless energy, into completing the final two years of his doctorate in dental sciences.

During a time when Kaye was not a driving passion in his life, the College of Physicians & Surgeons filled that gap. Those two years laid a strong foundation for his remarkable career in dentistry.

With the skilled hands of his grandfather, Vittorio, and the larger than life, embracing warmth of his grandfather, Benedetto, the boundless determination of his mother, Lina, and the open hearted kindness of his father Arturo, Art was perfectly suited to become a successful and popular student. At the same time, Art was blessed to have a faculty rich with talented instructors. During this time, he was not only vested with outstanding clinical skills, but with a deep pride in an industry that was arguably still in its infancy.

Throughout his long career as an educator, Art has consistently argued that what students are seeking from their instructors is not a "sage on the stage," but rather "a guide by their side." Art had several such brilliant guides at his side as a student at P&S, educators like: Ernie Sloman, Harry True, John Rhoads, Charles Sweet, Fred West, John Tocchini, B.C. Kingsbury Sr., Lyall Bishop, John K. Young, and many others.

The old building on Fourteenth and Valencia may have remained standing because of "termites holding hands," but on the inside, it contained an all-star cast of players. Starting, of course, with Sloman, and continuing with Kingsbury, who at the time was a member of the school's board of trustees and its treasurer; many of the future leaders of the dental profession were doing remarkable things inside this nondescript building.

Kingsbury was a strong proponent of the idea that P&S accept a total of eight students transferring in from V-12 programs around the country, most of whom were coming home to California. A future president of the American Dental Association, Kingsbury felt a special obligation to assist these new students.

Kingsbury was a master of prosthodontics, a specialty area of dentistry that focuses on maintenance and restoration of a patient's oral function, comfort and appearance. Lab work in dental prosthetics that P&S students had done in their second year was often done in the third year in most other four year programs. Thanks to Kingsbury and Tocchini, Art and his fellow V-12 transferees began to learn crown and bridge, some of the prosthetic work they would need to get up to speed in building appliances. "Kingsbury was so well versed in the field," Art recalls. "We were all very fortunate to have him as an instructor."

It wasn't just the area of prosthetics that Art needed help catching up in during that first year at P&S. "Courses of study never align perfectly from school to school, so we had areas we needed special attention to master," Art explained. It only encouraged him to work harder as he immersed himself in his studies throughout his junior year, while continuing his part-time jobs at the butcher shop on Saturdays and the boys club on weeknights. The loving embrace of family during this year when he was still twenty-one no doubt made a significant difference in his success.

Lina was a deep well of faithful encouragement. As for his father, Red showed his support by building a new room and study area for Art in the basement of their house on Potrero Hill. Not an easy task, considering he had to reconfigure the basement to accommodate his wine press and several wine barrels for aging his homemade product.

Art quickly made friends as well. Three of them were fellow V-12 transferees, Bill Allen from Washington University in St. Louis, Jim Lieb from Georgetown, and Steve Peck from Art's first dental school, Kansas City Western.

As Art recalls with a smile, his two closest friends, Allen and Lieb, could not have had more different personalities, "Bill Allen and I went to the greasy spoon on Fourteenth Street next door to the school for lunch each day, while Lieb would regularly go to the St. Francis for lunch. Lieb's aunt was heir to the Schrafft fortune." Schrafft, a Boston candy company begun in the mid-nineteenth century, grew into a large food service company, which owned a chain of restaurants throughout the Northeast, many of which were located in some of Manhattan's best locations.

All three men stayed close in the years after P&S. Lieb, Allen, and Art each entered practice as pediatric dentists mostly due to the influence of Dr. Charles Sweet, who chaired the school's pediatrics department. In fact, Bill Allen, Art's closest friend, helped him write many of those letters that Art explained later to Kaye, "never got mailed."

"Sweet was an extraordinary educator, who could motivate you to be better than you ever thought you could be," Art says. "He had this remarkable ability to reach you whether you were a student, a colleague, or a patient."

As a practitioner, he suggested if you treat a child like an adult and an adult like a child, you'll be successful. For children, that meant getting down to their height and not hovering over them. Children will act grown up if that is what you expect of them. As for adults, treating them like children meant giving them all the information they could possibly want. "An adult takes comfort," Sweet explained, "in understanding what you're doing and why."

Sweet was equally gifted in getting his students to do their very best. He motivated them with equal parts information, trust, and respect.

"Dr. Sweet came to me one day," Art recalled, "and said I have a special patient for you, and she needs your help. She has no secondary teeth under her four primary molars. The patient was just seven. I was asked to do gold inlays on all four of those primary molars. I cast these four inlays three to four times. By the time I was done, the inlays were like crowned jewels. They had to be perfect, and I knew that they were.

"Sweet called others in the clinic over to have them examine my work. It gave me a sense of pride and great accomplishment."

Hard work throughout the week made Friday evenings at Keneally's (the nearby Irish pub on Valencia between Fourteenth and Fifteenth Streets) all the more fun. Pictures in the P&S yearbook of these gatherings, known as the TGIF Club, "Thank God It's Friday," show a group of sixteen guys playing table shuffleboard and Art looking several years younger than most of his fellow students.

Art recalls going to the phone booth at Keneally's and calling his dad to ask if it would be okay if he brought home a couple of "starving fellow students." Red, who still made his living as a pastry chef at the St. Francis Hotel on Union Square, was a kitchen wizard. By the time Art—with Allen and Lieb in tow—would arrive at the Dugoni home, his friends were shocked by the dinners that awaited them. A roast leg of lamb and a chicken, and of course, it being Friday, the obligatory plate of fish. But for Lieb and Allen the best part of a visit to the Dugonis was Italian red wine and pasta.

Between school, work, and friends, that first year passed quickly. Art joined the student council and became a favorite with the student body and the faculty. At the start of his senior year, Art was elected, unopposed, as student body president. The seeds of a lifelong relationship with P&S and his fellow alumni had firmly taken root.

Along with Sweet, Art developed a close relationship with Dr. Harry True, the chair of the restorative dentistry department. "True loved me like I was part of his family," Art recalls. "I worked in his office on weekends in my senior year. I gave up my jobs at the butcher shop and the boys club because my workload was simply too great to continue. In the evenings, and on Saturdays, I learned a great deal working as his dental assistant. We were like a grandfather and grandson.

"I was very fortunate that he was always generous with his time. I had never treated a patient until P&S. When I began in the clinic, I don't know who was scared more: me or the patient?"

This was especially the case when it came time for Art to give his first local anesthetic. True was certainly the embodiment of Art's ideal of a "guide by your side."

In addition to his clinical wizardry, True was famous with his students for his long list of what they called "Truisms." These were sayings such as "It's not good enough unless it's the best you can do." Or, "One drop of ink will make a million think." The two forged a friendship that continued throughout the remaining years of Harry True's career and life.

Art found himself surrounded by a number of superb practitioners. The school's history of excellence in clinical dentistry is rooted in over a century-long tradition of alumni giving time back to the school by assisting students in the clinic. Mentorship has been a huge part of that success.

For Art, this tradition blended well with a pattern that began with Brother John McCluskey back at St. James High School and continued with Ernie Sloman and a team of great instructors. Art modeled his professional future on the wise words of Isaac Newton, "If I have seen further it's because I stood on the shoulders of giants."

Sweet and True were a great influence on Art. Leading by example, they created the awareness in him that educating future generations of dentists was noble and important work. Emerging practitioners are the lifeblood of the profession. Each new generation has an opportunity to shape the future of dentistry. As Art looks back on Sweet and True, he recognizes them also as pioneers of humanistic education. "Back then, the age of humanism in dental education was still more than thirty years off," Art explains. "But these individuals were very far ahead of their time."

One giant of the profession and a mentor Art had the privilege to meet as a student was Dr. Fredrick T. West, a 1917 P&S graduate, a pioneer in the field of orthodontics, and a former president of the American Association of Orthodontists. Art remembers him as both a doctor and an individual of great distinction. "For West, his word was his bond. Ortho was in its infancy but he was a man of great stature and integrity."

As Dr. Robert Boyd, the current Chair of Orthodontics at the school explains, "Fred West and Art Dugoni are the only two people to have earned both The William J. Gies Award for Vision (Innovation and Achievement for 'exceptional contributions to and support of oral health and dental education around the world') and the Albert H. Ketcham Memorial Award, given annually to 'an individual who has made a notable contribution to the science and art of ortho-dontics.' It's amazing to consider that these two giants of the profession were once teacher and student."

Two other key players in Art's years as a student at P&S were Dr. Lyall Bishop, a professor of oral surgery, and Dr. John K. Young, Chair of Pathology.

Art originally met Bishop during his time at Farragut Naval Training Base. "I had such a love of medicine," Art explains, "and Dr. Bishop appreciated that."

On his free days, Art would go to Bishop's practice area to help with extractions. "As a result, I'm pretty sure I did more extraction work than any of my fellow students...experience that would serve me well in the years immediately following my graduation."

Art admired Dr. Young's work in pathology because he was an inspiring teacher. "The whole field of pathology was new to me. And Young lit a fire under me to the point that I found it easy to get all A's in his course."

Young was a scientist with a PhD. He made Art realize, for the first time, that there existed a translatable environment between a particular science and its clinical application. Through Young, Art came to appreciate that pathology and other basic sciences had real meaning when applied to such things as peri-odontal disease. "When you bring science into the clinical world, it takes on an exciting new meaning. I have Dr. Young to thank for helping me to understand and appreciate that."

Years later, when he was once again a student, this time in a graduate program in orthodontics at the University of Washington, Art had an academic research-er ask him why his students didn't like him. Recalling the close relationship doctors Young, Sweet and True enjoyed with their students, Art turned to the professor and said, "You never take the time to go down to the clinic. Your students respect you as a scientist, but know that you are not involved in their clinical work, so they feel no connection to you."

As Art explains, "The vast majority of dental school students or residents will not become academics. Young, Sweet and True were examples of how that divide could be gapped between the dedicated scientist and the dedicated prac-titioner." It was a lesson that stayed with Art through his years of teaching and the twenty-eight years of his deanship.

All of these talented and generous faculty members found inspiration in the man who served as the school's dean from 1938 to the time of his death, in 1952. Art quickly realized Dean Sloman was the positive force that moved the institution forward. When Art's brother, William, age fifteen in 1947, started going regularly to the clinic to be his big brother's "guinea pig," Art confided in him, "One day I'll be the dean of this school." It seems that an abiding admiration for the sense of fellowship Sloman created at P&S, in which generations of dentists served as mentors to future generations of practitioners, was an important influence on Art's views as to the critical importance of educating young men and women who one day would create the future of dentistry.

* * * * *

In late 2012, Irwin Marcus, one of thirteen surviving members of the Class of 1948 sat down to discuss his friend of sixty-five years, Art Dugoni. He began by saying, "I think I was the first of his contemporaries to see the greatness in Art. There was nothing phony about him. He would have made a great leader in whatever profession he chose." At eighty-six, Marcus was admittedly, having to reach into the distant past to recall the work they did together during their final year as students at P&S. But some of their shared stories were still very vivid for him. As he recalls, it was just a few weeks after Art's election as student body president that Dean Sloman called Art into his office and told him that the printing of the student yearbooks had been running a deficit for many years that had now grown to $6,000. Art was stunned. This was a huge amount of money in 1948, when the minimum worker's wage was forty cents an hour.

The publication, *Chips*, was printed annually and each class paid enough to get their portion of the yearbook on press, but not enough to cover the entire cost. The staggering amount was the sum total of all those unpaid printing bills. A problem that Sloman, with his usual sense of humor, wanted to know what Art was going to do to fix.

Art's first thought was to wonder why he had ever been so foolish as to offer himself up for student body president. Of course, he knew that the problem was not of his making, but being the diligent young man who always rose to a challenge, he was determined to find a solution. After several days of thought, Art returned to Sloman and suggested that the school send a letter to each of its graduates asking for a small prorated amount to pay off the entire debt. Sloman wisely rejected that approach, explaining to Art his expectation to build a new school once he completed his hoped-for merger with Stanford University. He was not going to have Art, "chasing down alumni for their yearbook's old printing bills when we have something much bigger that will need their support."

Not easily deterred, Art came back with another plan a few days later. This time, he suggested raffling off a new 1948 Plymouth. Dr. Marcus remembers that the Plymouth auctioned off was from a dealership owned by one of his father's patients. As an aside, Irwin's father, a physician, was one of the last students to get a doctor of medicine degree from the College of Physicians & Surgeons.

"I can't remember what we paid for the car," Marcus says, "but we got a good deal." A safe guess is that a 1948 Plymouth at wholesale, new, cost $900, and today no one recalls what the tickets sold for. It was still a mountain to climb knowing that in addition to the cost of the car, the printing debt meant that nearly $7,000 would have to be made if the scheme was going to get the student organization out of debt.

With his usual zeal, Art leaned on students, faculty, staff and administration to sell tickets. Neither Art nor Irwin can remember how many tickets they personally sold, but Art can remember some of his classmates coming back to him with half their allotted tickets unsold. When Art told them he had sold double the allotted amount of tickets, they protested, telling him, "That's easy for you Dugoni, with the size of your family! You probably have over forty aunts and uncles living in North Beach alone."

While the exact math has faded over the years, it is known that the raffle met its goal. A very happy freshman, Thomas Moore, Class of 1951, won the new Plymouth, and a very happy Dean Sloman made sure that all those past-due printing bills were finally paid in full.

* * * * *

While at UMKC, Art turned to athletics, specifically playing for the basket-ball team, to escape the pressure of classes and his endless studies. But when he returned to San Francisco, he once more got involved in an old passion: oratory contests.

"One day, I saw the annual competition announced in the newspapers," Art said. "I wanted a shot at the prize money, so I went to Dean Sloman and told him that I needed the school to submit my name for the Hearst Oratory Prize."

Sloman was taken aback, but nevertheless amused. "We're a dental school," he exclaimed. "We've never had a student enter a competition like this before."

Art, quickly responded, "No reason we can't start now!"

Sloman, who always admired Art's seemingly boundless ambition, directed his secretary to prepare the necessary paperwork for the school's nomination of Art as their entrant in the contest.

"Because of Brother McCluskey," Art explained, "I first entered the Hearst Oratorical Competitions as a high school student. I gave over a thousand presen-tations in my professional life, and who knows how many lectures as an educa-tor, and my ease of presentation all started with those high school competitions."

Ease indeed. In the July 9, 1948 Bill Simons' column in the San Francisco publication, *The Monitor*, Simons wrote "About six years ago I participated as one of the judges in a speaking contest at St. James High School. I recall be-ing extremely impressed with a lad named Arthur Dugoni. I can't remember his subject, but I do remember his voice. It was a beautiful voice, clear and well-modulated, and he was easily the winner."

The night of the Hearst contest, Art asked several of his friends to come hear him speak. As luck would have it, Jim Lieb and Bill Allen walked in during the middle of his presentation, but Art stayed on task. "From up on the stage, I could hear their shoes squeaking as they made their way down the aisle search-ing for their seats."

Art would not let himself be distracted. His presentation was flawless in front of a sold out USF auditorium. There was a three-way tie for first place. The judges conferred for a second time and chose a Stanford student for first place, with Art coming in third. Nevertheless, Art was greatly pleased to win a hundred dollars, a huge sum for 1948.

The combination of an outstanding grade point average, his student leadership and oratory skills, made Art a natural choice for Valedictorian for the P&S Class of 1948. He used his valedictory address to caution his fellow students against developing a "9 X 9 mentality." As Art describes it to this day, "a nine foot by nine foot mentality overtakes your view of the world when you limit your professional life, and the larger world in which it exists, to the confines of your practice area." Art's message was to be cautious about the trap of practicing all the time because it greatly narrows your perception of the world. This was a defining statement that determined much of the universal view he had of his profession. It was a key motivating factor for Art's lifelong commitment to be involved in dentistry's various professional organizations.

Art began his address, true to his nature of not being a solo performer, by identifying himself as part of a bigger team: "I stand here tonight, the voice of thirty-two valedictorians of dentistry—each carries within himself a different feeling, a different message than I might express. However, I would find it difficult to believe that there is one of us here this evening who is sorry his course in dentistry is completed."

Taking the community, their chosen profession, and the larger world into account, Art says:

"We realize that the past four years have been filled with studies and hours of work and research and that perhaps, in many ways, we have neglected ourselves, our family, society, and our community. Remembering that we are part of the world and that we live in an age of social responsibility, rather than one of rugged individualism, we the class of 1948 promise to live in the world, not only as dentists aware of our professional obligations, but as citizens of this country and neighbors of the world.

"Our intention is not to bury our hearts and souls in the practice of dentistry so that we exclude all else, but rather to live, as well as to make a living. For the achievement of a career is not an end, but a means. A person may succeed as a dentist or a lawyer or a politician or a merchant, but fail as a man. To fail as a man is to fail in life, for the achievement of manhood is the ultimate purpose of living. If one gains all the rest and misses that, one has lost all."

Despite the male-centric language of his generation, this is a remarkably strong and prescient statement for a man just one month past his twenty-third birthday. In his closing paragraph, showing his typical oratory flourish, Art gives voice to a passion for his chosen profession that has influenced his entire professional life.

"Let us look to our profession…Let us give it the power and glory of high noon, the wisdom of evening, the peace of night, and the faiths of new mornings. I say, give it the best in us, for the best multiplied many times over shall return to us."

The days after graduation were a time of transition. He wondered about the graduation gift that had arrived from Kaye and he dreamed of the possibility that she might still be a part of his future. But, at that moment, their future was still more wishful thinking on Art's part than reality. For a young man with great ambition, the professional options were many. At that moment of uncertainty, Dean Sloman came forth with a suggestion.

Dean Sloman leading a meeting of the P&S Board of Trustees.

Harry True, who as Art recalls, "Treated me like a son."

B. C. Kingsbury, who pushed P&S to accept Navy V-12 students.

Fred West, one of several of the giants of dentistry who mentored Art.

Chapter Eight

An Officer and a Gentleman

Dean Sloman invited Art to his office to tell him the Navy had created a dental/ medical internship program for the first time. Art would spend six months at a west coast naval hospital, then be transferred to Bethesda Naval Hospital in Bethesda, Maryland, a suburb of Washington, DC.

Sloman had already prepared a letter of recommendation and told Art to head to naval headquarters straightaway because he knew there would be a limited number of slots available. As Sloman explained to Art, "The Naval Reserve is going to call you back in at some point in the future to work off the service you owe them for your years at Gonzaga and Kansas City Western Dental."

With letter in hand, walking down Market Street, Art ran into Gordon Ledingham, a P&S graduate from the class of 1947. He was working as an associate in a private practice in the city, but thought the internship sounded interesting and decided to go along with Art and put in an application of his own.

Art was accepted into the program and was quickly assigned to Oak Knoll Naval Hospital in Oakland in early August. Art lived on base, but was a short bus ride away from his home in San Francisco.

Work at the naval hospital was a very significant change from the work that Art had been doing at the P&S patient clinic. "It gave me a much stronger and practical medical background than I had gotten at the dental school," Art recalls of those six months spent at Oak Knoll. "A lot of the patients were recovering from injuries sustained during the war. There were complicated cases that presented a variety of different medical and dental challenges every day I was on duty."

It wasn't long before Art was also recruited as the captain of the naval hospital's basketball team. He got a hold of a Navy surplus World War II field ambulance, stripped it down and converted it into a team bus in which they traveled to other naval bases and nearby leading universities. Consistently, Art was the team's leading scorer.

Art quickly settled into a routine of long hours in the clinic, followed by his favorite release, a basketball game and or practice. It was at this time that Art, more confident and certain of his future than ever before, wrote that passionate eight-page letter to Kaye, finally and completely declaring his undying love for her.

To his great delight, Kaye responded expressing her certainty that they indeed had been meant for each other. So, Art took a bold step. Not wanting to ask for her hand in marriage by letter or by phone, Art flew to Spokane on a Saturday morning. Moments after he arrived at the airport, he was in Kaye's arms. As he placed a ring on her finger, he breathlessly asked, "Are you going to marry me or not?" At last, a couple again, the deal was sealed with a passionate kiss.

Later that day, when he went to Kaye's dad Russ to ask his permission, Russ said, "Did you ask her?" Art confessed that, of course, he had. Russ smiled and said, "Well that's a good start."

Later that night, Art and his future father-in-law were sitting on the front porch of the family home when Russ turned to him and said, "You'll never know true happiness until you get married." He paused for a time, and then with a wise smile and his understated sense of humor he added, "Then you'll realize it too damn late."

Art flew back to San Francisco and was back at Oak Knoll on Monday morning. The two young lovers decided to get married at the Groo family church in Spokane and set the date for February 5, 1949. The days between September and February, as Art recalls, flew past.

Not surprisingly, it snowed that day in Spokane. But that didn't seem to matter very much to either Kaye or Art, who only had eyes for each other. Photos of that day reveal a strikingly beautiful bride in a floor length gown of white and an equally handsome young man in a crisp Navy Lieutenant's uniform. Officiating at the wedding was Father James Linden, dean of the Law School and Art's favorite teacher during his year at Gonzaga, who had shown Art the quiet study room above the dorm where he had only that statue of St. Joseph to keep him company.

The ceremony took place on the campus of Gonzaga University at St. Aloysius. (Gonzaga is named in honor of St. Aloysius Gonzaga, the young Italian aristocrat who gave his life to care for victims of an epidemic that swept Rome in 1591.) That church had, in many ways, been a center of the Groo family's life since their arrival in Spokane.

With coats over their shoulders, Art and Kaye were photographed just after the ceremony standing on the top step of the church. Peeking through a church door window behind them is Lina, admiring the happy couple while smiling with delight.

It must have been a very special day for Art and Kaye's mothers. They knew for many years that these two young lovers were meant for each other. All their shared decades to come and the seven children born to this happy union, proved these two mothers right.

As Art said at a party in 2013, "In 1943 I met a young, drop-dead beautiful high school girl who took my breath away. Seventy years later, she still does."

After their wedding reception, Art and Kaye headed to Seattle. This 300-mile, five hour drive across the state of Washington was an ambitions undertaking for their first night together.

"We didn't get very far," Art explained, remembering their first night together as husband and wife. "We were twenty miles out of Spokane when I saw a motel and we stopped for the night. The next morning, Kaye complained about the sound of trucks going by all night. I told her that wasn't the hum of truck engines; that was me."

* * * * *

As planned, when Art began at Oak Knoll, he had orders to report to

Washington, DC following their February wedding. He used his military pay to buy a new blue Chevrolet. After seeing family in Seattle, San Francisco, and then visiting with Art's best friend, Bill Allen, in San Diego, the newlyweds began heading East through the deserts of Arizona and New Mexico and then the seemingly endless drive through Texas.

"We spent a night in Houston in a dive motel we regretted choosing and then pushed on towards New Orleans," Art said. "A couple of times along the way, Kaye asked to drive, but each time she did, I started giving her unwelcome advice. I suppose you could say that it was our first fight as a married couple. Kaye got pretty tired of my complaints about her driving. Outside of Lake Charles, Louisiana, she stopped the car in the middle of the road, threw up her hands and said: 'You drive!' She's been my 'navigator' ever since."

The problem with Art's driving, like that of most young men, was he kept refusing to stop. For years, Kaye complained that her only view of New Orleans was from the Huey Long Bridge traveling at fifty miles per hour, and that, as Kaye reminded him, was at night!

The trip used all of the two-week leave Art had been given before he was due to report to Bethesda. When they arrived in the DC area, they found an apartment in the basement of a large home in nearby Chevy Chase, Maryland. "It had no real kitchen, just a hot plate. But that was okay because neither of us knew how to cook," Art explained. "Most importantly, it was a place of our own, and that was what mattered most."

At Bethesda, Gordon Ledingham and Art met again. "The two of us were very successful because we had superior clinical skills and experience than the other residents, who came from schools all around the country. A number of the residents started asking us to help them with their cases, realizing that P&S graduates had a long tradition of excellence in clinical practice."

Years later, Ledingham, a man who proved time and again that he could quickly seize an opportunity when it presented itself, became one of the first dentists in America to advertise his services, and he created a chain of very successful dental practices.

At Bethesda, Art once again played basketball. His coach, "Fearless" Frank

Frates, who gave Art the nickname of "Brooms," because he consistently swept the backboard for rebounds, was also a graduate of P&S (1933). He told Art several years later that, if he had stayed with Bethesda for one more year, he was certain they could have won the Naval Championship. "Frates," Art explains, "was a career naval officer. He loved to golf, and he had enough clout with his superiors to win approval for a putting green to be built on the grounds of the naval base."

Bethesda was a postgraduate dental school. As Art says, "We were interns who had the advantage of working alongside dentists who were getting their advanced degrees in various dental specialties. Researchers and physicians regularly came over from the National Institute of Health and faculty from the University of Pennsylvania, including Louie 'the Root' Grossman, to lecture us on a broad range of health topics. I can still remember Grossman's presentation on culturing the root canals and using PBSC paste to sterilize the root. Two procedures he helped to develop and, at the time, they were perceived as being state-of-the-art, but in later years were proven to be ineffective. Nevertheless, Grossman was viewed, and rightfully so, as a legend in his time."

As a twenty-four-year-old, who still entertained thoughts of returning to school for his MD, Art was enthralled with the opportunities he was receiving to grow and learn during each day of his internship. Surrounded by scientists and researchers, Art became convinced of an increasingly brighter future for health care, one in which the impossible would soon become the possible.

If science was to enhance the health of all individuals through both prevention and treatment of disease, the secret most certainly would be found in molecular biology. Much of what we take for granted in today's healthcare was all just beginning to appear in the postwar years. It was during this period that researchers awakened to the reality that arterial blockage was undoubtedly related to diet and tobacco.

In 1948 the National Institutes of Health created a division specifically dedicated to dental research. "I was interested," Art recalls, "in the broader picture of health, and here were people talking about the prevention of disease and infection on a broad scale. It was exciting and inspirational for me to be a part of all this at such a young age."

Every aspect of life in Bethesda went well, save one: Kaye was miserable in Chevy Chase. "She had no friends," Art recalled. Determined to be both an officer and a gentleman to his bride, Art began to search for another residence and was delighted when he found what he believed would be an ideal apartment just a few miles east in Takoma Park, where several other naval officers and their wives lived.

"We moved into an apartment building that was owned by the Seventh Day Adventist Church," Art said. "Strangely enough, it had intercoms in each apartment that connected it to other apartments in the building. One night, I was snooping around the basement of the building and found all of these murals of female nudes buried under canvas cloths. It was part of my dental training from Dr. Sweet. He cautioned us to 'Always be suspicious and you'll always be alert.' The murals, of course, only deepened the mystery for me. Then, one night, Kaye and the wife of one of my colleagues called for a taxi so they could come meet us at the Bethesda officers' club for dinner. The cab driver picked them both up outside our apartment building and asked our wives: 'How's business girls?' It was over our dinner conversation that we realized that what prompted the driver's question was that the apartment building we were all living in had previously been a house of prostitution. We laughed a lot that night after we put all the pieces together."

Art and Kaye chose not to share the discovery of their apartment building's checkered past when Kitty and Russ arrived by train from Spokane a few weeks later to visit the newlyweds. After a week in the Washington area, Kaye's mom and dad decided they would take advantage of this once-in-a-lifetime opportunity of being on the other side of America and go see New York City.

Art very much wanted to see New York as well. So, he asked his commanding officer if he could join them, but his request was denied. "The night Kaye arrived in New York, having had no luck reaching me on our home phone," Art explained, "She sent a Western Union telegram to confirm their safe arrival. The next day, my commander changed his mind and told me to take a few days and join my wife and her parents in New York. I got in the car and started driving.

How hard could it be to find three people in the middle of New York City? Of course, I had no idea. But then, while I was driving, it occurred to me that the telegram she sent, while not stating where they were staying, was my only possible clue.

"I drove into Manhattan and my head was turning every which way to look at all the incredible sights, while keeping an eye out for the first Western Union office I came across. When I found one, I went in and asked if there was any way they could tell me where the telegram had been sent from. The office clerk looked for just a moment and wrote down an office in New Jersey near the Hudson River. He explained that every office had a code number imprinted at the top of the page, and that was how he knew. So, I went to that office; I think it was in Jersey City, and again I showed the telegram I had received and explained my situation. The office clerk had a record of the sender, Kaye Dugoni, who gave her local address as a motel in Hoboken. So, I went there. By then it was about eight in the evening; I went to the manager, and I suppose in my Navy uniform, I looked trustworthy. I got the room number and knocked on the door. I was proud of my detective skills, and she was shocked to see me standing there. She gave me what I think to this day is the world's most beautiful smile, and then she jumped into my arms."

Art and Kaye were both overwhelmed by New York City: The Plaza Hotel, Central Park, Rockefeller Center, the theaters, and the museums. "To both of us, it was a world of wonder. Kaye had never left Spokane except to go to Seattle, and for me, as a kid, a real adventure was a trip down to Menlo Park. Thanks to that cross-country drive, our view of America had greatly expanded, but nothing we had seen, including the nation's capital, had prepared us for the lights and excitement of New York."

* * * * *

After Bethesda, Art was assigned to Naval Station Great Lakes. Undoubtedly, it would be a surprise to many to learn that America's largest naval training facility is a thousand miles from the ocean. In fact, it's fifteen miles south of the

Illinois-Wisconsin state line and about thirty-five miles north of downtown Chicago. This massive training facility, founded originally on orders by President Theodore Roosevelt, has served the nation for over a century as the focal point for the training of US Navy recruits. At times, such as during the first two years of World War II, or the outbreak of war in Korea, the facility accommodated as many as 100,000 recruits taking part in the Navy's equivalent of Army boot camp.

Art continued his internship at Great Lakes and had, as he explains, "the opportunity to do incredible work." Many of the Navy's recruits came from rural communities and impoverished backgrounds.

"I had some eighteen-year-olds that needed every tooth in their head extracted. Yes, all thirty-two teeth. We would then make dentures for them. My clinical work was admired, and because I had excellent performance reports from Bethesda, they assigned me to a special small clinic to work on officers, their wives, and children. Kaye and I lived just a few miles from the base in Waukegan, Illinois, where Kaye worked as a medical technologist doing blood and lab work for a local hospital. We spent most of our free time getting to know the amazing city of Chicago."

It was when Art was at Great Lakes Naval Station that tensions between North and South Korea, as well as between the US and the Soviet Union and China, began to escalate dramatically. Art had not taken a leave for over a year, so his commanding officer, Admiral Curtis Shantz, called him in and told him to take thirty days and see his and Kaye's family in Spokane and San Francisco. They suggested that, after the leave, he would probably be given orders to ship out to a base somewhere in Asia.

Making $400 a month, Art explains, "I bought a new Buick and we headed to Spokane. I was quite a sensation there because I was dressed in a naval officer's uniform with one and a half stripes on each shoulder. We were there less than a week when orders came in saying that I had been assigned to the First Marine Division at Camp Pendleton Marine Corps Base in Southern California. I contacted my commander at Great Lakes to ask if I should leave immediately for Pendleton. I was told to stay put and enjoy the balance of my leave, because it might be my last for quite some time and that my formal orders would be sent with a date certain to report.

"But, when I got to Pendleton three weeks later, I was greeted by an angry Marine Corps executive officer who wanted to know 'where the hell,' I had been. My unit, by now, was halfway across the Pacific. Fortunately, those formal orders that arrived from Great Lakes showed that I reported on the date I had been given. That mix up in my orders was the only reason I spent the balance of my service time at Camp Pendleton, as opposed to on a carrier off the Korean coast or on the ground in South Korea."

At Pendleton, Art was placed under the command of Captain A.W. Borsum, who was an administrator, not a doctor. After a short period of time and evaluation of Art's records, he said to Art, "I'm not shipping you out to Korea, you're going to be my oral surgeon."

"That was when I told him," Art explains, "that his facilities did not meet the standard of modern day naval surgical practices. We had a vastly inadequate sterilization unit and no recovery beds, to name just two glaring deficiencies.

"Borsum told me to go down to the San Diego Naval Hospital, about fifty miles south of Pendleton, and see what they were doing. When I came back, I sketched out what the surgical suite and recovery areas should look like. In several weeks, it was built because things got done in a hurry on a major facility like Pendleton, particularly when there is a war on the horizon."

It was a good thing the remodeling was done so quickly because cases started coming in, not just service personnel returning from Asia, but others still stationed on or near the camp with fractured jaws, orbits and nasal bones resulting from auto or motorcycle accidents to bar brawls down in San Diego.

"Here I am, a twenty-four-year-old, doing oral maxillofacial surgeries and facing new challenges every day. I told Borsum that I was working on cases more complex than I had ever faced, and I was very uncomfortable because the doctors who were working with me in the clinic were officers that outranked me and were trained surgeons."

When Art discussed with the captain his discomfort over the situation, Borsum suggested he go to Santa Margarita Hospital on the nearby naval base and enlist the help of a new oral surgeon that had just joined the staff from the Mayo Clinic.

To Art's delight, he walked into the hospital and discovered that this new surgeon was Frank Pavel, who had been in the V12 program with him at Gonzaga.

"Frank and I started working cases together. I can remember meeting Frank in the private office an hour before surgery, going through textbooks to help us prepare for cases that we were about to face. It was both intimidating and exhilarating, and it's the kind of experience you can only get when staff and materials are stretched to the breaking point. You simply have to do the very best that you can.

"It was an amazing, but stressful time. Most nights, I stayed late at the clinic preparing for the cases I would be handling over the coming days. Still, I can't deny that I was relieved when, in the fall of 1951, the Navy sent notice that I had done the time that was required in exchange for my education at Gonzaga and UMKC, and I was to be honorably discharged.

"Before Kaye and I returned to San Francisco, I made the decision, once more, to go to medical school and pursue a career as a surgeon."

But, once again, Art's life took an unexpected turn. Back home in San Francisco, Art paid a visit to P&S to check in with Ernie Sloman. As you might suspect, Dean Sloman had a different suggestion about Art's next career move.

The new couple, both in uniform, at their new home in Bethesda, Maryland.

NUPTIAL MASS UNITES PAIR

A nuptial mass in St. Aloysius church united in marriage this morning Miss Katherine Groo and Dr. Arthur Dugoni Jr.

Double-ring wedding vows were read in a setting of white and pink roses. The Rev. James Linden was celebrant.

The bride wore a gown of white satin, fashioned with a long train, long sleeves pointed at the wrists and a sweetheart neckline trimmed in lace.

The full-length veil was trimmed in lace and fell from a Mary Queen of Scots headdress.

Follows Tradition

She wore pearls, a gift of the bridegroom and carried a pink and white arm bouquet. After the ceremony the bouquet was placed on the altar at Holy Names college, a traditional ceremony for brides who have attended that school.

Miss Patricia Groo was maid of honor for her sister. She wore a gown of aqua net over satin, styled with three-quarter length sleeves and a sweetheart neckline. Yellow flowers on her half-hat matched her colonial bouquet.

Bridesmaids were Miss Patricia Grenier and Mrs. Cyrus Kestell, also a sister of the bride. Mrs. Kestell wore blue net over satin, and Miss Grenier pink net over satin. Their gowns were styled to match the maid of honor's gown. They wore matching half-hats and carried colonial bouquets of roses.

The bride is the daughter of Mr. and Mrs. Russell P. Groo, E814 Mission.

Attending the bridegroom as best man was his brother, William Dugoni. They are the sons of Mr. and Mrs. Dugoni of San Francisco.

Ushers were Mr. Kestell and Ronald Etten. Music was by Gene Greif at the organ.

A wedding breakfast for members of the family and bridal party followed at the Francis Lester hotel.

A reception is planned for this afternoon at the hotel with Mrs. J. R. Brennen, aunt of the bride; Miss Jessie Johnston and Miss Mary Gallagher serving. Miss Marian Buckley is to be in charge of the guest book.

The couple plan to make their home in Bethesda, Md.

Art and Kaye, the newlyweds.

The Wedding Party including friends Ronald Etten and Patricia Grenier on either end, Patricia Groo, next to her sister Kaye, Father James Linden, Dean of the Law School at Gonzaga, Art, Mary Groo Kestell to the right of William Dugoni.

The newlyweds leave the church in Spokane with Lina close behind.

Chapter Nine

Moving Ever Faster

"John Tocchini has a practice in South San Francisco," Sloman began.

Art wondered silently, "Where in the hell is South San Francisco?" But he certainly remembered John Tocchini. In fact, Tocchini was so well thought of by Art, and his fellow students, they dedicated the 1948 issue of their annual yearbook to him: "In true appreciation of his loyal and valued services."

Tocchini was one of many alumni/faculty working part time or as uncompensated volunteers at P&S in what then was known as the Department of Operative Dentistry under the capable leadership of Dr. Harry True. Throughout the history of P&S this alumni/faculty corps sustained this private school that often operated on a razor thin margin between profit and loss. It was also this dedicated group of doctors that enabled P&S to establish its more than century-long reputation of producing highly skilled practitioners.

Tocchini worked at the school two and a half days a week, and then for the balance of the week at his practice. Sloman suggested that Art could switch off working as an instructor at the school part of the week and in Tocchini's practice the rest of the week. Tocchini's practice focused on all phases of restorative dentistry, but he had a special emphasis on pediatric care, which Art had gained experience in both at P&S and during his time at Great Lakes, caring for the needs of the base's officers and their families. This was well before pediatric dentistry became a boarded specialty–meaning the practitioner chose to limit their practice to a special area such as pediatrics, as opposed to being specifically prepared for that field.

During 1946, in Art's final months as a student at P&S, Sloman had secured four Quonset huts, post-World War II Navy surplus, which he placed on an empty lot P&S had purchased behind the school. One of those huts became a dedicated pediatric clinic, and it was there that Art first developed his interest in dentistry for children. Additionally, under the direction of Charles Sweet, the school offered a series of post-graduate courses conducted by Irwin Beecham and Fred West, all of which took place in these retrofitted Quonset huts. After completing several of these courses, Art joined the team as an instructor in advanced pediatrics and preventative orthodontics.

While Art was serving his second stint in the Navy, Dr. Sweet, one of Art's beloved mentors during his two years of study at P&S, became chair of the newly formed pediatric department. This served as an additional enticement for Art to return to P&S.

Art left the meeting with Sloman, however, thinking that this position with John Tocchini would be temporary and that he would still go on to get a medical degree in oral maxillofacial surgery. The income resulting from a part-time practice would help to support his further education and allow the young couple to buy their first home as well. Art knew this was a smart and practical choice. Additionally, Sloman's advice was difficult to set aside.

It was at this time that Art learned that his twosome was about to become a threesome. Kaye was pregnant with their first child, which, of course, made a significant change in their plans for the future. Over the next four years, Kaye and Art would have four more children. Certainly this was a time to put down roots, focus on making a living, and begin the process of building a lasting and successful career. With a mind now more clearly set on the practice of dentistry, Art jumped in with his usual determination.

As Art explains, "It was because of John Tocchini, who practiced both general and pediatric dentistry that I fell in love with pediatrics. We shared only Saturday mornings in the office together. Other than that, we rarely saw each other. When he was teaching at the school, I was seeing patients at the office, and then we switched for the balance of the week. It worked well, just as Sloman suggested."

For the first time in his early adult years, Art was making some real money and beginning to build a private practice of his own. Not long into developing his practice, Art decided to focus exclusively on pediatric dentistry. In 1952, he was one of the early dentists to step into that role.

* * * * *

Just ten weeks after his appointment to President Truman's Commission on the Health Needs of the Nation, Dean Sloman suffered a massive heart attack. After three weeks in the hospital, he was sent to Fresno for further rest with the hope that he could return to the school in early May. But, on the evening of April 30, 1952, the fifty-six-year-old dean suffered a second heart attack. This one proved fatal. The man who had done so much in his fourteen years to shape the future of P&S, and the profession of dentistry as a whole, was gone, and P&S was at a loss as to who would take his place.

The news hit Art on a deeply personal level. Art's affection for the late dean was ever-present, and ever-lasting. Sloman gave Art an opportunity to establish his qualifications at P&S when he first walked through the dean's open door in 1946. And Sloman's suggestion that he take advantage of the Navy's special post graduate program proved invaluable in shaping his future view of dentistry. Now, his entry into private practice and into teaching at the school was also the result of Sloman's thoughtful guidance. No single individual had a greater impact on the course of Art Dugoni's career than Dean Ernest Sloman.

Sloman's replacement was a longtime faculty member and a 1931 graduate of P&S, Ernest Frank Inskipp. A native of Bromley, England, he came to the United States in 1925. Like his predecessor, Inskipp had a devotion to the school that caused him to work long hours and worry endlessly about the financial stability of a school not affiliated to a major university such as Stanford. That was the merger Sloman had long hoped to make, but the details of a merger with Stanford ultimately eluded both of them.

Inskipp, a less charismatic, but nonetheless admired and beloved dean in his own right, served less than one year before being felled, as well, by a sudden and fatal heart attack. The great pioneer of orthodontics, Fred West, who had served as interim dean prior to Inskipp's appointment once again stepped in to fill the void, but personally had no intention of taking on the deanship permanently. Instead, the attention of the school's board now focused on Art's practice partner, Dr. John Tocchini.

Tocchini never doubted his devotion to the school's future, but was uncertain as to the financial practicality of taking on the position of dean. Tocchini asked Art what he thought he should do. He was making over $20,000 a year in his practice, and the deanship paid an annual salary of $12,000. Art told Tocchini, "You're more than capable of being dean, perhaps you can continue to practice at least one night a week and on Saturdays to supplement your income."

Tocchini spent the summer thinking about his next move. Meanwhile, he worked at a nearby shipyard on a boat he had been building for the past year. He told Art that if he needed to reach him by phone to please ask for Mr. Tocchini, fearing that should he ask for "Dr. Tocchini," the boatyard's owners might increase his fees.

After several more conversations with Dr. West, John Tocchini decided to accept the deanship, provided he could wait until after Labor Day, so that the work on his boat could be completed. In September of 1953 the San Mateo, California native became the fifth dean in the school's fifty-seven year history.

In one of his first messages to the school's alumni, Tocchini famously noted, "We have lost two great leaders because of heart attacks in the last two years. The board has now selected a younger and comparatively unknown man to be your dean. I suspect I was chosen because I've been told that I don't have a heart."

* * * * *

Just two years later, in his personal business life, Tocchini made another major decision: to build a new building that he would populate with other dentists. The new building was located at 225 Spruce Avenue in South San Francisco, just a half block away from Tocchini's original office, in a building owned by Horace "Sparky" Wald, MD, where he had first leased space back in 1938. Art was the first that Tocchini asked to take a space in this new building. Art agreed, but wanted to design an office where he could have more practice chairs. As Art saw it, "I'm teaching. I have access to the best new graduates, why not invite them to practice with me?" This was his first step in developing a group practice concept.

In this new building, Art decided he would identify himself solely as a practitioner of pediatrics. His new shingle told the story:

"Arthur A. Dugoni DDS, Dentistry for Children"

"This was the first opportunity for me to consider how I would design my own practice. I chose to create a central lounge/reception area with three practice areas: hygiene, surgical/dental offices, and lab area." This was the seed for a much larger group practice facility that Art would establish ten years later. All of this seems like a pretty standard approach, given the perspective of dentistry's modern era, but it was a big step away from the individual practice, single chair model, that dominated dentistry prior to the 1960s.

Art and his associates, Sidney Francis (P&S '54) and John O'Donnell (P&S '53) practiced in the Wald building, paying rent. They became individual practitioners in a new group setting in the Tocchini building on Spruce Avenue.

* * * * *

Art's involvement as an instructor at P&S was ongoing from the time of his return from the Navy. During this first decade of his professional practice, a pattern emerged that would become clearly defined with each passing decade of his long and remarkable career. Art had an insatiable appetite to take on new challenges. In each area he decided to enter into, he was constantly a man on a mission. He never allowed his interests or his attention to be deferred. The first of these challenges was his involvement in the development of a high-speed handpiece and the practice enhancement made possible by quadrant dentistry.

"As I was developing my skills as a teacher, the first area we decided needed changing was the speed of the dental handpiece," Art recalled.

"In 1950, a handpiece moving between 5,000 and 6,000 revolutions per minute meant a much higher level of vibration and difficulty for the practitioner as well as considerable noise and discomfort for the patient. We experimented with a system of larger pulleys and wheels that would increase the speed of the handpiece. Higher speeds could eliminate much of the jarring and vibrations for patients, and dentists, both of whom were subject to the problems of slower moving handpieces. The double pulley in the new handpiece, developed by the Midwest Company, took us up to 35,000 rpm. That was a substantial improvement, but we soon realized that this higher speed was just the tip of the iceberg."

By early December 1956, San Francisco newspapers were carrying numerous feature stories about an advance in dentistry that took drill speeds from 6,000 to 100,000 rpm.

And Art was pictured in many of those articles working on a young patient with this new, "almost painless" drill. Each article talked about a South San Francisco dentist, "Dr. Arthur Dugoni." In the *San Francisco Examiner* he was quoted explaining this new advancement in dentistry to the general public:

"These new instruments develop speeds of more than 100,000 revolutions per minute…They have ushered in a completely new era of patient comfort, due to the elimination of vibration. Used with a minimum of pressure and a brush-like motion, the patient is unable to perceive the cutting action…No claim is made for completely painless drilling, but increased speeds result in much less tension and fatigue for patients."

Between 1951 and 1961 the dental handpiece made incredible advancements leaping from 5K to 400K rpm. That changed the entire nature of restorative dentistry for two major reasons: one, it made patients far more comfortable allowing a practitioner to work on multiple teeth during a single appointment; two, the reduced vibration and higher speed allowed the practitioner to be more productive.

"In the Quonset hut, I had an ongoing clinical research workshop utilizing many different air driven handpieces," Art recalled. "We went from a heavy application of force to working with a feather touch. I was fortunate to be in the right place at the right time. I was teaching the full spectrum of restorative dentistry. This fed into my hunger to do more and to be more engaged."

The dental industry jumped into the pursuit of better and faster handpieces because it was clear that the future of dentistry was moving in this direction. With their funding and research capabilities, Art and his team of students tested and retested a variety of handpieces.

"It was an exciting time with eight different private companies developing, not just new higher speed handpieces, but the water cooling and particle evacuation systems essential to the operation of this new generation of handpieces. I was asked to evaluate a new water turbine handpiece by the National Institute of Dental Research and the ADA's research department.

"In a variety of clinical applications, I was a facilitator in the process, in many instances, being the first person to use this type of equipment." Art worked with a team of eight students on various approaches to the best uses of this new instrumentation. "We would respond to the manufacturers on their prototypes and telling them what changes we'd like to see."

During this exciting time, Art presented over seventy-five papers and lectures on the subject of high-speed handpieces. One of these presentations brought Art to the UCSF School of Dentistry. Attending the lecture was Dean Willard C. Fleming, who had been the school's dean since 1939 and who met with Art in 1946 regarding his possible transfer from UMKC into UCSF. A meeting, as previously mentioned, that did not go as expected and led to Art's first meeting with Dean Sloman.

Helped along with the advent of high-speed handpieces, quadrant dentistry (working on an entire section of a patient's mouth at the same time as opposed to a single tooth) was developing during this time, and there was a widening gap between what was happening at P&S in clinical application and what was happening in dental practices around the nation.

In teaching, Art was loyal to doctors True and Sweet and admired them greatly for their brilliant work and the contributions they made to dentistry. At the same time, Art knew that changes in the rapidly evolving field of modern dentistry had begun to pass them by. Art started teaching the new approach of quadrant dentistry. Doing three or four restorations at a time was not being taught in the main clinic, but back in the Quonset hut, it was. Utilizing one of the four portable buildings that Sloman had bought from the Navy, Art pushed the envelope forward, certain that this was the new direction in which dentistry was moving. Art created a specialty clinic with a total of twelve chairs. Quadrant dentistry and high-speed handpieces were here to stay!

"We would do a pre-restorative quadrant impression," Art explained. "I refined a technique, developed by Dr. Tocchini, to use custom matrix bands and an anatomical wedge that allowed us to duplicate the ideal anatomical form of the tooth that was originally there prior to cavity preparation."

Quadrant dentistry led to even bigger challenges that Art took on with his usual sense of confidence.

"It was not uncommon to have pediatric patients who needed multiple restorations," Art recalls. "Often, this work was more easily accommodated in a hospital. So, I worked with Tocchini on getting needed crowns prepped and completed on a simulation basis. I would take an impression of a child's mouth, then pour up and produce medal models. I would mount these models of their mouths on articulators, and then I would cut the crown preparation on the models. Then I fabricated the crowns on these models, so they were ready to be used at the time of hospitalization.

"The common aspect to all this work—high-speed handpieces, quadrant dentistry, crown preparation, and crown fabrication—was that the patient could be moved through the treatment process far more quickly. A lot of this was moving far too fast for some of my early mentors. I learned at an early age how easy it is to become mired in the past. It's a lesson I have tried to remember throughout my career, both as a practitioner and as an educator."

* * * * *

In the late '50s and early '60s, another aspect that became a hallmark of Art's career in dentistry started to take shape. He began moving "up through the chairs" in the San Mateo County Dental Society. In late 1959, he was elected president of the society, prompting South San Francisco's *Enterprise Journal* newspaper to call him "the youngster president."

For over four decades, Art served in a variety of dental associations and societies. From president of the California Dental Association to president of the American Dental Association; from president of the American Association of Dental Schools to president of the American Board of Orthodontics to president of the American Dental Association Foundation and to treasurer of the FDI (the World Dental Federation.)

Art decided early in his career that if you wanted to have input in the direction of your profession, you needed to be a part of the conversation that determined policy and set the course for future state and federal legislation and ultimately regulation. "If you care about matters that affect you and your practice, you should take a seat at the table and join the conversation," he would tell colleagues and students alike. "Don't complain about your state legislature changing the rules of your profession if you don't have the time or interest to join in the debate."

His inclination to assume a leadership role, of course, began much earlier in his life. At Gonzaga, at age eighteen, Art served on the student council, ran for student body president and lost his first election by one vote to a student who became a life-long friend, Mike Paioni. He also served as the editor of Gonzaga's student newspaper. Four years later, as previously mentioned, he served as student body president at P&S.

Some of this was a result of Art just being Art. Other factors were likely his immigrant upbringing, which constantly served as a reminder that being able to "take a seat at the table" and join in the conversation and the debate was both a privilege and an opportunity not to be ignored. In the old world, you were born into a ruling class that presented you with the right to speak on the topic of governance, or you were simply shut out of the process. In this new world, each individual had an opportunity to define their own role. The path was open to those who had the desire and the ambition to travel down that road. Art always viewed it as a privilege, and he treated it as such.

Another factor is that Art embodies many of the characteristics of what journalist Tom Brokaw called "the Greatest Generation." This is a generation of Americans who grew up in the years of the Great Depression and served their nation during World War II. FDR famously said, "This generation of Americans has a rendezvous with destiny." They most certainly did!

Brokaw, perhaps better than any other, described the men and women of this generation:

"It is a generation of towering achievement and modest demeanor, a legacy of their formative years when they were participants in and witness to sacrifices of the highest order. They know how many of the best of their generation didn't make it to their early twenties, how many brilliant scientists, teachers, spiritual and business leaders, politicians, and artists were lost in the ravages of the greatest war the world has seen."

Many of these characteristics are apparent in Art. Not the least of which is that striking combination of "towering achievement and modest demeanor." In spite of the loving embrace in which he spent much of his early childhood on Glover Street, he saw the bread lines and the job lines. Success never came easy, as his mother preached to all her children. But certainly it was there for those willing to work tirelessly to achieve success.

You can better understand Art's generation by watching some of the classic films of the 1940s and 1950s. In a genre called "film noir," Hollywood produced hundreds of movies in which a person of worth is faced with a moral dilemma, and the plot turns on his or her decision to follow the right or wrong path.

What began with his involvement in the San Mateo County Dental Society took root and blossomed in the body and soul of a tireless worker who came to see the betterment of his profession, and its role in society, as one of the key contributions of his life's work.

"I realized that this was how I would have the most positive impact on my profession," Art explained. "Attending the meetings of these organizations was essential to how we could preserve and enhance the profession. Not to mention promoting good oral health. In practice, these organizations serve not just the profession, but they are also critical to improving public health."

In an early example of public outreach, the San Mateo group under the direction of Drs. Robert John and Richard Burns, took an old bus and converted it into a brush mobile. The bus went from one county school to another, and entire families learned a lot about oral health and the prevention of oral disease because of these efforts. This was Art's first opportunity to see the dramatic difference that thoughtfully organized outreach programs can make.

In total, the San Mateo Dental Society had 300 members. "Of that number," Art says, "about forty of them made the organization hum." It was a reminder to Art that organizations move forward and achieve goals because of a select number of volunteers who make things happen. It took eight years for Art to move up through the chairs and become president of the organization. In doing so, he used all the personal and organizational skills that he started to cultivate back at St. James High School. Learn the names of your colleagues, and learn something about their families and their professional interests.

"People support people who they feel a connection with," Art explained. "When you cultivate those connections by doing little things like serving as a bartender at your local society's social events, you meet people," he explains. "Volunteer to make someone a drink, and you just made a new friend."

Back at P&S, often instructors would work until five and then head home. Not Art. Come seven in the evening, he'd still be working with students. There was always more to be done, more to be accomplished, more students to teach, reach, and inspire. Art never walked away from taking on bigger challenges. Just like those high-speed drills, Art's life was moving at an increasing speed. To his way of thinking, that was just fine.

As president of the
San Mateo Dental Society, Art
invited inspiring speakers like
Dr. Julio Lawrence Bortolazzo,
an early advocate for community
colleges as a "path out of poverty."

John Tocchini, Sloman's
successor as dean, and
Art's first practice partner.

Dr. Dugoni, '48 Displays New High-speed Equipment

Philosophy of High-speed Teaching for Undergraduates

By Arthur A. Dugoni, D.D.S.*

Our generation has been fortunate to live in an unparalleled age of scientific, cultural, and economic advancements. In dentistry there has been comparable progress, and foremost has been the development and utilization of increased rotational speeds. Modern dentistry in the eyes of public acceptance has achieved a new look. These significant ad-

* Assistant Clinical Professor of Operative Dentistry

vancements have stood the test of clinical application and have evolved beyond mere experimentation, and now function as standard, accepted procedures in the majority of dental offices throughout the country. The impact upon the dental profession, and the public acceptance and demand for increased speeds has aided in motivating the expansion of our

teaching program; however, the prime reason for including increased speeds in undergraduate teaching is the advantage of producing the highest quality dentistry with increased comfort to the patient.

Recently, the dental college received a gift of nine air turbines from the Ritter Dental Manufacturing Company. They have been installed in the special clinic section of the annex, along with the following six turbines on consignment as a high-speed research project: one Midwest, one Weber, one Starflight, and one Densco. In expanding our teaching on the use of increased speeds, the availability of such equipment has provided the main impetus. During the past few years, students have utilized equipment in the main infirmary capable of speeds up to 45,000 r.p.m. The main source of information concerning the equipment and techniques related to speeds of up to 300,000 r.p.m. consisted of lectures and demonstrations. It is now possible to provide the clinical approach to these increased speeds.

The junior amalgam special clinic has been expanded to include the present senior techniques in order to allow the conversion of the senior section to a high-speed course designed to acquaint the student with the thoughtful, correct use of increased speeds and the modern approach to multiple restorations. Working under close supervision of an instructor, the students will be familiarized with the increased efficiency and cutting action of the ultra-speed instrument. This will be initiated on full arch-mounted extracted teeth. The initial loss of tactile sense, due to the ability of the instruments to cut with very light pressure, will be redeveloped by continual practice. Instrumentation and procedures will be systema-

tized to complement their increased effectiveness. After sufficient laboratory experience, patients with carefully selected cases allowing the maximum of visual perception will be operated upon.

The following concepts relative to increased speeds will be developed:

1. More effective treatment planning and scheduling to take advantage of the increased efficiency. Patients will tolerate longer appointments, due to the decrease in the actual cutting operation.

2. Planned cavity preparations and procedures in advance are vital to eliminate unnecessary loss of sound tooth structure.

3. The combining of conventional speeds, variable speeds, and hand instruments to produce dentistry of the highest caliber.

4. Continuous water-spray cooling is essential for maximum pulp protection, efficiency of cutting and visibility. Techniques will be emphasized that include the utilization of auxiliary personnel and high-velocity suction.

5. Light, gentle pressure and continuous planing of the tooth structure is vital to produce a well-defined, smooth cut as well as control of temperature rise. Lightness of hand and decreased pressure lessens patient apprehension and affords the operator greater control, due to the lessening of physical fatigue.

6. The decrease in perceptible vibrations lessens the annoyance factors both to the patient and the operator.

7. The time saved by the use of increased speeds is only a very slight advantage when considering

(Continued on Page 39)

— 34 —

— 35 —

One of Art's early articles on high-speed technology.

On camera discussing high-speed technology, dentistry's "new frontier."

Chapter Ten
Taking a Different Path

Like those new handpieces, the 1950s seemed to move along at blinding speed. That's no surprise considering the rapid pace of change in Art and Kaye's personal and professional lives. By 1959, the young couple had five children. Steve, who was by then seven, was followed by Michael, age six, Russell, five, Mary, four, and Diane, three. Art and Kaye's growing family moved into a bigger home at 932 Rosewood Drive in San Mateo.

"Basically," Art says, "I was making a living restoring the cavities of children ages four to sixteen. In fact, in 1952, when I first entered practice, it was not unusual to have children at age six who needed a filling in every tooth."

But, by the late 1950s, there was a big shift toward prevention of tooth decay. In part, that change came about as a result of the debate over adding fluoride to municipal water systems. Another factor was increased awareness on the part of parents to what truly constituted good oral hygiene, including dietary and preventative measures against dental decay.

"I was enamored with orthodontics, and now I had the added encouragement of seeing the base of my dental practice beginning to change. I had patients coming to me who needed no work, and I thought orthodontics offered a lot of interesting challenges from the scientific, diagnostic, and clinical aspects of the work."

Art was taken by the science of moving teeth through bone. Pediatric dentistry was wonderful, but not the challenge he felt in the practice of orthodontics. There was also that oral surgeon awakened inside of him during those long working days at Camp Pendleton. If he could rise to that level of performance, certainly he could take on the challenge of pursuing a specialty degree in ortho-dontics with five children and at thirty-six years of age.

Art and the legendary pioneer in orthodontics, Dr. Fred West, had an on-going dialogue concerning the direction of Art's career. Art would speak of his interest in pursuing a future in orthodontics, and as Art recalled, West would say, "No! You're building a great reputation at the school, and one day you'll be the chair of restorative dentistry. You're going to follow in the footsteps of Harry True, perhaps even be dean of this school one day."

In 1960, Kaye became pregnant with what Art and she anticipated would be their sixth child. But, five months into the pregnancy, Kaye suffered a miscar-riage. "That was a life-changing moment for both of us," Art recalls. "The baby we lost was a little boy, and it was one of those times that makes you think life is just too short to not do what you really want to do."

But when Art went to John Tocchini to tell him that he was leaving the school to pursue a master's degree in orthodontics, Tocchini shrugged off Art's idea and said, "Art, I want you to stay here and chair the department of restor-ative dentistry. To that offer, Tocchini attached an $18,000 salary, a handsome sum in the early 1960s. Art gave the offer some thought. He loved teaching, and this was the department chaired by his old mentor, Dr. Harry True. Succeeding him would indeed be an honor!

Like every other crossroads Art ever confronted in his life, he prayed for the patience and wisdom to make the right decision. In the end, Art could not resist the more challenging path. It was an enormous leap of faith...leaving a successful practice and leaving teaching at P&S, turning down the chair of the department of restorative dentistry, and renting his home in San Mateo for a period of two years. Not to mention uprooting a family with five children, the oldest of whom was not yet ten, to resettle in Seattle and, once again, become a student. But, if he could indeed win acceptance to the University of Wash-ington's orthodontics program, he would take the plunge. Art knew he was at a crossroads, and he certainly had, as he had shown so many times before, the courage of his convictions.

After years of Fred West talking him out of leaving restorative dentistry, Art went to him and said, "You're not talking me out of this again. I'm going to be an orthodontist!"

Seeing that Art was determined to take a different path, Fred West wrote a letter of recommendation for Art to the University of Washington. "I had no idea until after I joined the program in Seattle," Art says, "that the University of Washington had 600 applications for their graduate program in orthodontics and a total of ten positions. It's not surprising, however, given the fact that it was probably, at that time, the finest orthodontics program in the United States. I didn't know it back then, but I was indeed at the right place at the right time."

As you might suspect, with his course now set, Art moved quickly. To start, he needed a buyer for his practice, so he picked one of the best and the brightest of his students in pediatric dentistry at P&S, Charles Bona, who was graduating with the class of 1961.

"This was a time," Art says, "when almost no one looked to sell their practice. But I did, and I sold it with all the equipment. I knew Chuck was honed and industrious, and a good Catholic boy as well." Art suggested that Bona send him $333 a month. Art had no set idea of what Bona's monthly payment should be, so he suggested a number, "I picked it out of thin air. I was thinking of the holy trinity."

In addition, Art had saved fourteen thousand dollars. The San Mateo house carried a mortgage of $25,000 and, fortunately, the rental price was able to cover the monthly payment. In addition, Art asked Chuck to send him money every month that came into the practice from his accounts receivable."

With the entire family in tow, Art left for Seattle several months before the program began, so he could find a home to rent and help get his growing family settled. He started by going to where he would feel most at home, far away from home, at the Jesuit church near the UW campus. The priest there helped Art find a rambling old house that had been built in 1900 in the city's Capitol Hill neighborhood.

The house had three stories with an ancient coal furnace in its basement that was half the size of Art's old living room back on Glover Street. The entire third floor of the house was nothing more than a large unfinished space. The house had a carport that Art suspected might fall down with the first winter storm that year. But the price for the home was right, and the location was three blocks from a Catholic school that was adjacent to the local church.

Art had a lot of work to do. He began by going down to the local pharmacy where he got the owner to give him a half-dozen old fountain stools that he took and recovered. He then went to the lumberyard and created a breakfast room bar in the pantry for a row of five kids. He bolted the stools' porcelain stands to the floor. After that, he attached the custom built counter to the wall. "Both Kaye and the kids loved it, and they loved that old house," Art recalls.

Next, Art tackled the carport. Not satisfied with the location of the existing carport in the rear of the house, he tore it down and built a new carport on the side of the house. Totally, the house in Seattle's then up-and-coming Capitol Hill neighborhood cost $18,000, a house which forty years later was worth over two million dollars. But, in the '60s, Art was unable to sell the house when he completed his studies at UW and prepared to return to San Francisco. He rented it instead and a year later finally sold the house for exactly the $18,000 he had invested in it.

Art prepared for the master's program in orthodontics, which he started in September 1961, with his usual vigor. Once one of the youngest students in dental school, now at thirty-six, Art was the oldest student in UW's graduate program. Even with a family of five children, however, he was still a force to be reckoned with, earning just under a straight-A average in his first full term.

Six months after Art began the program, he received a four-page letter from his old mentor, Dr. Harry True. It's a letter Art has kept for over fifty years. In it, True confessed that he "selfishly wanted to cry because we were losing you, but when I realized what was before you and knew you would make a grand success of whatever you would undertake, just like you always have, I began to be pleased and proud of you."

The letter meant so much to Art because he knew that his decision to leave restorative dentistry, as both a practitioner and an educator, had disappointed a lot of people, but his relationship with Harry True was much like the bond he had formed with Dean Sloman. These two giants in their respective fields had done so much to nurture and encourage Art's success. Both of these men served as role models for Art, and their kindness and caring about his professional future encouraged Art to always take the extra time to care about the careers of those following him. Art borrowed from their example and passed it forward.

In his second and final year at UW, John Tocchini came up to see Art and offered him the chairmanship of the school's orthodontic program. Dr. Forbes, who had headed the program at P&S, was leaving, and John thought Art was the perfect candidate to take his place. Art said he would consider it, and he went to the chair of UW's orthodontic department, Alton Moore, seeking his advice. Moore felt certain that Art would do well at any challenge he took on. Moore explained that he had come as a graduate student directly out of the University of Illinois when he took the helm of UW's ortho department. "Moore, who was a great educator in his own right," Art explained, "encouraged me to take the position, assuring me that I would find it both challenging and rewarding."

Art had the additional encouragement of knowing that Moore had created an ortho program that was well-regarded nationally by clinicians and educators alike. Art found the program both "stimulating and invigorating." Each night, Kaye would take Art's notes and type them up. In this, as in every challenge they faced, they worked closely together as partners in developing Art's career.

To Art, the most engaging aspect of UW's graduate orthodontics program was the way in which it tied in all the academic programs at UW that were master level courses…programs like child psychology and anthropology. Students additionally were required to take statistics to help in their own work and to interpret research studies in orthodontics.

Art applied his usual focus and determination to the program, getting up as early as four in the morning to study, and being rewarded with excellent grades. As he explains, "The program inspired me to do my best. My master's thesis researched the growth rates of children between the ages of three and eight in a total of 136 patients." Art took seventy-two points in the skull and tracked them over time to prove statistically that his assumptions were correct. His finished work cited over 120 articles and drew twenty-four conclusions. The thesis ran 400 pages, and is today enshrined on a shelf in the orthodontics department at the University of the Pacific's Arthur A. Dugoni School of Dentistry.

In the 1940s and '50s, orthodontics was primarily practiced on children ages eleven to thirteen. Art believed strongly from his pediatric practice experience that, in certain cases, corrective intervention should be attempted on children much younger. Art asked, "Would an orthopedist allow a malformed foot to continue its growth without intervention until pre-adolescence? Should we allow a child with a retrognathic mandible to be ignored until age eleven or later? I didn't think so, and today we practice early intervention."

Art graduated in June, 1963. He made the decision to accept Tocchini's position. After graduation, Art stayed through July and August working at UW, copying syllabi and preparing materials for the program he would lead at Physicians & Surgeons, now newly merged into UOP and renamed as the University of the Pacific School of Dentistry.

Art and Kaye returned to their home at 932 Rosewood in San Mateo, bringing with them the newest addition to their family, Arthur Jr., who had been born during their time in Seattle. The couple decided to name their sixth child after Art's dad, Arturo, who had succumbed to colon cancer in March 1962 at age sixty-four.

Red's decline came about suddenly. And, typical of the time, the dire nature of his illness was kept from him. Evelyn stayed with her father through most of his illness and neither Art, nor William, who was also in school completing his Doctor of Pharmacy degree, were able to make it home before Red slipped away.

Their mother, Lina, who would continue to be a powerful and influential presence in the lives of her children and grandchildren, lived nearly one hundred years. She never remarried, but rather remained a widow for the balance of her forty-one years.

Art in Seattle, a full-time ortho student and a part-time handyman.

Kaye happy to have a kitchen for six kids with one more on the way.

Chuck Bona, who took over Art's pediatric practice, at dinner with Art.

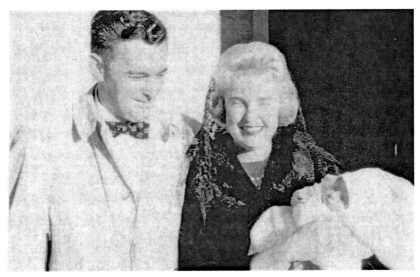

Art and Kaye with number six: Art Jr., after his Baptism in Seattle

Chapter Eleven
A Go-to Guy

It's easy, with the hindsight of history, to look back on the life and career of Art Dugoni and imagine that he led a charmed existence. That's more fantasy than a true representation of Art's life. Art was the ultimate alchemist, regularly turning lemons into lemonade.

Often, he was presented with unanticipated events and unwelcomed consequences. Through it all, his continued success was more a result of a deeply resourceful and powerfully creative mind. On a football field, Art would have been a remarkably agile running back who seemingly had his forward progress stopped only to break through and gain another ten yards.

Case in point, that "$18,000 a year position as chair of the P&S Orthodontics Department." An offer made by John Tocchini that would supposedly be waiting for Art when he returned from Seattle. It was the reason Art stayed in Seattle during the summer of 1963 preparing materials for his new position at Pacific's School of Dentistry.

Unfortunately, Tocchini did not have the same budget come August of 1963 as he imagined that he would have had when he discussed the position with Art more than a year before the merger with Pacific.

Upon his return to San Francisco, Art was offered a salary of $1,500 per year to chair the department part-time. That was utterly unfeasible for a man approaching forty with a home, a wife, and six children. Fortunately, the transition back to the Bay Area for both Kaye and the children went well. Art, a classic stoic male of his generation, was reluctant to share this bad news with Kaye. In Art's generation, and for all those that preceded his, the wife raised the children and maintained a lovely home, and the husband made sure that, when it came time to pay the bills, the needed money was on hand.

"I went back to Fred West for advice," Art recalls. "West described the decision as obvious, 'Do what you have to do!' he said. 'You've got a growing family to support and they're always your first priority.'"

To this day, Art is uncertain as to how or why John Tocchini missed his budget projections so badly…and why Tocchini didn't reach out to him prior to his return from Seattle to explain this new reality. But Art never blamed the dean, knowing that the merger with Pacific had completely changed all of his previous projections. And, undoubtedly, the dean had more on his plate than just one department and one disappointed faculty member. Regardless of blame, Art's plans were turned upside down.

It was time for a go-to guy to get going, so Art accepted the new reality and suggested that he work in the ortho department, as chair, two days per week. Of course, Art had a different definition than most of us as to just what two days a week meant. Since Art typically arrived at the school before six in the morning and did not leave until eight in the evening, he managed to put in close to thirty hours in his "two-day" work week.

Art didn't have the money to buy into a new practice, so he restarted his practice by sharing the office of Jess Henriques, who became another one of his many lifelong friends. Henriques, a general dentist, invited Art into practice with him at 100 Arroyo Drive. In time, Jesse and Art bought the building, and Art created his own separate orthodontic practice.

Remarkably, in less than a year, Art was onto a much bigger plan, this time to build what he called, the "Mayo Clinic of the west." Art pushed this plan forward by working long days at his practice and crunching numbers at night. In his typical fashion, one door had closed, so he pursued an alternative path with equal vigor. Certainly, there must have been periods when he felt discouraged, but Art's pattern was always to minimize any and all disappointments and put his considerable energies into the next opportunity.

To this new venture, in addition to Jess Henriques, Art brought along three of his old practice partners: John O'Donnell, Sid Francis, and Chuck Bona.

"Together," Art explains, "we built a group practice with multiple operatories, central bookkeeping, radiology, and much more. We brought in several additional practitioners who were all teaching part-time at the dental school. Totally, we had over fifty individuals counting staff, dental assistants, and dental hygienists."

Art knew that no matter how many hours he put into those two workdays, the only way he could bring stability to the department was to also provide a corps of other practitioners, working and teaching in the clinics, just as they once did back in the old Quonset huts. Somehow, Art made it work with the help of a strong volunteer group, by building a team that was dedicated to the success of the school's emerging orthodontic program.

Art stretched limited resources to the breaking point. Meanwhile, he was growing discontented with a job that was spilling over into three days a week and running forty hours for what, even in the 1960s was considered a very small amount of compensation.

"So, I went back to John Tocchini," Art says. "I told him that I needed more money and that the program needed more money as well. Further, I told him that the overall environment of the school was deteriorating. The students were unhappy, and I suggested that it was time that we begin to think seriously about developing a more humanistic model of teaching."

Graduating classes during much of the 1960s were often so embittered by their school experience prior to the days when the "humanistic model of teaching" was ushered in by Dean Tocchini's successor, Dale Redig, that they pledged to each other that they would never be active alumni involved in supporting the ongoing operation of the school's clinics, or the school's philanthropic endeavors. Both aspects, volunteerism and giving monetary gifts, had been essential to the school's success from its earliest days.

It's a phenomenon that Dr. Fred West attempted to describe in 1953 when he wrote, "It is positively amazing how our overcrowded and poorly equipped school attracts our graduates and the graduates of other schools to return and give of their time, knowledge, patience, energies, and good will just to help Physicians and Surgeons." In conclusion, he wrote, "Our loyalty, enthusiasm, and devotion to an ideal, our expenditure of time and money by faculty and alumni alike, our perseverance and stick-to-itiveness has impressed everyone interested and concerned with dental education."

Now, that esprit de corps was straining at the seams. And Art could see it all unraveling.

As Art explains, "John said, 'If you don't believe in me or my leadership, you're no longer chairman of the department.' But I think one of the underlying reasons for my removal was that when we built the new building on Mission Road in South San Francisco, several of the dentists in John's building came over to the new facility, leading, of course, to a loss of revenue for John."

Later that day, after their heated conversation, Art's secretary told him that Dean Tocchini had removed him from the faculty.

"I still wanted to be on the faculty," Art said, "but John would not accept my calls. John just told people, 'Art's gone.'"

The close relationship that Art had built with John over the years had unraveled. It was only completely healed decades later, near the end of John Tocchini's very long life. "We were friends once again," Art explained, "and that only happened because it was important to both of us that we put our past differences behind us."

For the first time since Art walked into Dean Sloman's office in the summer of 1946, with the exception of his service years in the Navy, Art's connection to P&S had come to an end. Financially, as it turns out, that was a good thing, because he now directed all of his focus into perfecting the group practice on Mission Road.

Construction of the project began in 1966. One building, 1131 Mission Road was a round one-story structure elevated ten feet above the ground with parking tucked beneath and surrounded by gardens.

Into the new facility, Art also brought in associates who kept 60% of the revenue they generated. Art provided for himself a spacious ortho office, with multiple practice chairs, followed by Bona's pediatric office, and offices for Henriques, O'Donnell and Francis. The second structure at the site, 1135 Mission Road, was a two story building designed as a rental operation.

Art managed the business part of the group practice. Including the original five partners, all told there were over fifty people working in the two buildings between dentists, hygienists, laboratory and x-ray technicians and support staff. This was a dental complex of unheard-of size and complexity for a group practice in 1965.

It was here that Art gained his first experience in management. Wanting to do his best in that role, Art began taking extension, off the main campus, leadership and business courses at the Wharton School and at Stanford University, and the Center for Creative Leadership, which, at the time, was located at Duke University in Chapel Hill, North Carolina.

Filled with a new entrepreneurial spirit, Art suggested to his partners in the new group practice that they begin buying nearby residential properties. They set up a fund to buy one house a year that were then upgraded and turned into rentals. Before long, this new entity, Mission Properties, owned sixteen homes, and, in time, became a multi-million dollar venture in its own right.

Art received no compensation for his management role in the group practice or the real estate investment company he initiated, and when he became dean of the dental school in 1978, new time commitments soon made it impossible for him to manage the practice and the business and run the school. He continued, on a limited basis, to see patients in his own practice until 1988.

Like each of us, Art's life was frequently caught in the crosscurrents of other events. One of the remarkable qualities he demonstrated over a lifetime was the ability to adjust to shifting realities and make rapid changes.

This pattern revealed itself in so many ways: From Art's push for high speed handpieces, to his belief in quadrant dentistry, and his pioneering group practice offices on Mission Road in South San Francisco. The pattern become more pronounced as Art eventually returned to the school and became a leader and national spokesperson for the profession of dentistry. In each instance, he showed himself to be, a go-to guy.

* * * * *

John Tocchini completed two major goals that Dean Sloman held at the time of his death in 1952. One was the affiliation of P&S with a major university. The other was to replace the old building on Fourteenth Street. After all, those termites could only be expected to hold hands for so long!

In 1965, just after Art and John's relationship fell apart, the school broke ground on its new home, the Webster Street campus. Two years later, the school moved into this modern facility in San Francisco's Pacific Heights neighborhood. At 113,000 square feet the school's new home nearly tripled the size of the old Physicians & Surgeons location. Constructed after the earthquake and fire of 1906 had destroyed the school's first building, the old campus had served as home to P&S for nearly sixty years.

In the late sixties, everything both inside and outside of the school seemed new. To a man of science born in 1912, John Tocchini found this all a bit overwhelming. He was well-liked by most of his faculty, but his relationship with the student body grew increasingly tense.

"John was brilliant in many ways, and, in truth, never got enough credit for what he did achieve," Art says. "It was John who was instrumental in securing the funding from both public and private sources to make the new dental school possible. He was, without doubt, very hard-working, but he wasn't prepared for the generation of students that came into the school in the 1960s. John enforced rigid protocols, and he would dismiss students for 'inappropriate behavior.' In today's terms, John would be described as old school."

Worst of all for Dean Tocchini was likely the stress that the still-new relationship with the university added to what was already viewed as a stressful job. In 1968, John Tocchini retired in a fit of frustration. Shortly after, he told the university's board of regents that he would like to rescind his resignation. The board rejected that request and the administration launched a search for John Tocchini's replacement.

After many years of reaching in-house for a new dean, Pacific chose to do a national search for the school's next dean. They found him at the University of Iowa, College of Dentistry where he chaired the department of pediatric dentistry.

Tocchini's successor, Dr. Dale Redig, brought a new style of leadership to an institution nearly seventy-five years old. For the new dean, the timing could not have been better. San Francisco was the epicenter of cultural change in the age of "flower power," and Tocchini and Redig could not have been more different.

Redig looked more like a television personality than the dean of a dental school. He was tall, lean, tanned, and had a confident easy smile. Like all other newcomers to the school, Redig was greatly impressed by the school's consistency in producing graduates with outstanding clinical skills. What Redig was not pleased with was the distinct undercurrent of a boot camp atmosphere in which faculty too often played the role of drill sergeants.

Redig introduced a new approach, one that came to be known as the "humanistic model of teaching." This concept applied to the teaching of dentistry was viewed, at the time, as revolutionary, but in coming decades was imitated by every other dental school in the country.

Redig's approach was both simple and innovative. Today's dental school students, he reasoned, are tomorrow's professional colleagues. Each one of them should be treated with the respect a colleague, albeit less experienced, deserves. While his deanship lasted less than a decade, this shift in thinking left a lasting impression on the school and became as integral a part of its philosophy as the pursuit of clinical excellence continued unabated. Dean Redig's successor, Art Dugoni, institutionalized this philosophy during his nearly three decades as the school's dean. Dugoni, in time, built on the humanistic model in ways that educators in 1970 could not have imagined.

As Art recalls, "John was constantly frustrated by the share of the school's operating funds that was taken away by the university. Dale was better-suited to work through the complex politics that always exist between the dean of any given school and the administration of the university. It's a push and tug where each side inevitably sees their needs as more important than that of the other side. But Dale changed this relationship to a University of Southern California budgetary model where you paid for a percentage of various aspects of the University's operations. Leaving more money for the dental school's operation was absolutely essential to building a better school."

Art remained in private practice during Dale's years as the school's dean. Nevertheless, Dale contacted Art and invited him to rejoin the faculty, and Art agreed to do so working one day a week in the orthodontic program, which by now had transitioned from an undergraduate to a graduate program. "There, I started the mixed dentition early treatment clinic for patients ages seven to ten," Art explains. "It was an expansion of the work I had always been passionate about, dating back to my doctoral thesis in orthodontics, the effect of treatment intervention beginning with children as young as age five and up to age eight."

In all their interactions, Dale and Art blended well. Later, as dean, Art built on many of Dale's initiatives. The two most recognized thirty-five years after Dale Redig left Pacific was the humanitarian model of teaching and the transition from a four year program to the creation of a three year degree program that encompassed the full four-year curriculum.

"When you take the long view of history," Art says, "Pacific was blessed to have both John and Dale as deans of the school. Both brought their own unique styles to the school. And both were imaginative and innovative in attempting to meet the challenges of their time.

Dale Redig, who introduced the humanistic model of teaching to the dental school and went on to serve as the CDA's executive director.

John Tocchini, with shovel in hand, breaks ground on the dental school's new Pacific Heights campus.

Honoring her retirement from Wells Fargo Bank, Lina is surrounded
by her brother Leo, daughter Evelyn, and a roomful of
co-workers captured in the mirror behind her two sons, Art and Bill.

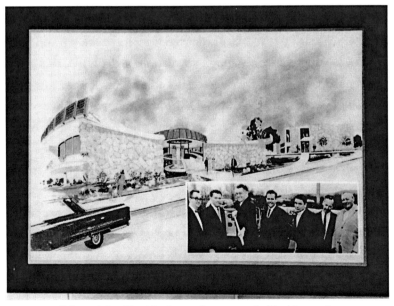

Memorialized in this plaque, Art surrounded by his practice
partners, breaks ground on 1131 Mission Road in South San Francisco.

Chapter Twelve

Waiting for Angels to Sing

Nine years after Dale Redig accepted the deanship at Pacific, he began to look for a position elsewhere in dental education.

At this time, 1977 and 1978, Art was very active in the leadership of the California Dental Association. Along with his old friend and fellow P&S student Bill Allen, they led a committee search to find a new executive director for the CDA. The committee reviewed all the potential candidates and developed a short list of three outstanding candidates.

"In our view, all three were well-qualified. Bill and I thought, at the time, that the other two were more experienced for the position, but they turned us down for a variety of reasons," Art recalls. "Dale Redig accepted the job and proved us wrong. Today, looking back on the transformation of the CDA that happened during his tenure as its executive director, it's unimaginable that anyone would have done a better job. Dale took the CDA from a 'mom and pop operation' to a major force in national dentistry. He moved us from offices in Los Angeles to Sacramento, where legislative action every year has such an impact on our profession. Dale remade the CDA into a force deserving to be heard in the process of state and national decision making."

When Dale Redig decided to leave his deanship at Pacific, he suggested two of his faculty members to the university as possible successors. One was Steve Cohen, chairman of the school's endodontics program; the other was Art Dugoni, a part time adjunct professor in orthodontics. Additionally, the school appointed a search committee that would report back to university's board of regents with its recommendations. That committee began a major search of internal and external candidates to fill Redig's shoes.

The complete list of candidates numbered over thirty.

Before interviews began, Dr. Cohen dropped out, suggesting that his col-league, Art Dugoni, was the school's best choice for dean. The list of potential candidates continued to fall. First thirty-two, then fifteen, and finally down to three. But, as the list of possible successors continued to dwindle, and Art went through several rounds of initial interviews, Art became more aware of the fact that he was very uncertain about assuming the job.

"Of course, my ego was pleased. This was the school I walked into in 1946 out of the University of Missouri. The only school in San Francisco that was willing to take a chance on me," Art says. "There was such a deep feeling of family here, and I had such a great love of this place and the people who worked here."

At the same time, as the 1980s neared, Art envisioned a different life for Kaye and himself. In the thirteen years since his return from Washington state, his orthodontic practice had become one of the most successful in the Bay Area, with an income exceeding 200,000 dollars a year and with the return on his investments all doing well, he was advised by his accountant that if he was to be offered what Dale Redig was currently earning, approximately $50,000 per annum, he'd find himself in a tight financial spot. By 1981, Steve, his oldest child, would complete his advanced degree in orthodontics and be ready to take over the practice.

"One of the top officers of the university came down from Stockton to my office in South San Francisco in order to assess my interest in the position. I told him that in the coming years, Kaye and I were planning to live a portion of each year abroad. Our thought was to live a month in London, then come back and practice for five months. Then live a month in Paris, come back to practice, then a month in Milan and so on. By then, Steve would be a part of the practice, and I could start to pull back.

"So, I kept telling them that I wasn't sure I wanted the job. Deans back then generally did not move from school to school. Most leaders would groom their successors. And universities looked to promote from within.

"The remaining three candidates went through a round of three interviews each. Even when it came down to that final three, and I was still on the list, I simply wasn't sure that this job was the right fit for me."

Today, that all seems a bit unimaginable. Just like how close Art came in 1943 and again in 1950 to following a path into medicine as opposed to dentistry. But in 1978, his deanship and leadership of organized dentistry was all unwritten history. Standing at the crossroads of destiny, Art's future seemed not nearly so certain.

Art knew when he got a call late on a Friday afternoon inviting him to a lunch with Pacific's president, Stanley McCaffrey, at San Francisco's Bohemian Club the following Monday, that it was most likely that the position of dean was about to be offered to him.

"When I sat down on Saturday with my lawyer and accountant to write down the pros and cons for both me and my family," Art says, "the cons were a lot longer. So, Sunday morning, Kaye and I went to church to pray and ask for God's guidance. I was looking for a sign. I did not know what that sign might be, I was just hoping for something. After mass, we went up to the altar in front of the statue of Mary and Jesus and we again prayed for guidance."

McCaffrey, who grew up in Whittier, California, a part of the greater Los Angeles area, was a boyhood friend of Richard M. Nixon. He worked as a member of Nixon's staff during the future president's eight year service as vice president under Dwight D. Eisenhower, and he was a top staffer during Nixon's unsuccessful presidential race against John F. Kennedy in 1960. McCaffrey left politics and took over as the president of the University of the Pacific in 1971, a position he held for sixteen years.

At lunch that Monday with McCaffrey, Art was offered the same salary Dale Redig was currently earning.

"For me, that was a non-starter," Art says. "I explained that I can't make that work with a family the size of mine and that I was making more than four times that amount in my practice. I thanked him for the offer, and I got up to leave. McCaffrey took my arm and told me to sit back down.

"Then he said, 'Art, what would make this work for you?'"

"To me, it was obvious," Art explained. "If you can't do money, you have to give me a chance to practice."

At first, McCaffrey was resistant to that idea, explaining to Art that the university did not allow its deans to continue in private practice. In the end, it only worked because President McCaffrey saw that there was no financial alternative for Art but to practice a minimum of two days a week plus Saturdays.

As the lunch neared its conclusion, Art realized that he had committed himself to taking on a very big task for a relatively small amount of compensation. "I thought maybe I would hear angels singing their approval," Art remembers. "But there were no angels."

At the same time, Art felt deeply honored by his selection. Thirty-two years earlier, he had walked into the old building on Fourteenth Street for the first time. Now he was about to step into the shoes once filled by Ernie Sloman and other distinguished educators and practitioners. Art was about to become the seventh dean in the school's eighty-two-year history. He could not help but be honored and moved by that fact.

Later that day, driving home, Art was wondering how he would explain his decision to Kaye. He knew she would support, as she always had, any career decision that he made. At the same time, it was more than understandable if she had her doubts about his choice. After all, he was himself uncertain about this new direction his life was taking.

There was no way of knowing that night that during the twenty-eight years he spent as dean of the dental school he would become known to his peers as the "Dean of Deans." That early in the next millennium, he would be the first sitting dean of a dental school in North America to have the school renamed in his honor. That night, he could just think about what he would need to do to make the numbers work, manage his practice, balance the books, and pay for the higher education costs for all seven of his children.

Five years into Art's deanship, Art went back to McCaffrey and said he should be getting $65,000 a year. McCaffrey agreed with Art, but told him that he didn't make that kind of money. Ten years into his deanship, in 1988, Art reached a salary of $100,000 per year.

It all changed quickly in that first decade after he had trepidatiously accepted the deanship. By then, Art's practice was doing well, principally because he had his two daughters managing the business and his son Steve working as a fulltime partner. Equally satisfying was the fact that the role of dean suited Art, and he was growing as a leader and educator in ways that he never imagined.

"Every job that I had, such as heading up the CDA," Art says, "I suggested, after completing my term in office, that people be paid for their time. Home mortgages, school tuitions, medical costs and so much of life's every day expenses simply can't be paid with good intentions. Having a separate source of income should not be a prerequisite to serving in any leadership position."

A big part of how Art made it work was rooted in the fact that he and Kaye came from humble backgrounds. They were children of the Great Depression and the two of them always knew the value of a dollar. As his investments outperformed his expectations, his practice continued to thrive, and his compensation increased, Art and Kaye finally found themselves blessed with an increasing amount of financial security. This was an unaccustomed situation for a man who, at an earlier time of life, had one pair of pants that he hoped would make it through another winter and a woman whose father ran a modest business that used a cigar box as a cash register.

Angels may have not sung that afternoon when President McCaffrey offered Art the deanship, but his work proved to be more rewarding than he had ever foreseen. Looking back over his record number of years as dean of the dental school, Art felt blessed to have chosen this path.

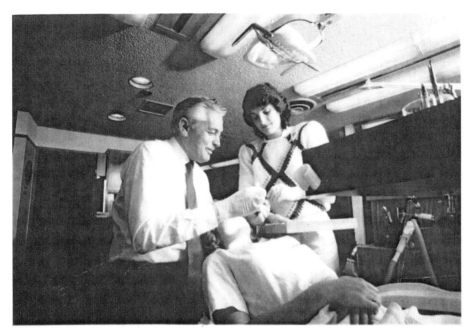

Still seeing private patients, six years into his deanship, Art is
pictured here in 1984 with Donna Zocchi, his dental assistant.

Chapter Thirteen

"Art, Be Fair"

When Art stepped into the role of dean in 1978, you might say that the man and the moment met. Over the next twenty-eight years, thanks to his tireless dedication and a devoted faculty and staff, Art transformed the school from a distant point of light on the edge of the Pacific Coast to the very epicenter of dental education. He turned a unique three-year degree program into an admired model of efficiency and he made the humanistic teaching model in dental education the gold standard.

Harry Truman famously put an engraved motto on his desk that said, "The buck stops here." Art placed an index card that he folded back and leaned against a desk lamp. It was a short statement, but one that strongly resonated with him. It said, "Art, be fair. Power corrupts."

That simple statement says a great deal about Art's view of leadership. Art embraced the concept that serving as dean offered him the chance to build a better institution. But he never viewed leadership as a chance to dictate to others. Rather, it was an opportunity to collaborate with colleagues in setting a better path for the school and all the constituents it served.

For Art, the deanship was 5% privilege and 95% responsibility. His least favorite part of the job was terminating a staff member or informing a student that their academic performance made their continued pursuit of a degree in dentistry impractical. The part of the job he loved was being able to mentor and inspire. Throughout his deanship, there was a countless number of students, staff, faculty, colleagues, even fellow deans who tell almost identical stories about how Art, "made me better than I ever thought I could be." As Dr. Michael Alfano, who today is the Executive Vice President of New York University, explains, "When I became dean of NYU's College of Dentistry in 1998, I made what many thought of as the obligatory pilgrimage to San Francisco to ask Art how he built the kind of institution he had at Pacific."

Perhaps that sense of caring and commitment that Art brought to his deanship was rooted deep inside the boy who wondered if he should pursue a life in the priesthood. After all, he devoted a lot of his energy and thought to providing motivation and inspiration to others.

Art was determined to lead with his own unique blend of compassion and consensus. He may have chosen not to devote his life to the church, but this was no doubt a reflection of his years of spiritual practice. Art was imbued with the notion that we are all imperfect creatures. Often, however, he thought: "What would God want me to do in this situation?" Given that inclination, it's easy to understand why a small sign reminding himself to "Be fair," was such an important aspect of doing a good job. Silently, he often told himself to, "Do the right thing!" It was a burden he carried happily.

* * * * *

Art began his deanship in much the same way as he has tackled every other job throughout his life: by making a list. It is a deceptively simple approach that has always served him well. As Art's oldest daughter, Mary, who spent many years working in his orthodontic practice explains, "I don't think there was ever a time that dad has not put together a 'to do list.' Even on family vacations, he always had a list of things that he wanted to accomplish. His kids and his grandchildren have always teased him about these lists, but you might say the joke was on us because, as the years went by, many of us started making 'to do lists' of our own."

In his first full year as dean, Art created a fifty-point program of various goals that he wanted to accomplish during his tenure. Some he hoped to achieve in the short term, other goals he knew would take many years to accomplish. For Art and the institution that he led, there was no looking back.

Art took on a variety of objectives simultaneously with what his brother Bill told the school's in-house publication, *Contact Point*, was his, "Tremendous drive. Whatever there is to accomplish, he tackles it."

First and foremost, Art had to address the politically sensitive aspect that exists in any institution when a new leader seeks to make change. "When you look at a school and consider its future," Art explains, "the need for change or improvement does not mean that you are being critical of what happened in the past. Different opportunities present themselves at different moments. If you keep looking forward, you will capture those moments. It's not so much about the past as it is about the future you're hoping to create. I never doubted that in following Sloman, Tocchini and Redig, that I was standing on the shoulders of giants. We so often measure past leaders against standards that simply did not exist during their time. That's foolish and unfair. In their own way, these three deans of the school made tremendous strides forward. I could not have accomplished what I did if it was not for the solid work and tireless efforts of my predecessors." Art explained his approach as persistently working for evolutionary change that, in time, would create revolutionary results.

"You start with faculty and work your way down from there. Faculty has to share your vision or you're creating a two-headed dragon that will never speak with one voice.

"You must practice patience and never lose sight of the fact that you simply cannot change everything all at once. Whenever you get people excited about change, you'll find that everyone wants their area of the organization to be first. Did we improve? Yes! Did we do all that we could have done? No! In truth, it's like the old adage, 'How high is up?' You never get all the way to perfect; it's simply the direction you want to travel in. Just like being a lifelong learner, it's not a destination you'll ever reach, but rather the direction in which you're traveling."

* * * * *

Today, it is long forgotten by many, but Art came to the deanship during difficult economic times. The years of the late '70s and early '80s were tough on

Americans. In the rearview mirror, that difficult economy doesn't look all that painful, but it was painful enough to drive a sitting president, Jimmy Carter, from office when he ran for a second term against former California Governor Ronald Reagan, who won the election in a landslide.

That economic downturn, which stretched through most of Reagan's first term, led to the worst financial crisis private and public dental schools faced in the second half of the twentieth century. From Georgetown in the nation's capital, to Washington University, in St Louis; Loyola in Chicago, and many more, it was a time of great uncertainty.

As Art's successor, Dean Patrick Ferrillo recalls, "When I first became dean at Southern Illinois University, during the 1985-86 academic year, we went from graduating 450 applicants to less than 150.

"Some dental schools had one applicant per seat. Several dental schools during those years closed their doors never to return. Today, the situation is totally reversed. There are thousands more applicants to the sixty-four dental schools in America than there are available seats. In surveys of desired fields of study for a future career, dentistry has been at or near the top in recent years.

"During this time when dental school student populations were sinking, and when many dental schools were closing, a reality particularly true of schools like Pacific's that were divisions of private universities, Art expressed his unshakeable confidence in seeing a brighter future for the profession. He had the wisdom to recognize that the profession of dentistry was stronger than economic downturns, an AIDS crisis, and other impediments to the profession's growth."

Today's thriving dental profession was a distant dream in the 1980s. However, at a time when more practitioners were leaving the profession than coming in, Dugoni insisted that the current state of affairs was a momentary setback on a longer road to a more vibrant profession when enhanced technology would allow for areas of growth previously unimagined.

It was all part of a bigger picture to Art who has, in all things, thought of the glass as being half-full as opposed to half-empty. As Kathleen O'Loughlin, the current Executive Director of the ADA explained, "Art's devotion to the profession has been unparalleled." And that devotion clearly led to his being unmatched as a voice of optimism for dentistry's future.

In fact, soon after Art became dean, the HIV panic broke out in three American cities: New York, Los Angeles, and San Francisco, being hit the hardest. As dean of a dental school operating a number of clinics serving a large and diverse patient population, Art found himself at the epicenter of that crisis.

"Meeting the problem head-on meant marshaling and coordinating the resources to make substantial changes in how we operated our clinics and labs," Art explains. A major overhaul of clinic procedures was needed, particularly with enhanced attention to infection control protocols and procedures.

Art, as you would suspect, didn't shy away from the enormity of the task. Rather, in typical fashion he met it head-on. As O'Loughlin, who has known Art for well over twenty years explains, "His capacity to work hard and work long hours always amazed his colleagues, including everyone at the ADA."

Art's work ethic is perhaps best captured in his own words: "The difference between good and great is you simply outwork them. Eight hours to work, eight hours to sleep. What do you do with the other eight hours?"

For Art, on most of the days of his nearly three decades as dean, those "other eight hours," were spent on the job. Art would regularly share with his students his belief that they should guide their professional lives by the Five B's:

Be on time.

Be there.

Be involved.

Be disciplined.

Be balanced in your life.

Throughout it all, Art had a sixth "B." One that he kept mostly to himself and faithfully adhered to through every crisis he faced as dean: "Be fair." It was an abiding belief that served him well and helped to define his legacy.

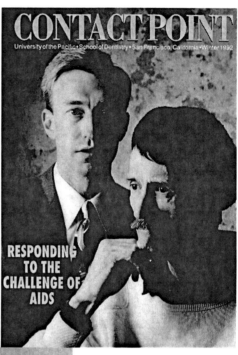

Changing times: Two covers of the school's publication Contact Point: one announcing the selection of Art as the seventh dean in the school's eighty-two year history; the second, focusing on the impact of the AIDS Crisis on treatment procedures.

Art, the man with the endless "to do list," always made time to visit with his students.

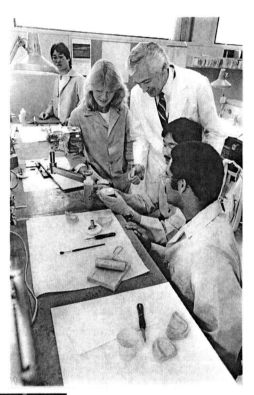

Jim Lieb, Kaye, and Art—as they often did when together—sharing a laugh.

Chapter Fourteen

Camp Dugoni

For Art, striking a balance between personal life, family life, and professional life has always been difficult. Even for a man unafraid of working eighteen-hour days, there is only so much that can be done inside the space of twenty-four hours and only one place any one individual can be at any given time.

Art reflects the traditional values of his generation. Mom stayed home and raised the kids, while dad went out and made the money that supported his family's needs. Art and Kaye embodied that lifestyle. And in conversations with their children, it appears clear that this arrangement worked well for them.

Mary Dugoni, Art and Kaye's fourth child, remembers her dad often coming home after ten each evening. "We knew when dad got home that it was time for us kids to be in bed," she says. In most cases Art's only day at home was Sundays, which always began with the family going to church. After church, as Mary explained, "Dad had such a long list of chores for everyone to do that when he was home we used to ask our mom why he couldn't work on Sundays as well."

After Steven was born in 1952, three and a half years after Art and Kaye wed on that winter afternoon in Spokane, four more children followed in rapid succession. Art and Kaye's family started out with three boys, Steven, Michael, and Russell, followed by two girls, Mary and finally Diane, who was born in 1957. Over the next five years, Kaye suffered two miscarriages. During the couple's time in Seattle, their sixth child, Art, was born in December 1962. A short time after, in February 1964, James, who calls Artie, his "Irish twin," was born. With James, who also refers to himself as "the caboose," the Dugoni family was complete. Art's brother William, and his wife Patricia, had ten children and Art's sister Evelyn had three. All totaled Lina, who, as the grandmother of twenty had an unexpectedly full house, was affectionately known as "Nonnie."

Not long after Art, Jr. and James were born, Art and Kaye moved the family south from San Mateo into a rambling '60s ranch style home at 302 Atherton Avenue in Atherton.

As Jim Dugoni describes it, "The Atherton home was a sports center: basketball court, monkey rope, trampoline, swimming pool, slide, and much more. The front of the house was beautifully manicured as a mini-baseball field where we played wiffle ball, basketball, volleyball and croquet."

Steve, Mike and, Russ had their hangout behind the carport. Diane and Mary held court in their own portion of the house, and Artie and Jim, two boys under the age of ten might appear anywhere at anytime as they added to the frenetic pace of daily life at "Camp Dugoni."

But rarely on a summer or weekend day were there just seven children at the home. Kaye, understandably, thought that busy children required less individual attention than bored children, so the children were always welcome to invite their friends to the house. Both Jim and Mary remember all their friends thinking of Kaye as a "second mom." William's widow, Patricia, who called her sister-in-law, Kaye, the "most generous woman I have ever known in my life," fondly remembers summer days when she'd bring her kids over to play in the pool. "Can you imagine," she says, "a woman with seven children of her own inviting your ten kids over as well?"

But that was a typical day at Camp Dugoni, where Mary fondly remembers her mother's habit of watering the plants on summer mornings. "Mom would be out in the flower beds in the morning smoking a cigarette in one hand and holding a green water hose in the other hand. It was her quiet time, and as crazy as the house could be during the rest of the day, we knew that this was her time and we all left her alone."

It has long been said that opposites attract and in so doing they create a couple in which the sum of the parts is greater than either one individual. That appears to have been the case in the operation of Camp Dugoni. Art was the organizer, and Kaye set boundaries, but never over-managed the children. Kaye apparently was a master of the fine art of organized chaos. With a house filled with children, she had to be. Art, if he could, would talk the flowers out of the ground, Kaye would give them a little water every day and then let nature do the rest.

"Mom was not a disciplinarian; noise did not bother her," Jim explains. "She was the neighborhood mom. She would load up the fridge and the freezers with casseroles and treats." There was always something to eat at Camp Dugoni, where Kaye specialized in a variety of Irish dishes from stews to pies. "I don't know if Mom ever planned supper for fewer than ten," Jim adds. "It really was more like running a camp than running a home."

While Kaye was the master of Irish cuisine, most weeks brought a visit to Camp Dugoni from Lina, who allowed no one in the kitchen while she prepared her Italian dishes. "Nonnie," Mary explains, "would take the bus down from San Francisco, get off at the nearest stop in Atherton, and walk the nearly two miles to our house. She'd make a huge meal, stay for a couple of hours, and walk back to the bus and head home. She was a sweetheart. She had two rules, no one in the kitchen while she was busy preparing our food, and no rides back and forth to the bus." Independence was important to Lina and she safeguarded it well into her nineties.

"Everything fell to my mom," Mary explains. "Volleyball, basketball, croquet, it really was an endless summer camp. Dad's contribution was bringing home the newest and the latest toys and gadgets. I'll never forget the two mini motorbikes that he brought home that, unfortunately, wound up at the bottom of the swimming pool."

Looking back on her years growing up, Mary, now with children, and grandchildren of her own, better sees the push and pull of daily life that shaped the lives of her parents. "I think there was a part of Dad that wishes he could have lived several lives all in one. He loved the school, loved his profession, and loved his family. Dad rarely came to one of our games. Mom never missed one. And, up until the time she got ill, Mom never missed one of her grandchildren's events either.

"The wonderful thing about my dad," Mary adds, "was when you needed advice, he was always ready to listen and thoughtfully help you through whatever issues you were facing. I think that was the part of him that made such a wonderful educator and mentor. He would patiently talk you through a problem and help you to see a different approach."

Jim Dugoni's fondest memories came not from their days in Atherton, but during vacations at the lake:

"The greatest times we spent as a family were on our summer vacations up at the cabin on Lake Almanor. Led by Mom, who was the great card player in the family, we'd set-up multiple tables in the kitchen and living room to play Spades, Hearts, Gin Rummy, Backgammon, and Cribbage, to name just a few. Dad would always participate and especially enjoyed playing cards with all the kids.

"Using Dad's list, our days would usually start out with me, Artie, and our friends spending a couple of hours moving rocks and raking leaves in the backyard that led down to the beach. Then, just when the weather would start to get windy on the lake, we would finally get to go out and waterski on choppy water. Despite our seemingly well-reasoned arguments to the contrary, Dad's philosophy always won out—first you work hard, then you play hard."

Jim agrees that his dad was "legendary for his use of hand-written 'To Do' lists." On each one, "Dad would place hand-drawn check-off boxes. Routinely he would post those lists on the refrigerator door for all of us kids to see."

Artie recalls his dad coming home late and leaving early for work. "But he would always leave post it notes for us saying things like, 'help mom with the dishes, rake the yard, and clean up the pool area.'" Just to make sure that Art Jr. got the message, his dad stuck a post-it note to his forehead early one morning before leaving for work. That day he made sure to get his chores done before his dad got home.

Artie also remembers, as does every one of the other Dugoni children, that his mom had an open door policy to friends and friends of friends. "Mom was always happy to welcome our friends. It's no wonder she was a second mom to so many of the neighborhood kids. And Dad always had a new way to make us all healthier. I still remember his 'Power Pancakes;' they tasted awful."

* * * * *

For a family of seven children, Art and Kaye were blessed with a mostly happy and peaceful home. But that peace was shattered in June of 1981 when at a post-graduation day party at a friend's house, Artie tumbled down a flight of concrete steps. His friends surrounded him as he laid unconscious on the ground. What they did not know at that moment was that Artie had just suffered a near-fatal brain injury.

Two pieces of good fortune most likely saved Artie that night. The first was the result of good timing, the other was the result of another tragic accident that had happened just a few miles away earlier in the evening. The first was that the mother of Artie's friend, who was hosting the party, was a registered nurse and she arrived home from a late work shift shortly after Artie's fall. His friends thought he had just been knocked out cold, but the mom spotted a slow but steady flow of blood coming from his left ear. That indicated to her that a brain bleed was occurring and she rushed inside to call an ambulance.

The tragedy earlier that evening was a motorcycle accident near Stanford Medical Center, which had caused the brain trauma team to assemble. When Artie arrived, the trauma team was split, so that he could be attended to immediately.

After the drilling of holes in Artie's skull proved unsuccessful in relieving the swelling, the surgical team took the more radical step of removing the side (temporal bone) area of Artie's skull, knowing that failure to relieve the pressure caused by a swelling brain would most likely prove fatal.

Art's sister Diane was the first to arrive at the hospital. She had gotten a call from one of her brother's friends at the party that Artie had fallen and been taken to Stanford Hospital. Not knowing the severity of the accident, Diane drove over to the hospital in her parents' station wagon, reasoning that Artie might want to lie down on their way home. Not until she arrived at the hospital did the critical nature of his injury become apparent.

For a girl in her early twenties, the next hours were agonizing, knowing that her kid brother's life was hanging in the balance. Her parents had just left, shortly after attending Artie's high school graduation ceremony, for Lake Tahoe, and that added to her feeling of dread. To Diane's great relief, her sister Mary arrived not long after Artie's surgery had begun.

At about that time, Art and Kaye were awakened by a loud knocking on the door of their cabin at a resort where they were attending a weekend seminar put on by Art's colleague and close friend, Jim Pride. Jim had left the faculty of the dental school to start a highly successful organization he named The Pride Institute.

The person banging on their cabin door turned out to be a deputy sheriff, who informed Art and Kaye that they had a member of their family in the ICU at Stanford Medical Center.

"We both thought it was my mom," Art recalls. "But when we reached Stanford by phone, we learned for the first time that it was Artie. We found out that he had been admitted with a head injury and was in surgery at that moment. It's at a moment like that when parents need to remind themselves to keep breathing.

"I woke up Jim Pride and said we needed the use of his plane. Jim said 'Let's get it done.' The pilot was located and we headed to the airport and were flown back to Palo Alto." They arrived at the hospital just as the night sky was giving way to the start of another day.

"We could see down a long hallway," Art explained, "that there was a doctor in a white coat talking to our girls. Both of them were crying. Kaye and I took a deep breath. The doctor looked at me angrily as Kaye and I approached. He began by saying 'Your son has no right to be alive; I'm not sure that he'll come out of his coma, and I don't know what he'll be like when, and if, he comes through his post op period.'

"I was taken aback and pretty angry with this young resident surgeon's tone, but I knew my first responsibility was to comfort Mary and Diane, who had just spent the entire night at the hospital and were sick with deep worry about their brother."

"They all seemed quite certain that Artie may not walk again or function normally," Mary adds. "It was terrifying news for two young girls in their twenties to hear."

It had all happened so quickly; a stunning turn of events, given the fact that less than twenty-four hours earlier, the whole family had gathered to celebrate Artie's high school graduation. Now, it appeared that all of Artie's promise for a bright future had been taken away in one careless moment.

"It still makes me cry to this day, Diane says. "I was so proud of him that afternoon and all that he had accomplished. The next morning, I wrote out the lyrics to Bette Midler's song, *The Rose*, and was going to give it to him when he came out of his coma."

Three days passed as Artie slept quietly in his coma, unaware of the turmoil he had caused and all the love that he had stirred. Kaye's deep faith sustained her. She refused to believe that her son would never walk or speak again. Art spent many of those long agonizing hours whispering in his son's ear, "You will be fine, you will come out of this whole, we love you, we love you, we love you."

Family, friends and classmates filled the corridor outside of Artie's room awaiting news and praying for a miracle. Art held Kaye's hand and they took strength from each other and from their shared faith. For a man who was accustomed to creating order out of chaos, there was little else he could do. A quiet and reassuring smile for all those friends and family that kept flowing in and out of the hospital was all Art had left to give.

"When Artie did awaken," Mary says, "he looked straight at my mother and said, 'Hi Mom.' He was some sort of a miracle for sure, and my mother, who refused to believe that there would ever be anything wrong with him, held onto her faith and never allowed herself to believe that he would be anything other than fine."

Today, happy and successful at 51, Art and Kaye's sixth child remembers those days in recovery. "Someone was with me almost every hour of every day. I was in the hospital for a couple of weeks. Things got better much more quickly than the doctors ever thought possible. My only complaint was having to wait for my hair to grow back!"

Three months after the accident, Artie arrived on time at Stockton to begin college at the University of the Pacific. To this day, he still has those lyrics that

his sister wrote down and placed in his hand thirty-two years ago:
"It's the heart afraid of breaking
That never learns to dance.
It's the dream afraid of waking
That never takes the chance.
It's the one who won't be taken,
Who cannot seem to give,
And the soul afraid of dyin'
That never learns to live."

Camp Dugoni buzzed continually with an accustomed level of frenzy. The winds of chance were always close at hand. But, as Artie's accident proved, the Dugonis' family life also vibrated with an undercurrent of love, faith, and solidarity that, whenever challenged, always proved unshakeable.

Never a moment's peace: five sons in Atherton,
with James, Art Jr., Michael, Steven, and Russell.

Camp Dugoni Take Two: some of the next
generation of Dugonis, with Kaye, Art, and Russell.

Full house: Art and Kaye's seven children pictured in descending order of birth, starting from the right, Steve, Michael, Russell, Mary, Diane, Art Jr., and James.

Can you tell it's the Seventies? Diane and Mary pose with their dad.

Chapter Fifteen

Several Briefcases, Many Goals

In June 1985, Art celebrated his sixtieth birthday. Entering life's seventh decade, most individuals begin to slow down, shorten those "To Do Lists," and plan more time for relaxing and enjoying life outside the office.

That certainly was not the case for Art. In fact, his sixties was the start of a twenty-year period that would largely define his legacy. Between his deanships, presidency of the CDA, the ADA, several other professional organizations, his anchoring of Lifetime Medical Television's program, *Dentistry Update*, and much more, Art was in a perpetual state of motion. During this period, he was approached about assuming the presidency of the World Dental Federation, FDI, several other dental school deanships, plus the presidency of the University of the Pacific. Ultimately, he turned these and other positions down. But, no matter how far his travels took him, whether relatively close, Sacramento, or Stockton, or relatively far, Chicago, New York, Europe or Asia, his heart was still left in San Francisco; the place where he was raised, close to where he and Kaye raised their family, and where the dental school had for so many decades served as his home away from home.

You could say that during this incredibly busy period of his life, as the expression goes, he was a man who wore many hats. In truth, however, Art's secret was that he was a man of many briefcases. Between the deanship, the CDA, the ADA, the FDI, corporate boards, professional organizations like the Santa Fe Group, his own orthodontic practice, and his real estate and business investments; Art managed it all with the help of five essential ingredients. First, Kaye, a partner who brought balance to his life and family; second, a staff of assistants that kept him on task and managed the blizzard of paperwork he produced on a daily and weekly basis; third, son Steve, and daughters Mary and Diane, allowing him to rest assured that the thriving orthodontic practice he had begun continued to run soundly and profitably; fourth, Art's superhuman ability to work countless hours coming into the school often at six in the morning and leaving for home well after ten at night; and fifth, his gift for organizational management as exemplified by the fact that he divided his many jobs between many briefcases. Leaving for Chicago for a week of meetings at the ADA, he'd grab his ADA briefcase, heading for Stockton to meet with the university's president he'd reach for his Pacific briefcase, and so on. As Art says with a relaxed and easy smile, "those different briefcases helped me to keep all those different jobs straight. I trained myself to focus on one project and carry that project however far it needed to go. It was when I was coming up in the CDA that I started keeping different briefcases for different organizations. Without the discipline of being self-organized, none of it would have worked."

Art is quite certain that his motivation to excel was instilled in him by his mother. "She saw in me the potential she could have had if she had been born a man, born an American, and been blessed to receive a quality education. I'm certain that she put that drive into me. When I was a teen and girls would call, I'd have my mom answer and say, 'Art's not here.' I was always multitasking... taking on what needed to be done, and then setting up a time schedule to get it done."

As Art recalls, "Starting in high school, I found I was more productive if I got up at five and did two hours of work before leaving home. That habit continued through my education. After school, I would go over my notes for the day, but leave the actual studying until the next morning. I was also blessed with a nearly photographic memory, so I could see written information in my mind and absorb it much more quickly."

Whether it was a memo to staff, a member of his administrative council, or an article for a professional journal, Art claims that he could see the whole document in his mind's eye, and therefore, dictating what he wanted to say was a natural outcome of that special ability. This is one possible reason why Art was so adept at turning out volumes of documents.

Art made good use of a staff of assistants. He would come out of a meeting and issue ten different memos an hour later. "It was a gift that I could see what I wanted to say. I have no doubt that, for me, the gift of a clear and powerful memory paid great dividends."

In addition to his long hours, his ease with written communication appears evident in the fact that colleagues and staff consistently tell of a shared experience in working with Art in which a follow-up memo, letter, or report came to them well before they expected it to arrive. Several of his fellow dental school deans had a running joke comparing experiences on whether Dugoni's summary report of their meeting, a note of thanks, or other materials, would reach their desk before they returned home. Nearly always, it did.

Of course, much of this occurred well before the age of the Internet. When Art's staff moved from posted to electronic transmission, his response time became that much quicker.

Tere Hanson, who served as Art's executive assistant in 1991 and worked for him for a period of twelve years says, "He was more organized and aware of details than any human being I have ever met in my life."

"Art's nightly routine was to talk into a transcriber," Hanson explains. "On my staff, I had two clerical assistants. It took both of them the better part of an entire workday, every workday of the week, to transcribe the flood of letters, staff memos, directives, lectures, and more that he would dictate every night. It was not unusual for both of them to be typing all day.

"I used to wonder, when does Art ever sleep? We would leave the office every evening at five thirty or six and come in the next morning to find another stack of voice tapes waiting to be transcribed."

In all aspects of his deanship, organization was essential. As Hanson explains, "filing was the key to working successfully with Art. He had a system in which everything went into a binder, and then he would go over individual binders with each staff member, which allowed Art to track the work of each of his administrators."

Dr. Craig Yarborough, who, as associate dean for admissions and later the school's development department, was a long time member of Art's administrative council. He remembers well the blizzard of paperwork that became infamous during the Dugoni years.

"We used to joke that before Art the Mojave Desert was known as the Mojave Forest. We were all amazed at his work output," Yarborough says.

"He had an incredible capacity for details, and more amazingly, a memory for those details," Hanson adds. "From my vantage point, I could see that he tirelessly gave 150% to every aspect of the dental school."

What most impressed Hanson was the volume of work that Art was able to complete. "If I didn't know better, I would have thought he was three people."

But what most fascinated Tere Hanson was simply, "The way his brain worked." As she explains, "It was true that Dr. Dugoni would visualize what he wanted to say in a memo. He could digest a huge amount of information and turn it around quickly. To be in my position and watch that massive flow of information was an unforgettable experience."

What most impressed Hanson and what she remembers most fondly was the human side of this very busy, very productive man. "He always wanted to know about everyone at the school: the students, the faculty, and the entire staff. His memory for personal details astounded me and everyone else. When he walked around to the different departments, offices, and classrooms, he would ask about people and issues they might be confronting at the time. Everyone thought that he must have worked from notes, but I knew better. What actually happened was that group administrators would comment to him about a staff member facing a family illness or personal difficulties, and he would follow up when he saw them. It could be the executive associate dean or a member of the building's maintenance staff; to Art, they were all part of his family, and he cared about everyone equally, regardless of their position."

Perhaps even more amazing was the fact that at school alumni events, Art would remember facts about people's lives from two, three or more years prior.

"He would see alumni and remember health issues they had confronted, the birth of a child, the start of a new practice and other details," Hanson recalls, "and people would ask me how he did that. How could he possibly remember? I would smile, shake my head, and say, 'I have no idea.' It was just a remarkable experience."

* * * * *

Clearly with all that Art wanted to accomplish both at the school and in his profession, his relentless drive, his organizational skills, his interpersonal skills, communication skills, and more, served him well.

"I always had a passion for the school, but I probably took it to an extreme. With so many early days and late nights, I got to know the school's cleaning and security staff very well. And working those kind of hours sends a powerful message to everyone else on your team that you don't just talk the talk, but you walk the walk."

Dr. Patrick Ferrillo, remembers when he first came to the dental school how impressed he was with the dedication of both the faculty and the staff.

"At Art's request, I conducted a mock accreditation visit to the school in 1992."

Pat had both served as a consultant to the commission on dental school accreditation and had just recently gone through his first accreditation site visit as dean of the dental school at Southern Illinois University. Pat recalls that Art, who he was meeting for the very first time, had brought his entire leadership team into the session for the purpose of motivating them as they prepared for the school's site visit. After a session that ran into the early evening, Art invited Pat to join him for dinner.

As Pat explains, "After dinner, when we returned to the school, I noticed that Art's leadership team was working late, so I asked Art what they were doing at the school long after they should have left. Art explained that they were work-ing on the changes that we had discussed earlier in the day. I knew, at that mo-ment, that Art was one of those unique leaders who truly knew how to motivate the people on his team. They had a commitment and a level of enthusiasm that was inspiring to see."

One of Art's administrative team, Dr. Eddie Hayashida, associate dean for administration, says he never saw himself as an administrator, but Art saw those qualities in him.

"I became accustomed to being on the receiving end of the paper mill that, as so many others have said, was legendary during Art's deanship," he explains. "Art was always feeding us articles and information about our area of study or practice. I was reading stuff that Art sent me during the week on my Saturday nights and Sundays at home. I was giving up my weekends to keep up with all those materials, but I knew that whatever sacrifices I made for the job, Art was always doing more.

"I learned a deeper sense of personal responsibility because of my years with Art. You always knew that Art would not ask you to do anything that he would not do himself. Whether that was picking up trash in the hallway or working on a presentation until midnight. Deeply ingrained in Art is the commitment to lead by example and he did that in every aspect of his work."

The depth of Art's dedication to his work was only one reason for the increasing loyalty that he earned from his staff with each passing year. Another aspect was his growing celebrity in the field of dentistry.

Dr. Roy Bergstrom, a Chicago native, and Art's associate dean for business and financial services, saw a parallel between Art and his constituency, in this case the faculty, staff, students, alumni, and friends of the dental school, and the two Richard Daleys, father and son, both famous former mayors of Chicago. Roy explained, "The reason people kept electing and re-electing Richard J. Daley, back when I was a kid growing up in Chicago and then in more recent years his son, Richard M., (the longest serving mayor in the city's history) "was because everyone thought they could have been elected to any office they wanted. But rather than seeking state or national office, they chose to continue to serve the people of Chicago.

"After Art had spent ten years as dean of the school, along with his term as president of the CDA and then the ADA, plus his work as a national spokesperson for dentistry, all the impact he had on his profession gave people the feeling that he could have taken any job that he wanted. The fact that he wanted to stay at the school made people feel better about their choice to be part of the school as well. Art began his deanship as a respected member of the school's faculty and ended it as the most respected and recognized name in dentistry."

* * * * *

But before Art grew into the role of being a leader, both in dental education and the profession itself, he had a daunting "to do" list that he had created for himself at the dental school.

Many of today's savvy leaders of schools, colleges and universities, carefully select a signature issue that becomes the legacy for their deanship or presidency. Aware of a variety of political and logistical constraints, one could say that they are more cautious in how they allot their time. As was the custom of leaders of his generation, Art simply could not think in those terms. He took on whatever he thought needed to be addressed and simply pushed forward with his usual brand of determination. If not for his great personal charisma, this pattern of constant action would likely have drawn many detractors. Yet, Art, sincere, open, and fervent in his beliefs, was more like a force of nature. Once he set his mind to a task, he pursued it with unabated vigor.

Dr. Burton Press, Art's predecessor as president of both the CDA and the ADA, said, "Art could write a book on how to give more than any one is expecting you to give. In fact, that is what he always did. He had an incredible number of gifts, but most of all, it was the power of his personality that consistently allowed Art to get people to sit up and pay attention. That was, in my opinion, the source of his influence, both in dental education and organized dentistry."

* * * * *

Not surprisingly, one of his early objectives in reshaping the school was to improve the level of classroom presentation. In Art's time as a member of the school's faculty, and for decades before then, the majority of teaching faculty at a school of dentistry were dentists actively running a practice. To a certain degree, that was always a great strength, but having little, if any, instruction and preparation in the fine art of teaching left both the educator and the student at a disadvantage.

Art, as we have seen, had a lifetime passion for communication. It was a quality that first flourished when he was a boy at St. James High School and continued to reveal itself as he moved up through the ranks of his profession.

Art greatly valued the lasting impact of communication in all aspects of life, particularly in education. He always thought of the teacher's ability to reach and motivate a student as an essential aspect of creating outstanding caregivers, and perhaps most importantly, individuals who would pursue the ideal of being lifelong learners. But just as the lesson that truly effective salesmanship was something that came down to the "last three feet," (the distance between a seller and a buyer) the effectiveness of classroom learning comes down to the connection an educator is able to make with his or her student.

The long tradition of a demanding system of learning that dominated dental education for over a century was the belief that success in learning was the student's responsibility. If an educator followed a prepared course syllabus, presentation skills were not considered. Attentiveness and application on the part of the student were all that were required for success. Art, as you might suspect, did not share that belief.

In an interview Art gave after being chosen as president of the ADA, he explained that, as a dean, it had always been his desire to, "Create an atmosphere that turns people on to learning. As an educator, my responsibility is to inspire and motivate students and faculty to be continual learners. *When you cease to be a student, you cease to be a competent dentist.*"

In other words, what started in elementary school, continued in secondary school, and on into college, dental school, and graduate school, never really ended in Art's view of life. Therefore, it is incumbent upon educators, along each step of a maturing student's path, to do what they can to not only educate, but to inspire.

One comment on the power of a teacher, written by mid-twentieth century Israeli educator Haim Ginott, so resonated with Art that he had it copied and distributed to his faculty every year. His long-held belief that a teacher can serve as the essential inspiration for a lifetime of learning was to Art both an honor and a sacred responsibility.

"I've come to the frightening conclusion," Ginott wrote, "that I am the decisive element in the classroom. It's my personal approach that creates the climate. It's my daily mood that makes the weather. As a teacher, I possess a tremendous power to make a student's life miserable or joyous. I can be a tool of torture or an instrument of inspiration. I can humiliate or humor, hurt or heal. In all situations, it is MY response that decides whether a crisis will be escalated or de-escalated and a student humanized or dehumanized."

The expansion of the humanistic teaching model, introduced during the administration of Art's predecessor, Dr. Dale Redig, and then perfected during the Dugoni years, marked a dramatic shift throughout dental education. It was a turning point that redefined how dentistry was taught and how students in pursuit of a DDS were viewed.

The fact that instructors who were first dentists and second educators had dominated dental school faculties for generations made perfectly good sense. It helped to create students who had a strong grounding in clinical patient skills, and from a practical financial perspective, dental schools, which had always operated on a razor thin margin between profit and loss, were able to produce competent dentists and balance their books by having part time, and predominately volunteer, staff, most of whom were alumni. It also encouraged a system in which practicing dentists could recruit students in taking an entry role in their profession by sharing in one of their instructors' practices. This integration had a very positive impact on Art's development as a practitioner, as seen first in his part-time work while still a student, in the dental office of Dr. Harry True, and the invitation he received to join the practice of Dr. John Tocchini after he completed his second stint of service in the Navy.

As stated, however, the inevitable drawback to this approach was that many of these instructors had neither the training nor the patience to work with novice students. That lack of both qualities led to an atmosphere that too often teetered between teaching and abuse. Legions of dental school graduates left school and never looked back: many of them vowing never to participate in alumni events or contribute to their alma maters, having been so mistreated prior to earning their degree.

Students who took a class from a young Dr. Dugoni in the 1950s and '60s also recall an instructor who could, at times, be less than considerate to his students. Occasionally, he would impatiently hurl an eraser at a student who was doing anything but paying attention in class. But Art evolved rapidly and recognized that the pervasively thoughtless behavior toward future generations of practitioners had to change if the profession was to move forward recognizing the contributions to the field that would one day be made by the next generation of practitioners, educators, and researchers. Once convinced that there was a better path, Art, in time, became one of the nation's leading advocates for a more humane approach to dental education.

That desire on his part created many new directions that would forever change the face of dental education. From white coat ceremonies for students who had completed their first year of classes and were about to begin work in the school's public clinics, to including students in administrative decisions that had never been contemplated before Dugoni. To Art, the logic of this approach was self-evident. The future of the profession (as we'll see in greater detail in a coming chapter) will eventually be placed in the hands of these students. Art believed that when those new to the profession were disrespected, that all-too-obvious fact was ignored. Art graduated into a profession in the late 1940s that was still viewed by many as a trade. When he retired his deanship nearly sixty years later, dentistry was viewed as a learned profession responsible for the oral health of billions of people around the globe. Art played a critical role in creating that change.

* * * * *

Another long-term goal Art set for his deanship was that the school would become better known throughout the dental profession. A key component to accomplishing this was getting faculty, staff, and students into leadership positions in the profession, with a particular emphasis on involvement in the American Dental Association and the California Dental Association.

"Every time you have a faculty member, a staff person, a student or an alumnus, involved in one or more professional organizations," Art explains, "you raise the school's visibility among colleagues and related professionals. There is simply no substitute for that level of involvement."

Art, as in all things, of course walked the walk: first with his long affiliation with the California Dental Association and later as president of the American Dental Association.

Dr. David Nielsen, one of Art's seven associate deans, is a P&S graduate, who went to work for the ADA, and was recruited by Art to return to Pacific in 1980. Charged with oversight of the school's postgraduate and community programs, Dr. Nielsen also provided oversight for the school's alumni association. Between his years at the ADA and his experience working closely with Art as he moved up through the chairs at the CDA and the ADA, Dave Nielsen gained a unique perspective into Art's dual roles as a school dean and an emerging leader in the field of dentistry.

"In 1984, Art became president-elect of the California Dental Association," Dave explains, "and in 1985 he became the president. It was the job of the president-elect during the twelve months prior to assuming the presidency, to make at least one meeting of each one of the thirty-two component dental societies throughout California. It was a logistical nightmare juggling Art's schedule, but by car, plane, and train, Art actually made it to every one of those chapters. I'm not certain, but I don't believe any other president-elect was able to accomplish that entire circuit. The very last one of those component society meetings on Art's schedule was Humboldt County, which met in the small picturesque town of Arcata. The drive up the California coast was over six hours in each direction, and there was no way we could carve out that kind of time from his schedule.

Art reached out to his old friend, Dr. Jim Pride, to once again make the impossible, possible. Jim offered Art the use of his private plane and pilot to get him up to Arcata for the event. About forty-five minutes from landing, the single engine plane ran into some heavy weather and the pilot decided that, in this particular case, he would be better flying beneath the storm clouds, rather than attempting to travel above them.

"When Art returned home safely," Dave recalled, "he told me about this hair-raising adventure they had as he sat next to the pilot who was flying just above the tree tops. Art decided that this was the last time he would take a small private plane to get anywhere in a hurry. But he did make it up to Arcata that day, and they loved having him there."

As part of preparing Art for his visit to these component societies, Dave Nielsen did some advance research and discovered that the school had alumni in almost every one of the state's component societies. "Weeks prior to his appearance, Art reached out to these alumni with a personal invitation to come to the event, and on the day of the event, he made a connection with each one of them before the meeting."

Ultimately, every step that Art took on the long path to the pinnacle of his profession was built on a previous step. He knew that he would never have a powerful alumni base supporting the school's philanthropic goals if he did not make and maintain these all-important connections. Additionally, 1984 was a time when the dental profession was in the midst of a crisis of confidence; Art brought an important and refreshing perspective to dentists, first throughout California, and later throughout the nation that, as Dr. Nielsen explains, was delivered in four parts:

"First and foremost, Art spread optimism and confidence about the future of dentistry. This was a profession with a bright future and, in spite of recent difficulties, this was a great time to be in dentistry. Second, educating tomorrow's dentists is at the core of the profession's future. Third, research done by recognized universities was essential to dentistry's future as well. Research is how the profession grows into new areas of practice such as dental implants. Fourth, it is essential to give something back to your dental school. Art recognized that a lot of dentists had a visceral dislike for their old schools, having felt mistreated as students. But in the age of the humanistic teaching model, all that was changing. Art stressed that supporting your dental school helped to elevate the profession as a whole."

* * * * *

One of Art's early priorities was to build on the three year model for receiving a DDS degree, a program initiated at the school by Dale Redig. Rather than "apologizing for the fact that we were graduating students in three years, rather than four," Art explained, "I wanted to use it as a benefit unique to Pacific." Today, Pacific is still the *only* school in the nation that graduates students in three years, rather than four.

As one of Art's long-time admirers, Kathleen O'Loughlin, the current executive director of the ADA, says, "It has always amazed Art's colleagues in dental education that he was able to succeed so significantly with a three year program."

Certainly, few leaders in dental education would have ever anticipated that graduates of a three-year school would have nearly 100% success on state board licensing examinations.

But, no matter how Art pressed the case for the quality of the school's unique three-year program, he faced skepticism regarding the comprehensive nature and quality of the academic program. More troubling, Art saw that there was a prejudice in graduate and advanced placement programs when Pacific students presented a three-year transcript. So Art, as usual, had a bold idea. He decided to reconfigure the school's three-year transcript into a four-year transcript.

In reality, the school covered a four-year program in three years, so why should a student's transcript not reflect that? The three-year program was not accomplished through the use of academic shortcuts or less rigorous standards, but principally by following a radically different school year calendar, one that did away with long summer and winter session breaks.

Art was determined to see Pacific recognized for achieving and maintaining a high level of success, and part of that was building on the school's long tradition of clinical excellence. He knew, from 1946 on, when he first stepped into the patient clinic at P&S, that its real magic was a devoted team of faculty who were current practitioners (just as he had been for three decades) who were also alumni. All of them viewed the school as an integral part of their lives and their profession. Now, he wanted to go the extra step as he steered the school toward a more solid academic footing.

"Pacific today," Art says, "has over a century-long tradition of leadership and mentorship. The humanistic model that Dale Redig began complemented that bond between practitioner, teacher, alumnus, and students seamlessly. Everyday our faculty works in the clinic, they have a chance to touch the future of this profession. Today's teachers won't be caring for patients in the second half of this century, but the students they are working with will do exactly that. And, I believe, as future instructors and mentors, they will give a part of their professional lives to helping prepare the practitioners of the twenty-second century…a third century of service for the private dental college that Dr. Charles Boxton began in 1896."

* * * * *

The challenges he faced, both as a dean and a leader of his profession, stretched on much like they would for anyone standing at the start of a long country road trying to envision what lay ahead on the distant horizon. Committing to a long journey is an act of faith. It's easy to lose your sense of direction along the way. But Art was steadfast in his determination not to lose sight of his many goals. He never turned away from his belief that every road inevitably leads to a potentially brighter future. Turning visions into reality required a combination of wisdom, faith, organizational skills, and a willingness to work long hours. Luckily for his school and his profession, Art had all these gifts and more.

Dr. David Nielsen: keeping up with
Art was just one of his full-time jobs.

The crew of Dentistry Update turn Art's office into a television set.

Lina's adoration for her son shines through in her eyes.

Art kisses his first grandchild, Mike's daughter, Christine, in 1981.

Chapter Sixteen

Consensus Builder

There is an old expression in academia that the only thing harder to move than a faculty is a cemetery. Simply stated, change does not come easily to any institution.

Art, a great admirer of the work of Machiavelli, was fully aware of this reality. One of his favorite quotes from the sixteenth century philosopher's masterwork *The Prince*, explained perfectly a leader's dilemma.

"It ought to be remembered that there is nothing more difficult to take in hand, more perilous to conduct, or more uncertain in its success, than to take the lead in the introduction of a new order of things. The innovator has for enemies all those who have done well under the old conditions, and lukewarm defenders among those who may do well under the new."

At the time he assumed the deanship, Art was a practicing orthodontist, additionally he had done extensive work in pediatric and restorative dentistry, gained a master's degree in orthodontics, and as proven in his massive doctoral thesis, he had an abiding respect for the rigors of both academics and research. Further, Art had been an instructor with over two decades of teaching experience behind him. Perhaps most importantly, he had proven his business acumen in the formation of a very large professional group practice, a practice that in size and scope was arguably two-to-three decades ahead of its time.

Through the wisdom he gained working in close association with three of his predecessors, Sloman, Tocchini, and Redig, he knew that leading the dental school would require all the talent and enthusiasm he could bring to the job.

You can be a creative and energetic dean, but no number of "to-do" lists and long-term goal planning will ultimately bring about change. To accomplish the sweeping reforms he envisioned and to create and institute new approaches and programs, Art would need to bring to the process his unique ability to reach and motivate people, and perhaps most importantly, to build consensus.

"You can't bring any group to a consensus without first making them aware of the big picture," Art explains. "By our nature, we focus narrowly on our specific area of work. I never accused anyone of not understanding the bigger picture, I just attempted to describe an issue in a broader context."

Art believed that bringing forth all the available and relevant information on any given subject meant every discussion would have well-informed participants, hopefully making a consensus easier to achieve. This was an underlying reason for the paper blizzard that descended from the dean's office during the Dugoni era. Wise decision-making was a direct result of a well-informed staff.

"In almost any institution," Art explains, "Staff, faculty, and students, are first concerned with how changes affect their specific area and interests. It's unwise to stifle that conversation. Because, I can assure you, if it does not occur when you're in the room, it will occur as soon as you step out. After I would make my case for whatever program or approach I thought we should consider, I would write on my pad KYMSS, that was a reminder to myself to *'keep your mouth shut, stupid.'* When I was tempted to cut off debate, or even stop someone in mid-sentence, I would look down at my pad and remember that people are not ready to bend until they first believe that they have been heard. Rather than interrupting, I would circle KYMSS on my note pad and remain patient. There were times that I drew a dozen circles before the discussion was complete."

Dr. David Chambers, associate dean for academic affairs throughout the twenty-eight years of Art's deanship, attended countless meetings with Art, both privately and as part of various administrative councils. "I always felt that Art wanted stable solutions so that everyone would win," he explained. "Art always hoped that you would walk away from the table as committed to something as he was. His aim was always to find a true solution. He knew you couldn't get that by talking; it happens by listening. Art uses listening to build relationships."

Dr. Chambers, like all of Art's professional colleagues, easily reveals a deep fondness for his former boss. Only half-jokingly he adds, "Art will listen to you until you agree with him."

Everyone who worked with Art mentions that he would have a gesture in which he would put his hands out in front of him and then draw his fingers back towards himself. This was Art's way of saying, "Tell me what you think, give me more details."

"You must draw your staff into the conversation, because if they are not partic-ipating, you cannot get them to join you in reaching a consensus," Art explains. "I would say I'm going to propose this. Is it a good idea, or bad idea? Tell me what you think. Once they were engaged and they had told me what they want-ed, I'd say: Okay, can I count on your support?"

The inner dynamic that moved Art forward was the hard-driving engine in-side of him, which was consistently masked by a presence of outward calm and gracious warmth. To have redefined his profession and impacted the teaching of dentistry for generations to come, there was a lot more to the man than his charm.

As a lifetime lover of sports, particularly as seen in his passion for playing basketball, Art knew that teams follow leaders who inspire them…leaders who believe in the potential of each team member to excel. In terms of that game, Art was always ready to take a shot, but understood the critical importance of being able to pass the ball as well. When you played with Art, on or off the court, he made it crystal clear that, in his view, every member of the team had an im-portant role to play. That deep respect for others was ingrained in his character beginning with his childhood.

His mastery in leading a conversation, no doubt, led everyone on his staff to conclude that he could have won any office he sought. Other deans and lead-ers of professional associations felt much the same way. Dr. Burton Press, who served on a variety of committees with Art over the many years they were active in both the CDA and the ADA, came to admire what he called Art's "gentle persistence."

"I'll tell you this about Art," Dr. Press adds, "If he had decided to enter the priesthood, he would have been elected the first American pope."

Art's easy charm might have led many to conclude that he was a "go along to get along," kind of guy. But he clearly was not. Dr. Chambers, who came to Pacific in 1971 to serve in Dale Redig's administration, marveled at the different styles of both men.

"Redig and Dugoni were equally important in redefining the school's future. Redig was a surgeon, he came in and made the changes that had to be made, Art was a physician, a healer, and he made the school whole again."

Redig, you might say, was an example of the old adage, "You can't make an omelet without breaking a few eggs." Art was always considered something of a magician in dealing with the sensitive aspects of human relations, because he had an uncanny talent for coaxing eggs out of their shells.

As Art explains his management style, "I came into a lot of organizations with an agenda, not in pursuit of something that impacted me directly, but something I felt needed to happen."

In any and all of his leadership roles, Art did not push for modest change or incremental improvements, but often seeking to make bold strides. Reminiscent of the hard-driving basketball player, avoiding turnovers and moving the ball forward was priority one. Taking a hard hit by way of criticism was, to Art, simply a part of playing the game.

So, for example, in 1985, when he served as president of the American Board of Orthodontics, he stepped into the difficult issue of asking why 90% of oral surgeons were boarded in their specialty but only 18% of orthodontists had gained the same level of accreditation.

Art began with a simple question, "Why are we not able to do that as well?" In response, he was told, "We've always done it this way."

Of course, as you would expect, Art would not accept that line of reasoning. "I challenged the status quo by asking, 'Why can't we approach this differently?' How about if future practitioners started in school by selecting a case that they would be boarded in? We talked about every issue that made it difficult to be boarded in seven years after entering practice. In a short time, it became clear that the system itself needed an overhaul."

That is revealing as to Art's approach in navigating an array of tricky topics and sensitive issues. As the ADA's O'Loughlin explains, Art's desire to achieve consensus did not exclude those moments when he took a direction opposed by every other person in the room. But he was always sanguine about such moments. "Art can read a room," O'Loughlin says, "better than anyone I've ever met. He's spot-on in understanding people. He's always an active participant in every conversation."

Perhaps that innate understanding of what others are thinking is at the heart of his ability to shuffle the cards, without disturbing the deck…making change while balancing the needs of entrenched interests.

"What Art values," David Chambers explains, "is not being right, although usually he is, but that's not his goal. What he really values is the group moving ahead together. Art leads, not just from the front, but from the center, and anywhere else in the group."

A large part of what Art did throughout his career was to follow the path once suggested by the great writer George Bernard Shaw, who famously said, "Some men see things as they are and ask why. Others dream things that never were and ask why not."

Dreamers, for all they are admired, particularly with the benefit of the wider perspective of history, tend to have targets painted on their backs. Regardless of your talent for building consensus; if you're frequently asking, "Why not?" a fair amount of criticism is bound to come your way. Art successfully deflected much of that criticism with his relaxed humor, frequently prefacing his proposals as, "Another crazy idea from Dugoni!"

Art was happy to take any amount of criticism, so long as it began a dialogue and got people thinking about taking a new approach. He was one of those very rare individuals who, in most cases, could successfully separate his ego from his goals. Once again, moving the ball forward was worth the sharp elbows he encountered along the way.

One such "crazy idea," Dugoni raised early in his deanship was a proposal to purchase a building on Post Street, seven blocks from the dental school, to provide space for student housing. Individuals in and out of the administration thought this was a preposterous notion, after all, as many alums suggested, "It wasn't needed in our time." But in 1980, during a time of dramatic inflation, coupled with declining dental school enrollments, Art saw housing as an important benefit that the school could offer. This was particularly beneficial since Art had launched an ambitious student recruitment effort going after promising students in western states that, at the time, had no dental schools: states such as Arizona, Hawaii, Nevada, and Utah, to name just four.

One of Art's overarching expectations for his deanship was the transformation of the dental school from a regional reputation to an institution of both national and international stature. An important step in reaching that goal, particularly given the financial realities of the time, could be accomplished by providing student housing.

Art sat through many meetings where the choice of investing in student housing was questioned. Many suggested that students could arrange to stay with friends or family in the area, not realizing that Art's long term plan was to eventually bring students to Pacific who were leaving family and friends a thousand or more miles behind.

In the end, Art prevailed, convincing both the school's foundation board, his executive committee, and the university's president and board of regents that this investment in student housing was part of a bigger vision for the school.

The student housing building, purchased and refurbished for $3.5 million, served the needs of countless hundreds of students over a period of three decades, and became a valuable asset for Pacific, selling in 2013 for $27 million. This was nearly a nine-fold increase over the property's purchase and renovation cost.

But Art, as you might suspect, had many other "crazy" ideas, two of which were the creation of a maxillofacial surgical program, a specialty that treats a variety of diseases, injuries and other problems of the head, face, neck, and jaws; and on Pacific's Stockton campus, the development of a facility and program to educate and train oral hygienists to fill staff shortages in dental offices throughout Northern California.

One of Art's boldest innovations was creating an undergraduate program in conjunction with Stockton to offer undergrads options for fast track educational programs that, for gifted students, allowed them to complete college in a two- or three-year program and then get their DDS at Pacific in just three years. Nearly all those qualified opted for the three plus three option, however a large percentage that elected and completed the two plus three program graduated valedictorians. The success of the program surprised many, but not Art, who was quick to remind people that, when he graduated from dental school in 1948, he was just a few weeks passed his twenty-third birthday.

Dr. Robert Christoffersen, who served as Art's executive associate dean, explains that Art had, "impeccable intuition." Never hesitant to enter the fray, Christoffersen says of Dugoni, "When he knew something was important to the school, like the addition of the maxillofacial surgery program, or the creation of an oral hygiene program, he drove with a relentless sense of purpose toward that goal. Many times, the administrative council told Art to give up on the acquisition of Highland Hospital's oral maxillofacial surgery program, but he persisted in his belief that this was the right move for the school."

But through all the long hours of discussion and debate, as Christoffersen points out, "Art remained loyal to his team. In public, he was always supportive of them."

"When ideas are challenged," Art explains, "that is when they prove their worth. If they can't stand up to objections and criticisms, perhaps they were not very sound positions to begin with."

In time, the oral hygiene facility was built on the Stockton campus, and that program was launched shortly before Dugoni left the deanship, and the acquisition of Highland Hospital's oral maxillofacial surgery program was completed as well. In both cases, Art's quiet persistence as a determined consensus-builder eventually brought about success. He coaxed the eggs out of their shells and left nothing broken.

Another "crazy idea" that grew into one of Art's crowning achievements was offering a degree program in International Dental Studies, (IDS). This creation was emblematic of two important threads in the fabric that make up Art's life: First, as the son of immigrants, Art was forever in awe of the struggle of his grandparents and parents in establishing their lives in a foreign land where the language, customs, and culture were all unknown to them. Second, was the increasing level of international issues in dentistry that Art was exposed to through his work with the ADA and the FDI, the World Dental Federation.

At the time that Art pushed for a program that would accept students from around the world who wanted to practice here in the United States, there were four programs already in operation at the University of Southern California, University of Pennsylvania, Loma Linda University, and New York University.

One of the many assignments that Art entrusted to Dr. David Nielsen was oversight of the new IDS program that welcomed its first students to the school in 1987.

While the program, Nielsen explains, was in place at other schools, Art brought his own unique twist when he decided to integrate IDS students into as much of the school's curriculum as possible.

"Art was a huge advocate of how much students from around the globe were bringing to our program for American students," Dr. Nielsen explains. "In the first six months, IDS students study on their own. In the next six months they integrate into classes and clinical work with the school's second year students and then in their second and final year they are fully integrated into the third year DDS program for all students."

Culturally, this integration has immeasurably enriched the school's entire student body.

As Dr. Nielsen explains, "Different cultures would look at the same problem and come up with different approaches and solutions. A good example of that is the extraction of a tooth. The IDS students helped to bridge the gap between what we do here in America and what the rest of the world does.

"Additionally, the program has reshaped our international outreach and enriched our linguistic abilities. In China and India, the world's most populated nations, where there are multiple dialects, the IDS students were always of great help."

One student, originally from Southeast Asia, who became one of the refugees known as the boat people after the fall of Vietnam, went through the IDS program and established a practice outside of Fresno where over ten thousand

Hmong people (an Asian ethnic group originally from a mountainous region of China, Thailand, Laos and Vietnam) now live. About three years after he graduated, he told Dave Nielsen, "I never speak English in my practice. I've been able to get into the local schools and speak to the Hmong children and families about dental hygiene."

"This is just one example of cultural influence the program has had," Dr. Nielsen explains. "Several of our graduates have left America and gone back to their country and raised the level of care. We'll never know the many ways this program has improved the oral health of thousands of people around the world, but I have no doubt that it has done just that."

The IDS program has always been relatively small. It started with just seven students and today offers 22 seats each year for which there are over 700 applicants.

"I had the idea, but I did not make it happen," Art says. "I have a lucky star. I pick the right people and they made me look good. That's exactly what happened with IDS."

Another critical area in which Art worked closely with Dave Nielsen was in the expansion of alumni outreach to many of the western states where Pacific had a growing number of graduates. The expanded student base that he pursued in the 1980s became the expanded alumni base of the 1990s.

"Art felt," Dr. Nielsen explains, "that our obligation to the students was to be there for them after they graduated. He would often say, 'you're going to be a student here for three years, but you'll be an alumnus for life.'"

Together with Art, Dave Nielsen would travel throughout the Western states to meet with various alumni associations. "Art would stay involved in their lives, always asking questions like: 'How is your family?'"

As you might suspect, this created a renewed bond between these graduates and their school. As the years went by, dozens of them sent their sons and daughters to Pacific.

"Our alumni events would parallel with the annual meeting of a state's local dental society," Dr. Nielsen explains. "The goal was to develop lifelong relationships with our graduates…a bond between institution and student all built on the bedrock of what Art referred to as the 'Pacific family connection.' I would say faith and family were huge motivators for him. Art brought those values to this institution."

One more of Art's concepts for the school was to initiate a post-graduate education program entitled Advanced Education in General Dentistry.

"When I became dean, I realized there should be more opportunities to grow as I did when Sloman directed me into the Bethesda Graduate Medical Education program at the US Naval Dental School," Art explains. "Originally, students went into practice or graduate programs. Graduates going into advanced education programs have grown dramatically in the last decade. This has given the graduate many more options after obtaining their DDS."

To his former students, Art gave the same advice he gave to so many of his colleagues throughout a sixty-plus-year career, "We serve our patients best when we are committed to lifelong learning."

* * * * *

Perhaps it has been in his vision of philanthropy (a topic discussed in detail in a later chapter) that Art encountered his most significant resistance. In Art's view, philanthropy has always been a needed ingredient in the advancement of both dental education and research.

A little over two years into his tenure, in an address to the school's alumni association delivered on January 30, 1981, Art laid out certain themes that persisted throughout the balance of his deanship. In his address, "Dreaming the Dream: Our Future Greatness," he pointed out that, traditionally, the cost to educate a dentist had always been considerably higher than the annual tuition fees charged per student. In spite of rises in tuition costs, there was still a significant gap ($10,000 in 1980 for example) between each student's tuition and the actual cost of their education.

It was incumbent upon graduates that they give back to an institution that did so much to support them and make them successful professionals serving their patients and earning a good income. Turning to the audience, he said, "Just think, there are 300 of you in this room. If you would each pledge $10,000 over five years, which is only $165 per month, you will have raised enough money to fund the entire student housing facility of $3.5 million."

Three examples of educational enhancements to the school's offerings were International Dental Studies, IDS; the Advanced Education in General Dentistry, AGED, and the Stockton campus based Dental Hygiene program.

To Art, there was no greater force for good then the application of focused intention. He recognized, as he often said, that what separated good schools from great schools was the size of their endowments.

His abiding faith in philanthropy led him to accept his last position of leadership, as the president of the American Dental Association's Foundation, to introduce one last "Crazy Idea from Dugoni." His hope was to create a billion dollar plus endowment for student scholarships. But this time, the great builder of consensus could not convince dental school deans across the nation to come to a collective agreement on how the initiative would accrue and distribute its scholarship funds, even though it was agreed that donors could designate gifts for use by specific institutions.

Art, as you might suspect, viewed it differently. In his view, every push for a greater act of philanthropy spurs an awakening in new donors to join the cause of investing generously in the future of the profession.

Art, by now in the ninth decade of his life, pursued the idea with his usual vigor, meeting with dozens of deans and foundations individually, working and reworking the concept in the hope that it would succeed. While it fell short of its goal, the foundation campaign raised over $600 million and spawned an untold amount of individual giving that went directly to individual institutions and programs.

In the example of the ADA Foundation, we can see, once again, Art's limitless ambition…his habitual drive to move the ball forward. To all who worked by Art's side, his energy, persistence, and focus was a thing of wonder. Arguably, there was never any real magic in turning so many visions into realities. It was the combination of hard work and endless patience. None of that comes easily; Art's array of talents only made it look that way.

The Silver Fox: Art where he spent countless hours,
consensus building over the phone.

Kaye, the first lady of the ADA.

Art waves as he rushes past.

Chapter Seventeen

Students Are the Future

It's not possible to understand Art's work as an educator without an appreciation for the deep respect that he held for each and every student. This respect could well be rooted in his struggles to get a degree in dentistry while the long shadow of World War II fell upon every aspect of American life.

While he no doubt came to appreciate the time that he spent at the University of Missouri, Kansas Western Dental School, he was certainly not there by his own choosing. Further, the cold greeting he received in 1946 from Dean Fleming and the UCSF dental school that suggested he might have to start his entire quest for a doctorate in dental surgery all over again, undoubtedly created the lasting impression that the hopes and hard work of any student can be quickly dashed upon the rocks of institutional indifference.

It was not until Art stepped inside Dean Sloman's office in the old P&S building that he was introduced to a different view of what the school/student relationship could potentially accomplish. Sloman, by his very nature, was a humanist well before the term was popularized.

Dean Sloman's influence on Art's perspective of what a positive model of dental education might look like is immeasurable. But it is reasonable to conclude that they fit well with Art's immigrant sensibility of what the promise of an American education could represent. As Lina Dugoni knew well, and relentlessly impressed upon her children, access to a quality education was the great American equalizer. Family name and social status could, of course, ease one's path to success, but ambition, intelligence, and hard work, coupled with educational opportunities could lead to great success regardless of your pedigree.

In the modern era, Pacific's School of Dentistry welcomed 140 new students to its three-year degree program joined by a relatively small group of students enrolled in other programs such as Orthodontics, IDS, AEGD, Oral Maxillofacial Surgery, and Hygiene. Therefore, at any given time, the school had a total of less than 500 degree and doctoral candidates. During Dugoni's deanship, the applicant pool, which dipped only during the early 1980s as enrollment in dental schools declined nationwide, rose steadily, averaging more than twenty applicants for each available seat. Art often said to his students that they were "the best of the best." And he treated them as such from their first day at the school to their last.

Prior to the start of each school year, which for Pacific with its unique three-year program occurred in the second week of July, Art would spend several hours in his office studying the student files of each new student. His rare ability to remember faces, names and personal facts led to amazement on the part of first-year students, as their dean already knew the name of each new student and the school where they completed their undergraduate studies.

When asked why he felt it was important to be able to do this, Art explains, "I took the time to know something about each student before they began the program because, in truth, every one of us wants to be recognized."

In fact, Art followed that same path in a variety of professional encounters. When assigned to a committee within the CDA, ADA, or other professional organizations, Art would review any and all printed materials regarding his fellow conference participants. His diligence was rewarded by legions of admirers. To Art's way of thinking, if each and every student and colleague is a person of importance, what better way can that sentiment be expressed than by the simple, but deeply meaningful, act of recognition?

Students who attended Pacific during the Dugoni years all tell a similar story about the close connection that they felt to their dean. Even with his busy travel schedule, particularly in 1988 and 1989, when he served as president-elect and president of the ADA, he made time for his school's students.

Early in his deanship, he initiated monthly student meetings that grew into what were later called "brown bag lunches." Of course, Art, who had a seemingly endless thirst for information, instituted regular meetings with staff and faculty as well, in which he would often ask, "What would you do differently in your job if you had the chance?"

At the same time, Art was keenly aware that any leader who expressed a willingness to listen to any and all concerns needed certain ground rules to keep that input from devolving into a series of personal gripe sessions. Art's two principal caveats were simple: one, if you present a problem, present a possible solution; and two, always remain confident in your ability to effect change.

Art has often reminded adults who were ten, twenty, or more years beyond the completion of their education that a "dental school is a building with the future inside." He has always seen every one of his students not just as future practitioners, educators, researchers, and in some cases, all three, but equally important, as future leaders of their communities. For decades, Art has shared with nearly every audience his mantra that, "At Pacific, we build people, who along the way happen to become doctors." Art was keenly aware that producing doctors who were practitioners, researchers, and educators, but also engaged in the success of their profession and the life of their communities, would have a lasting effect on the future.

In the area of student participation in the overall governance of the school, Art's logic was simple and direct. Any organization is only as strong as its weakest link. Students shut out of any substantive involvement in their school's decision-making process will inevitably be dissatisfied with their education and one day resentful of their alma mater. Just as a reminder, only a decade or two before Art assumed the deanship, classes graduating in the '50s and '60s had students pledging to one another that, in the years to come, they would never support the school with their time or treasure.

Today's graduates are tomorrow's benefactors. Deans who dismissed or marginalized the importance of the student body's role in their own educational process unwittingly placed their school's future in jeopardy.

Art's vision has been proven as correct time and time again. The philanthropy that one day would play an essential role in the opening of a new school facility in 2014, principally came from the students who graduated during the twenty-eight years of his deanship. The future needs for the school in 2050 will more fully be in the hands of the Class of 2020 than the Class of 1980. Art's hope was that the creation of an unshakeable tradition in building a strong humanistic model would help assure the school's continued success.

* * * * *

One of the students of the Dugoni years, Nader Nadershahi, who graduated from Pacific in 1994, is today executive associate dean, as well as the associate dean for academic affairs at the Dugoni School of Dentistry. During his years as a student, Dr. Nadershahi served two years as class president and one as student body treasurer.

"I remember that there was always a strong culture of support and expectation to be involved with leadership and determine the future of, not only our school, but the profession itself," Nader explains. "Art's administration was sincerely interested in listening to feedback and input from all of us. Part of the humanistic culture at the dental school was displayed in how we were treated as colleagues in the decision-making process. Students were given a voice in every committee to ensure that the perspective of all major stakeholders was considered."

Dr. Nadershahi remembers well those student leadership lunches with Dean Dugoni and his executive administrators, in which courses were evaluated along with the availability of outreach opportunities.

"We were always listened to respectfully and provided with the support to pursue appropriate solutions or approaches to improve the experience of the students and patients at the school's public clinics."

Dr. Nadershahi also recalls that the development of the now-successful SCOPE (Student Community Outreach for Public Education) program came from one such discussion in which some of his classmates had an interest in developing a more formalized outreach program. With the support of both Dean Dugoni and faculty members, a small group of students began forming relationships in the community to provide education and minor services for pediatric and geriatric patients throughout San Francisco and the East Bay.

In later years, the SCOPE program was recognized nationally as a model of effective student outreach.

After being in private practice, and later after returning to the school as a Group Practice Administrator, there are a few things that stand out in Nader's recollections of Dean Dugoni's constant support and inspiration.

"First, he would meet with us as a group, along with the associate dean for clinical services, Dr. Ron Borer and later Dr. Richard Fredekind. During these discussions, he was interested in hearing our concerns, or any ideas we had for making improvements to patient care or the management of the students' clinical education. He reminded us continuously of the importance of the role we played in maintaining the culture of the school, since the clinical faculty, staff, and students looked to us as leaders and role models in the delivery of patient care and clinical education. He understood that the behaviors we modeled would be taken by each student and transformed one day into their future professional practices."

But, no doubt, here as well, the personal charm of Art came through. Dr. Nadershahi, looking back on the many years he has known Art, calls him "a multiplier." Explaining that, "He consistently brought out the genius inside an organization by encouraging each individual to give 120%.

"Art was always gracious in his words of encouragement and support in making sure we understood that the role we played was important and vital to the success of our students. Art made sure that we all felt valued and appreciated for what we did. During his quarterly brown bag lunches with the students, Art made a point of mentioning how much our hard work was reflected in our GPAs, (grade point averages) and what it meant in the school's overall ranking of its educational program. He worked hard to help us feel like we were fully informed of what was going on in the school and that we were directly connected to the school's overall mission and the true measure of its success."

* * * * *

Art pushed successfully for students at dental schools across the nation to have an expanded role through the American Dental Association's House of Delegates.

As the ADA's Kathleen O'Loughlin explains, "Today, students hold five seats in the ADA's house of delegates, which is a larger delegation than several states can claim. I think Art's lasting legacy will be cementing the change in creating a humanistic philosophy in dental education. Students are motivated by a sense of accomplishment, and Art had the wisdom to understand that truth. Putting students on a school's finance committee was unheard of prior to Art Dugoni."

But to Art's view of the institution he inherited and the one that he envisioned in the future, this made perfectly obvious sense. "I wanted our students to always be aware of the financial realities that administration faced in the school's operation. Empowerment begins with transparency."

The school's tradition known as "brown bag lunches," started with Art meeting with eight students for lunch in his office. If you wanted to know more about how your school functioned, attending those luncheons was a great way to find out. It was also a good way to bring questions directly to the dean. As previously explained, Art's one ground rule was, if you came with a problem, attempt to present a possible solution as well.

"I strongly suggested," Art explains, "that all the associate deans and group administrators be in attendance at our brown bag sessions. The aim was to have students and student leaders of each class tell me what was going on in their classes and in their clinical work. Problems that arose were never set aside. I told the students that, during the coming week, they would get a written response with the decision of the school's administrative council.

"It was important to all of our students to know that they had the opportunity to engage faculty and administration on issues of concern, to make sure everyone felt they were a part of the process."

In his relationship with students, Art was driven, as he was in every other aspect of the school, to move forward with a shared awareness that a consensus had formed. As always, he accomplished this with a willingness to listen. He also chose wisely to hear from a class representative for each of the school's different class years. That way the voices and concerns of first year students would not be overlooked simply because third year students had a better idea of how to communicate with faculty and department chairs. Working in harmony with each class was, to Art, an essential measure of the overall success of the school.

"People like to say in real estate that the most important thing is location, location, location. In effectively motivating people to perform at their highest level, the critical component is communication, communication, communication," Art explains. "Let students know that they are essential to how we define the process of learning. When you successfully communicate to them that their success determines the school's success, everyone wins."

One more aspect of Art's formula for maintaining open channels of communication with his student body was holding twice-annual dinners in one of the school's seminar rooms. To these dinners, Art invited a group of sixty, made up of all student class leaders, department chairs, and students who held leadership positions in various dental societies. Art recalls the key to each dinner's success was to limit them to two hours and keep the participants focused with the use of time limits for each individual.

"The dinners created a greater sense of fellowship between faculty, staff, and students and were an important part of expressing our humanistic model of education in practical terms," Art explains. "Department chairs were a little concerned, at first, that these dinners would devolve into gripe sessions, but for the most part, they were remarkably positive, with all participants taking away a renewed sense that we were holding to our joint intention of creating our nation's best dentists graduating from our nation's best dental school."

Dugoni had, perhaps, an unparalleled passion for communicating with students. As he neared his eighty-ninth birthday, years after his retirement from the deanship, he continued to speak to first year classes at the Dugoni School of Dentistry. In one speech he has delivered many times, "Road Signs on the Road of Life," he shares this wisdom:

"You will become the future of this profession, and you will be one of the most affluent members of your community. The environment of your school was designed to bring out the best in you. Being at this school means you are committed to service above self. If we have not grown you to be committed to your patients, your community, and your profession, then we have failed."

Referring to the dental school's rich traditions and history, Art explains, "More than one hundred years ago, a group of citizens and practitioners came together determined to change the trade of dentistry into the profession of dentistry. Bringing science and education into dentistry. It took dentistry nearly seventy-five years to go from a trade to a respected learned profession."

Art was determined to inform his students that their profession, which had been built with such care and dedication, would be in their hands. "We have gone," he said, "from ignorance to understanding because of the standards and quality of education, practice, and our clinical and scientific efforts."

He was keenly aware of the corrosive nature and the corruptive influence that knowledge and money can present. He cautioned students to treat their patients with respect and to commit themselves to the highest levels of performance. What will destroy a reputation and any profession, could be found, as Art frequently suggested, in the words of Gandhi who cautioned against: "Politics without principle; Wealth without work; Business without humanity."

"My mother," Art told his students, "lived to almost one hundred years of age. Do you know why? She had a good dentist. Treat your patients as you would your mother, your father, your sister, or your brother, and you will always do your very best."

Near the end of his years as dean, Art told a class of graduates, "I've been privileged to touch over 7,000 lives through my work at the dental school. Living a life that matters happens by choice. Grab life by the ears and take it dancing. Make every day a masterpiece."

The loyalty and admiration in the voices of countless graduates during the twenty-eight years of his tenure is powerful testimony to his success. Art put his students first, and in turn, they did the same for their dean.

Art Dugoni and Nader Nadershahi.

Art and Dr. Cindy Lyon. Lyon was instrumental in the
creation of the Stockton Oral Hygiene Clinic.

Art and Dr. Ron Redmond. Ron's wife, Margaret, is seated to Art's right.

Art and Craig Yarborough.

Art, as Dean Emeritus, hoping to inspire
more future leaders of dentistry.

Chapter Eighteen

The Art of Leadership

As we have already seen, there are countless reasons why Art Dugoni would be considered an exceptional leader.

Without an overview of his leadership style as a whole, it would be difficult, if not impossible, to understand the oversized footprint that Art has left in the fields of dental education, research and practice. Of the many facets of his life, his leadership abilities will undoubtedly be at the heart of his legacy.

Not only was Art willing to dream dreams that many were often quick to ridicule as grandiose or impractical, but he had the courage to speak, write, and campaign for many of those dreams.

In his comfort with "sticking his neck out," we see one of the key components of Art's leadership style, a willingness to take risks and make bold decisions, all while moving his beloved school and his profession forward. Maintaining the status quo was not in Art's essential makeup. He probed and poked at possibilities. Additionally, he used his ravenous intellectual appetite in search of information to seek new ways to improve programs. He drove every individual, regardless of rank or position, to perform at his or her highest level.

As Dr. Nader Nadershahi experienced, both as a student and later as part of staff and academic administration, Art brought out the best in everyone.

Nadershahi's earlier reference to Art as a "multiplier," is from a term popularized by the 2010 leadership book, *Multipliers: How the Best Leaders Make Everyone Smarter.* As Nader explained, "He encouraged you to give 120%. He accomplished that by genuinely caring deeply about every individual, regardless of his or her role in the institution. Through Art's passion we connected to the school more deeply. How he integrated us as students into the operational aspects of the school is just one example. Because of the way we were treated, we felt we were in the best school in the world. Clearly the spirit that Art encouraged permeated the school."

In the book by Liz Wiseman and Greg McKeown, "multipliers" are described as individuals who have a unique ability to encourage growth and creativity, not only from their staff, but virtually everyone that they encounter.

You can find Art's leadership qualities described in highly recognizable ways in a number of best selling books on the subject. Art himself has had a long fascination with the topic as seen by the fact that one entire bookshelf of his office is filled with books on leadership. Further, as he always suggested to faculty, staff, and students, he followed his own advice to act as a "lifelong learner."

In addition to his passion for books on the topic of leadership, Art made time, as previously mentioned, to take courses in leadership and management at such distinguished institutions as Stanford University and Penn's Wharton School of Business in San Francisco.

Art ran his administrative team meetings as an openly democratic system. "I made it a point to meet with every member of the faculty and staff, and in every meeting I would ask, 'If you were dean for a day what would you do?' But, when Art was convinced that the time was right to move forward, he was comfortable making a decision even if, at the time, his was the only voice in the room to move forward.

"In my appointment book," Art explains, "I would block out an hour or two every week and put it down as 'MBWA.' That's an acronym for 'management by walking around,' a term popularized by management consultants, Tom Peters and Bob Waterman. To me, it is essential for a good leader to know all his people."

Dr. Jason Calvert, a graduate of the class of 2000, told of a surprise encounter he had with his dean, "During my freshman year, I would come to school early and practice preps in the simulation lab. One morning, I entered the empty second floor locker room and heard some shuffling a few rows over. I noticed a silver-haired man in a suit picking up trash. An instant later, I realized it was the dean." Later, in a note he wrote to Dean Dugoni, he said, "Not only do you 'talk the talk,' you 'walk the walk.' Your passion for Pacific is greatly appreciated."

Unbeknownst to others, Art always had a destination when heading out for an MBWA. He would ask his staff to give him the name, for example, of everyone on the second floor. He wanted names of spouses, children, and wanted to know if someone was facing a difficult situation at home. It could be the illness of a child or a spouse, or the loss of a family member. Good news was important as well…the son or daughter who just got married, won the college scholarship, or perhaps their school's science fair.

As a leader, Art was keenly aware that no one leaves their personal life behind the moment they step into the workplace. To Art's way of thinking, if you were going to cultivate a humanistic model in the workplace, then that has to start at the very top with the dean.

"My message to faculty, staff, and students was that we were family," Art says. "That only has real meaning if you live that message. Knowing people's names and knowing something about their families and their personal accomplishments is an essential part of saying that you care. Humanism and caring are inseparable. We have staff members who have accomplished remarkable feats. Duke Dahlin in our business office, for example, took off time to train for swimming the English Channel. When he achieved that goal, it arguably had nothing to do with his daily job, but he had justifiable pride in what he had done, and we, as his extended family, had great reason to celebrate along with him."

In Art's blending of family and team, as we'll see in his ADA inaugural address, once again, sports has helped to play a defining role in Art's view of success. He experienced team coaching that could turn a mid-level team into champs and the opposite effect, where a lack of motivation and inspiration could diminish a team's cohesiveness, drive, and confidence.

What is particularly interesting in studying Art's approach to leadership is how many best-selling books on leadership skills read as if they used Dugoni as their model.

Most striking perhaps is Jim Collins description of "Level 5" leaders in his best selling 2001 book, *Good to Great*. "Level 5 leaders are a study in duality,"

Collins explains. "Modest and willful, humble and fearless." Further on, Collins writes, "Level 5 leadership is not just about humility and modesty, it is equally about resolve, an almost stoic determination to do whatever needs to be done to make the company great."

Level 5 leaders most often serve as a bridge, taking a company or organization from good to great. In the modern history of the dental school, there is little debate that Dale Redig inherited a proud but troubled institution and steadied both its will and spirit. A dispirited staff, faculty, and student body was raised up by a new style of humanism that, at the time, was foreign to most other professional schools.

Principally, however, "Dale Redig changed the culture of the school as it pertained to the treatment of students," explains retired University of the Pacific's Provost, Phil Gilbertson. "Art took that model of humanism and made it part of the school's culture. From senior faculty to the maintenance staff, Art showed concern and respect for everyone who was a part of his school."

"Dugoni seized on the concept of humanism and perfected it," his successor, Dean Patrick Ferrillo points out.

The impact of Level 5 leaders reaches well beyond their tenure. As Collins explains, "Level 5 leaders set up their successors for even greater success…They display a workmanlike diligence — more plow horse than show horse."

Mark McCormack, the author of numerous books on business and leadership, including the bestseller, *What They Don't Teach You at Harvard Business School*, published in 1986, explains, "reduced to its essence, there really is only one management principle that works: Do unto others as you would have them do unto you. This is the Golden Rule…Unfortunately, few of us practice it as well as we preach it." McCormack says, "Working harder (or at least as hard) as everyone else gives a manager credibility. Without credibility you cannot lead people."

In understanding Dugoni as a chief executive, it's apparent that acting kindly and thoughtfully were essential ingredients to his leadership style. Remember that three-word note Art wrote to himself that stayed on his desk for the twenty-eight years of his deanship: "Arthur, Be Fair."

Art lived by the Golden Rule. None of his faculty, staff, or administration can recall outworking him, even as he approached age eighty. He was tireless. Never interested in receiving accolades so much as taking a long view of every area of the school's function with an eye toward improving it.

In a speech he delivered many times, "The ABC's of Leadership," to students at dental schools across the country, Art said, "I have often been asked what is the difference between individuals who are good at what they do and those who become great at what they do. In my mind, it's simple. The people who become great just outwork everyone else. It does not mean that they spend more hours at what they do. It is that they are more productive in the hours that they do spend. They use their time efficiently; they are not paralyzed by analysis; they gather information, make decisions, and then take action.

Art clearly demonstrated in his leadership that he lived by those words. He would take in written information and spoken advice from faculty, staff, students, colleagues, and his administrative team. Having consumed all of what he saw as the available information, he would move forward. The purpose of information and insightful analysis was ultimately to create balanced and reasoned decisions.

Dugoni's leadership skills are universal as seen in The Dalai Lama's 2009 book *The Leader's Way, The Art of Making the Right Decisions in Our Careers, Our Companies, and the World at Large*, in which he describes the six perfections that characterize effective leaders: generosity, ethical discipline, patience, enthusiastic effort, concentration, and wisdom. "A leader who possesses these traits," his book suggests, "has a distinct ability to affect others in profound ways."

Generosity: "Most leaders of successful organizations are, in fact, modest people who attribute good results to their team and who generously reward their employees for a job well done."

Art was not only generous in praising his team; he had a consistent record of being the first person to reach into his pocket to provide financial support. That support ran the gambit from supporting individual efforts to raise money for a cause that was important to one or more of his staff, such as cancer research, to consistently giving generously to the school itself. It was one more way Art led by example.

Perhaps, most importantly Art was always generous in his sharing the spotlight. As his growing reputation threatened to crowd out his support team, both at the university level and in a variety of professional organizations, he regularly pushed others to center stage. Art viewed his promotion of their work and accomplishments as part of his continuing effort to, as he explains, "inspire people to do things that they never knew they could do."

Ethical Discipline: This is represented by adherence to "a set of deeply held moral beliefs."

For Art, his faith-based upbringing, his education, and his home life all led back to the idea of shouldering personal responsibility. His relationship with his Catholic faith, though rarely mentioned, clearly grounded him with a deep sense of responsibility to his family, colleagues, and chosen career.

"Patience: In the case of anger, it is not the ability to suppress it but the ability to remain calm in the face of it that counts. To do so requires great patience, which is achieved only by training of the mind."

There are several myths that developed over the years regarding Art. One is that he was always a patient man. In truth, like most young men, Art could grow impatient at times. As seen previously, there were times as a young faculty member that he was less than the perfect image of a humanistic educator. But Art practiced patience and, like so many other qualities, in time, he perfected the ability to stay patient. As an educator, a dean, a businessman, and a leader in his profession, he was often tempted to allow his patience to dissolve into frustration, but as so many who worked beside him during his deanship and years as a leader of organized dentistry will attest, Art came to be thought of as the calm at the center of the storm.

Enthusiastic Effort: Art intuitively knew that a critical aspect of leadership was exhibiting enthusiasm for the work ahead. As Art once explained, "It's one tenth leadership and nine tenths team. You might be a catalyst, but it is the team that makes it happen. Without the team helping to create the message and the vision for the institution, any team leader is merely the sound of one hand clapping."

In his many lectures to students about leadership, making an enthusiastic effort was an essential ingredient. "As soon as I started practicing," Art explained in one of those talks, "I went to a San Mateo County Dental Society meeting. I found out that they were going to have a barbeque, so I volunteered to run the bar. This is a very strategic position because it provides the opportunity for you to meet everyone. Go to every meeting and sit with different people each time. Do not always sit with your friends, but meet different people. You need to obtain the directory of your local dental society and learn the names of the members. Please know that everyone loves to be called by their name, and they are flattered when you remember their names. It is necessary to prepare yourself for leadership. Thomas Edison once said, 'Good fortune is what happens when opportunity meets with preparation.'"

Concentration: This quality was evident in Art almost from the beginning. He was dogged in his approach to school work; whether that was preparing for his high school classes or taking on the financial concerns of the World Dental Federation. Art, by his own admission, had a seemingly endless supply of both energy and focus. Whatever concentration was needed to see his way through a challenge, he would consistently rise to the task and will himself forward.

The ability to focus on what was truly important defined Art's style of concentrated effort. An important reason why he often told students, as detailed previously, to never forget the "Five B's of success: Be there, Be there on time, Be involved, Be prepared, and Be balanced in your life."

Wisdom: This last of the six distinguishing qualities can be seen in Art in so many ways.

Perhaps it is best revealed in the widely recognized stature Art held for decades with his fellow dental school deans who commonly referred to him as "the Dean of Deans." No one could have summed up that quality better than Dr. Michael Alfano of NYU, who was earlier referenced for his comment, "When I became dean of NYU's College of Dentistry in 1998, I made what many thought of as the obligatory pilgrimage to San Francisco to ask Art how he built the kind of institution he had at Pacific." What Dr. Alfano was echoing was the belief held universally by Art's peers that he possessed a deep well of wisdom, which he shared generously with all.

* * * * *

In the book, *Leading with Kindness*, authors William Baker and Michael O'Malley, express their belief that, "good people consistently get superior results." The authors argue that, unfortunately, this is often a neglected aspect of leadership. But a leader who shows genuine care and interest in the lives of his or her staff can make a remarkable difference in the success of any organization's output.

Baker and O'Malley suggest that kindness is evidenced by: compassion, integrity, gratitude, authenticity, humility, and humor.

In conversations with staff, department heads, faculty, students, colleagues and others who encountered Art's approach to leadership, all six of these virtues are mentioned frequently…A likely reason why so many developed a fierce loyalty and fondness for him.

But the story of Art's kindness as a leader does not end there. It extends to how he nurtured everyone he encountered. In the overall success of an organization, this is arguably the most important aspect of all. Baker and O'Malley refer to it as "four qualities that great leaders are able to instill in others: self-confidence, self-control, self-awareness, and self-determination." In interviews with his administrative staff, Art's ability to nurture these qualities is consistently mentioned.

Art was a deep well of support and direction for a countless number of individuals, both in and out of the dental profession. Many turned to him for his wisdom and support and always found him giving.

It's important to realize, however, that through loyalty to his team, Art Dugoni earned their unstinting support. In discussions about success and leadership, Art has often credited his team for "making me look good." But that was only part of an ever-evolving symbiotic relationship.

Like the wise financial investor Art proved himself to be, he was also wise in how he invested in relationships with his administrative team, his colleagues, his faculty, students, and staff.

Dr. Bill Harman was a key member of Art's administrative team, originally recruited by Art out of the Chicago headquarters of the ADA. Starting in the 1980s, Art worked closely with Dr. Harman in turning the ADA's SELECT program into a groundbreaking success. (We'll look at that program in detail in the next chapter.)

Harman, who earned a doctorate in education, as opposed to dental surgery, served at Pacific for seven years as assistant dean for admissions and student services. He remembers fondly the one-on-one time he spent in Art's office... One-on-one sessions that he referred to in later years as "Dean's Lessons."

"Nearly every time I'd meet with Art, he would tell me about an issue, concern, or problem that he had encountered. He usually would ask how I would handle it, and then we would discuss it. He would gently add items to consider, all of which led to a solution that was fair, preserved the person's or the organization's self-esteem, and usually brought us all to the next level of excellence. I looked forward to my meetings with Art, as I knew my skills and abilities would improve each time he shared his knowledge and wisdom with me."

In 1997, when Dr. Harman made the decision to accept the position of associate dean for admissions at Baylor College of Dentistry in Dallas, Art sent him a two-page handwritten note in which he expressed his gratitude: "I am sad that you will be leaving, because I not only value your dedication, skill, and superb performance, but also your friendship and good counsel. You have been a valued and extremely productive member of the team...I have observed with pride and silent applause your growth over these past seven years...I gave you your freedom to run, and you accepted the challenge with a run to the finish line as a winner."

The successful confluence of Dugoni's and Harman's success in helping to turn around the precipitous drop in dental school enrollments is a perfect example of Art identifying a talented individual and using him to achieve results that perhaps neither of them might have thought possible when they first met.

It is an example of what is likely Art Dugoni's most significant legacy: "L'Importanza Della Famiglia." In his cultivation of Harman and countless others, you see Art's view of the extended family. That family, in a broad sense, could extend to hundreds if not indeed thousands who felt a deep connection to Art.

A wise family knows that they are always at their best when they work in harmony. Art Dugoni as a leader was a maestro of unity. Any team he coached, played not as individuals, but as a unit. A wise family and a wise leader would have it no other way.

Art with the love of his
life, Kaye Dugoni.

The family gathered in 1994 to celebrate Lina's 90th Birthday.

Art appeared on the cover
of numerous professional
publications, invariably as
an advocate for change.

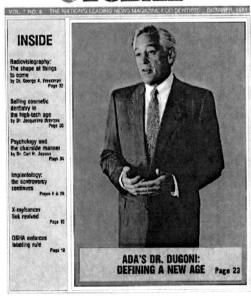

Chapter Nineteen
Leading Organized Dentistry

Voltaire famously said, "Every man is the creature of the age in which he lives, very few are able to raise themselves above the ideas of the times."

Arguably, Art Dugoni is one of those rare few. His decades as a leading voice for the profession of dentistry would support that argument. In each of his leadership roles, while certainly he addressed the issues of his day, he was doggedly a futurist.

From the moment he stepped onto the national stage from California and concluding with his leadership of the ADA's foundation, Art spoke about a profession with a bright and promising future. This was particularly empowering and uplifting throughout the challenging years of the 1980s.

Art brought a blend of immigrant tenacity to his leadership roles, combined with the boomtown mentality infused into the heart and soul of so many native San Franciscans. A philosophy that suggests we're always tougher than the toughest times, and with patience and persistence, we will eventually strike gold!

To Art, the importance of participating in various associations representing organized dentistry was obvious. "The only way we can influence the future of our profession," he said repeatedly, "is to be involved in organized dentistry."

Art's leadership skills, boundless energy, and seemingly endless dedication to his profession led him to the presidency of the California Dental Association, CDA, in 1982; the American Board of Orthodontics, ABO, in 1985; the American Dental Association, ADA, in 1988; the American Association of Dental Schools, AADS, in 1994, later renamed the American Dental Education Association, ADEA; and the American Dental Association Foundation, ADAF from 2003-2010. Additionally, Art served as Treasurer and board member of Federation Dentaire International, the FDI, from 1992 to 1998, but chose to decline the opportunity to serve as its president, a decision we will examine more closely at the end of this chapter.

When Art took on his first dental organization leadership role, the presidency of the San Mateo Dental Society in January 1960, he was thirty-four. Starting young and blessed with a long life, Art stepped down from his final leadership position, as president of the ADAF in 2010 at age eighty-five: a remarkable span of over fifty years.

Art took over as president elect of the CDA in 1981, when, with the help of Dr. Nielsen, he visited, as previously mentioned, each of California's thirty-two component dental societies. The added benefit to the school and its philanthropic efforts, as discussed in the next chapter, was Art's year as president-elect and the following year as the organization's president, which allowed him to reconnect with Pacific alumni throughout the state of California and elsewhere.

During Art's two-years as the CDA's president-elect and president, the organization's executive director was Art's predecessor as dean, Dale Redig. Dr. Redig had taken on the daily operation of the CDA at a time when it was actually two organizations preparing to merge into one. It was apparent that the association could do a more effective job for all its constituents as one body than as two separate organizations, one representing Northern California, the other Southern California. Redig did a masterful job at keeping the CDA on task and blending staffs where certain redundancies were bound to cause a degree of discord. At first, the new state organization made its home office in the greater Los Angeles area, but it was then decided to place the unified CDA headquarters in Sacramento, where the state legislature, and state government as a whole, cast a wide shadow over the regulatory aspects of dentistry in the nation's most populous state.

"Dale took us from a 'mom and pop shop' to a thriving dynamic organization. I can't imagine anyone who could have done a better job," Art says.

While Redig built a strong administrative organization, Art focused on energizing the participating member base, the majority of whom were active practitioners. In his role as CDA president Art established many themes that carried through to his term as president of the ADA just seven years later. Art challenged virtually every organization that he was a part of with this simple question: "Are we going to be a do nothing, or do something organization?" In 1982, in an article he wrote for the CDA Journal, Art delivered a no holds barred message on the perils of inaction, first presented, as he so often did, with an amusing anecdote:

"There's a story about four people whose names were Everybody, Somebody, Anybody, and Nobody. There was an important job to be done and Everybody was asked to do it. Anybody could have done it, but Nobody did it. Somebody got angry about that, because it was Everybody's job. Everybody thought Anybody could do it, but Nobody realized that Everybody wouldn't do it. Consequently, it wound up that Nobody told Anybody, so Everybody blamed Somebody."

Art went on to say, "In the last few years, a virtual fetish has developed about what is known as the 'laid-back style.' (Personally, I've always thought a day without a crisis in need of your attention is a total loss.) A fondness for this casual, easy-going approach to life has penetrated our professional lives as well as our private lives. But there is a significant difference between composure under pressure and simply being disengaged."

For those who do not recall, in post-Watergate America, and just three years after the nation's retreat from Vietnam after the loss of over 47,000 in combat, the late 1970s was a time marked by a deep sense of personal and economic disillusionment. Hoping to put that sense of malaise behind, voters created a landslide call for change in the 1980 election of Ronald Reagan.

But one event does not erase a slide begun many years before, and there was a pervasive sense of uncertainty in California and across the nation that continued through the early '80s. That sense of uncertainty helped to define this period of "laid back" culture. The thinking being that all these problems are bigger than any one of us, so perhaps it was best to just lay back and let someone else do the heavy lifting.

Of course, as he was indicating in the article to his fellow CDA members, appropriately entitled "Investing Ourselves in the Future," laid back was simply not an Art Dugoni trait. "Where there is little risk," Art told his fellow members, "there is little reward, and where there is no risk, the best possible outcome is breaking even."

To get a sense of how direct Art was in going after those members of the profession who would choose to just wait for "Somebody," to do something, he warned, "If we rest on our laurels, we're liable to get knocked on our rears."

In no other message did Art better explain his philosophy of active participation. "I believe that one of the most serious challenges the CDA faces today is the need to communicate and to motivate the unconcerned, the uninformed, and the uncommitted within this profession."

In his message to the CDA, you can see the Art Dugoni who weekly made a "to-do" list for each of his seven children, and the dean who instilled in his administrative team the attitude that standing still was the first step in falling behind.

As you will soon see, in his work with the ADA, and every other organization, Art's message and the thrust of all his efforts followed the same course. It's a sentiment that can best be summed up as a plea for reason on the part of those who shared in the profession of dentistry: people who have made their living in this field and are invested in the profession's success, need to be involved. Art Dugoni asked his colleagues the same question President Reagan asked the American people, "If not now, when? If not us, who?"

Rallying his fellow CDA members Art wrote, "Rarely a day goes by without a front-page headline predicting economic doom and gloom. Dentists are bombarded with publications heralding busyness problems, bankruptcy, and credit difficulties."

Reading this, it's small wonder why dental schools at the time were beset by a steep decline in student applications.

But, in a classic example of Art's unique ability to lighten any message with humanism and humor, he borrows a line from a famous political columnist of the time and concludes with a question:

"Who are these individuals who make all these dire predictions and guide our political and economic futures? What is the expertise of these people? Art Buchwald said it succinctly: 'Economists are like the guy who knows one thousand ways to make love, but doesn't know any women.'"

This is vintage Art, never accept defeat; we are always greater than our problems. Particularly when the many voices of organized dentistry speak as one!

Of course, that ideal can be a goal post that stands far off in the distance. To Art, the enormity of the task was never an acceptable reason not to try.

Dr. Chuck Wilson, who was president of the CDA back in the early 1970s and then served years later as Art's vice president at the ADA, remembers the struggles that he, Art, and their contemporaries had in getting members at both organizations to take more active roles in their associations and the dental profession as a whole.

Dr. Burton Press, who as mentioned previously preceded Art as a president of both the ADA and the CDA explained: "The great majority of dentists don't have the time or interest to serve in organized dentistry. Art and I must have shared some of the same genes, because both of us strongly believed that if you wanted to have a say in the future of your profession, you had to have a seat at the table."

Art has often told the story of early in his career attending a dental conference and walking past a conference room where a state board of California group was meeting on determining future policy related to licensure. The panel, Art was surprised to see, was made up of regulators and legislators, but not one member of the dental profession. Art walked in, took one of the dozens of empty seats that had been provided for an audience that never appeared, and stayed for the balance of the meeting.

"I simply could not believe that here was a discussion," Art explains, "that was being held regarding rules and regulations about the dental profession, and not one person in attendance, other than some of the board members, had a doctorate in dental surgery. I decided, at that moment, that I would spend a considerable part of my life encouraging my fellow practitioners to take a seat at the table when the future of their profession was being discussed. Without doing so, how could we ever hope to have a voice in the creation of our profession's future? For several years, I attended every board meeting and sat in the front row."

Art returned with a similar message in his December 1988 inaugural address as the new president of the ADA. "Dentistry has a very bright future, provided, as active participants in our profession, we choose to do something as opposed to nothing. Coming soon," he assured a record gathering in Washington, D.C., "there is a new golden age of dentistry, but only if we are prepared to guide the forces of change with commitment, competence, and compassion."

More than thirty-five years before Art became the president of the American Dental Association, he attended his first meeting of the San Mateo Dental Society. He had just joined John Tocchini's pediatric practice in South San Francisco, and he wanted to meet fellow practitioners and learn more about the challenges their practices were facing.

One long-term goal Art set for himself early in his deanship was for the school to be better known throughout the dental profession. A key component to accomplishing that was getting faculty, staff, students, and alumni, into leadership positions in the profession with a particular emphasis on involvement in the ADA, the CDA, and their component dental societies. It took time to fully develop, but, before long, Pacific was casting an increasingly recognizable presence across a wide spectrum of state and national organizations.

To date, Art is the last individual to be elected to the ADA presidency unopposed. When asked how that occurred, Dr. Mike Perich, a one-time practicing dentist in Northern California, who left his practice for a full-time senior administrative position at the ADA's headquarters in Chicago, explained, "Art ran unopposed because the people who served with him on the ADA board all thought they would not do as good a job as Art, so why would they want to run against him?"

As Perich explains, Art made it a point to get to know the administrative staff of the ADA, who eagerly anticipated his having a chance to lead the organization. Typical of Art's hard driving style, he spent his year in office focused on many of the critical issues that dentistry faced at the time.

One other unique aspect in Art's background explains why he is also, to date, the last dean of a dental school to serve as president of the ADA. "No one has brought together the academic, clinical practice, and research aspects of dentistry better than Art Dugoni," explains Dr. Craig Yarborough, "and a large part of his achieving that prominence was his stature, both as president of the CDA, and as an officer of the ADA."

Additionally, as Dr. Press points out, the reader would be wrong to assume that this was achieved without a considerable amount of personal charm.

"One of the principle reasons Dugoni was a unifier," Press explains, "was the simple fact that he knew everyone by name. So many other colleagues and acquaintances of Art's were floored by how he would remember people's names and the names of their spouses. I used to think he could do an act on Johnny Carson's *Tonight Show*. His ability to remember names and faces astounded all of us."

Art, as we've seen, was relentless in the pursuit of his goals. But equally important in his decades in leadership of organized dentistry was, as Burton Press points out, "the power of his personality. Art was able to get people to sit up and pay attention to the influence of organized dentistry. He was truly one of a kind!"

* * * * *

Many of the critical challenges that Art faced in the first ten years of his deanship were the same challenges that other dental practitioners at the time faced. These were problems that revealed themselves in the steep decline of student applications and subsequent closure of seven dental schools; the unanticipated challenges that the AIDS epidemic posed for both patients and practitioners; and an economy suffering first through inflation, followed by a steep recessionary period.

In an interview conducted in his Chicago office two months prior to the start of his term as ADA president, Art told Dr. Noel Maxson, editor of the *Chicago Dental Society Review*, that he welcomed a "time of change and challenge." These challenges, Art suggested, "will provide us with an opportunity to shape a different future."

The lengthy article by Maxson wonderfully captures the pressing issues Art was facing when he took office. As always, Art did not see the "glass as half empty, but rather as half full." Maxson began by asking, "What is the impact of AIDS on our profession?"

Art responded, "The way the profession handles the AIDS issue can enhance the dentists' professional image and improve the quality of care delivered. AIDS has increased the dentists' awareness of the need for infection control. It has required the development of appropriate infection control systems within the dental office."

In a comment that shows just how prescient a leader Art could be, he adds, "The disease will increase the public perception of the dentist as a total health-care provider by demonstrating an awareness of the patient's overall health and health problems. This will require a change within the profession, and it will occur slowly as dentists get over their fears about the disease and get on with the responsibilities and commitments of the profession to their patients. In the interim, AIDS will become a very polarizing issue within the profession. It will require dentists to evaluate their relationships and commitments to their patients, as well as to evaluate their roles within the profession."

Maxson then went on to ask about the closure of dental schools such as Georgetown, Emory, Loyola, Oral Roberts, and others. Art, by then, had already been deeply involved in the process of reversing the trend of declining student applicant pools.

"Dental schools," Art explained, "have reduced the number of places in freshmen classes over the last two years, in response to changes in the applicant pool, and this reduction has helped to maintain the quality of first year students. Since 1978, dental schools have reduced first year enrollments by nearly 31%, but even with this voluntary reduction, the applicant-to-first-year-enrollee ratio is only 1.24 to 1. This is of great concern to the profession."

To respond to the issue, Art had already been involved in the creation of programs both on the state, CDA principally, and national level at the ADA. As he explained, "The profession has responded to the problem by establishing the SELECT Program. One of its main goals is to encourage the nation's brightest and most capable youths to consider careers in dentistry and to provide them with accurate and realistic information on the future of the profession."

Ultimately, Art sought to create, not only resurgence in student enrollment, but in the growth of dental practices nationwide. In his view, there were clear indicators of future promise that would not mark the trends of the1980s as an omen of doom for dentistry, but rather as an era of transition from which the field would emerge playing a more vital and prominent role in the nation's health than in any prior decade.

"The adult population is increasing in number," Art explained, "and a greater proportion will retain their teeth for a longer period of time. We will have approximately 52 million more adults ages eighteen to seventy-four, with teeth, who will be at dental risk in the year 2000 than we had in the year 1975. This does not include the increased number of elderly over age seventy-five.

"There is an increased demand for the treatment of periodontal disease, cosmetic dentistry, orthodontics, orthognathic surgery, facial pain diagnosis and treatment, veneering, bonding, and dental implants. The need for dental care will continue to increase, but there will be a change in demographics, procedures, materials, techniques, and the scope of services practitioners will offer."

Art Dugoni, the same individual who made a bold decision in 1960 to sell a restorative practice and move his family to Seattle so that he could get a degree in orthodontics, more than twenty years later was on a national stage sharing his thoughts on the future growth of dentistry. He concluded, "The most significant impact in dentistry will not be the technological changes, but the demographic changes. The dental needs of an elderly population, which is growing significantly, will become a major challenge for the dental profession. Elderly patients will need dentists who have been trained to provide extensive geriatric care to patients who have extensive medical problems and are on multiple drug therapies. The increasing affluence of the elderly, coupled with their greater sophistication and higher levels of education will demand of the dentist more sophisticated dentistry, especially in the areas of peridontics, endodontics, orthodontics, restorative dentistry (especially root caries), and fixed prosthodontics."

In an era when dentists felt besieged by uncertain change and dental schools faced uncertain futures, Art was both bold and correct when he said, "This is an exciting time for our profession, a time of change and challenge. These challenges will provide us with an opportunity to shape a different future."

Finally, when asked what his number one goal for his presidency would be, Art responded, "To create an appreciation and an understanding within the profession of the importance of belonging, contributing, and being involved in the activities of our profession. The benefits of membership must become exceedingly clear and relevant to every member, and the need for involvement must assume a high priority within the membership."

* * * * *

During this, arguably Art Dugoni's most important professional address in a decades-long career of public speaking, he turns again to the life lessons he learned both as a high school and college basketball player. Here, the game serves as a parable for committing yourself, and your organization, to taking decisive action.

"Those of you who are basketball fans will remember the great John Havlicek of the Boston Celtics - Mr. Perpetual Motion! He was the standard by which all other basketball players were measured. He was the soul of the sports expression, 'He came to play.' He was committed and responsible, and he embodied the qualities that organized dentistry must have if we are to emerge as winners in this era of challenge and change. John Havlicek was a work horse, not a show horse. He subordinated his ego to the goals of the team. Unafraid to take risks, he was willing to lay himself on the line. One sports writer described how Havlicek would play anywhere—forward or guard, starter or sixth man; he did not care, just so he could play – 'shifting back and forth at a moment's notice, running—always running—yet, never seeming to break a sweat'…And that is the way we all must be.

"Consider John Havlicek's example—his energy, his belief in teamwork, his play-to-win attitude—and consider these questions: in the year to come, will you come to play? Will you go for the goal, even if it seems beyond your reach? Will you try to make a difference?

"I sure hope so, because you are it! The profession is in your hands, and if you are willing to pay the price of leadership, of commitment — if you are willing to come to play — then the future can be truly fantastic! Can you imagine what we could accomplish if all of us put aside our differences, our provincial thinking, if we concentrated our efforts on what was best for this country, our patients, and our profession.

"Let me ask you: What are you personally going to do in the area of membership recruitment and retention? One of our major challenges. Will you take some risks with me? Will you put yourself on the line and commit yourself to making every dentist you know an active player on our team? Will you reach out to young dentists whose participation in organized dentistry is decreasing? Will you dismiss them as rookies, or value them as colleagues? Will you focus on the concerns we share with them, or on our differences? Will you pass the ball to them? Or will you hog it?"

Art Dugoni has always projected an image of being a quiet, patient, consensus-builder. But in this passage of his address, delivered in front of many of his profession's most influential members, Art shows a different side. He speaks with the passion of a coach readying his team for a critical game…Inspiring his colleagues to play at their highest level…Not to settle for the ordinary, but to strive for the extraordinary.

Dugoni is not about to shy away from delivering a motivational message. He asks fellow members to do more than "talking issues to death or passing them on to a yet another committee." This is not the rhetoric of an individual fearful of ruffling feathers, but rather someone seizing the moment to accomplish change and see progress achieved.

"Choose a job you love, and you will never have to work a day in your life. If you do not love what you do, you will never go the extra mile, work the extra hour, or dream up a new idea. Passion leads to persistence. Persistence leads to loving what you do — and loving what you do leads to excellence."

Dr. David Nielsen, who was a close observer of Art's leadership of the CDA and the ADA, stressed that "the message that Art first honed in 1982 became the core of a set of beliefs that he would continue to preach through his tenure at the CDA, as well as his presidency of the ADA, and throughout other leadership positions. Art's message to his colleagues was that they should embrace their profession, and embrace the role education plays in securing a promising future for dentistry. Quite simply, he was the right person at the right time."

Among longtime practitioners, Dr. Nielsen explains, Art was subject to the general distrust that existed toward dental school deans because of the brutal nature of dental education back when they earned their degrees. At the same time, however, Art's insistence that the new humanistic model for dental schools was here to stay was quickly winning believers.

It was that generation of practitioners, many who were in their prime when Art was leading the CDA and ADA, who could not see themselves as ever supporting their old dental schools.

"Art was very active with the state boards," Dr. Nielsen continues, "and he got hygienists approved for expanded duties. He organized support, and his members became increasingly responsive. A lot of his success was his ability to attract good people to support his efforts."

Dale Redig at the CDA and Tom Ginley, at the ADA, both executive directors, were also instrumental in his successful tenures. In much the same manner that he succeeded in his deanship, Art was always keenly aware that a supportive staff was essential to any leader meeting and exceeding his goals. Just as he did at the dental school, Art took the time to learn the names of all the people who kept complex organizations like these running smoothly.

"With the ADA in particular," Dave Nielsen stresses, "finances were a real issue. I believe Art was the first one to do an in-depth analysis of the association's budget. In fact, budget was always Art's way into an organization." Art developed an expertise in identifying and cultivating non-member sources of revenue, and he left every organization he led in a stronger financial position."

Art made countless presentations throughout his years of leading organized dentistry, but in all of these, he was keenly aware that, in order to take the steps between promise and accomplishment, a lot of small victories had to be won. Art never forgot that leadership, like creativity, is 1% inspiration and 99% perspiration.

"In our time in office," Dr. Chuck Wilson recalls, "What Art and I had hoped to bring to the ADA was a wide-ranging discussion of the issues confronting the profession."

Those issues included the cost of education, expanding the body of the organization by expanding its membership, and seeing that those practitioners who were members played an active role. This was also a time when the profession was integrating third party payers and there was, as Dr. Wilson recalls, "much room for improvement."

During Art's tenure, the ADA had a continuing debate about the role of dental hygienists. Additionally, as Dr. Wilson recalls, "we had an ongoing conversation about what role various allied professionals can play in the delivery of oral health care, particularly among underserved populations. These boundaries regarding patient care are issues that continue to this day.

As Art and key ADA personnel together expanded the visibility of both the organization and the profession, an increasing number of manufacturers wanted to have the ADA's stamp of approval for their products.

"If we didn't have the sufficient capabilities in-house," Dr. Wilson explains, "we would get a university research team involved. We wanted to make sure that product standards remained rigidly controlled. We were proud of the fact that our recognition could not be bought, but had to be earned."

Art and Chuck Wilson recall that, prior to their time in office, there had long been a huge chasm between the ADA and the American Association of Dental Schools. "There was just a lack of communication," Dr. Wilson recalls. "Numerous groups worked in isolation, and there was a certain arrogance that has vanished largely over the years."

One of the inescapable realities was the simple fact that so many dental schools' facilities were falling apart. In the 1960s, the federal government poured millions of dollars into these schools in the form of grants and direct aid, but now, twenty years later, those schools that had not taken advantage of this assistance were in very bad shape.

It was one reason that the timing could not have been better for a dental school dean to lead the ADA. It is interesting to note that not another dental school dean has been elected as president of the ADA since Art's tenure, nearly thirty years ago.

* * * * *

Another major area of focus during Art's ADA leadership was establishing a higher level of public understanding of oral healthcare in the overall health of the nation. The role that modern dentistry plays in society today is radically different than it was when Art entered dental practice in 1948. Much of that change came in areas that he began addressing early in his career. And, in seeing the broad sweep of industry change during the second half of the twentieth century, you gain an additional appreciation of Art's impact on the profession. Of course, that changing role was much what Art anticipated when he boldly sold his practice in the early 1960s and returned to school for a graduate degree in orthodontics.

Near the end of his ADA presidency, Art's visibility as a spokesperson for the profession of dentistry had grown to such an extent that he was approached by members and staff of the ADA urging him to do a public awareness campaign that would involve his anchoring of a regularly scheduled program called, "Dentistry Update," on Lifetime Medical Television. The program was typically done in two segments, one being a panel discussion on a topic impacting the profession and what these changes would represent to the patient, and a segment done on location, usually in a practitioner's office involving new treatment approaches. Art hosted the panel discussions and introduced all segments of the programs. Additionally, Art worked with a production team to create a series of twenty second public service spots on the importance of maintaining good oral health, broadcast on both local and network television programs.

Some of the programs were filmed on location, some in New York City, and some were done in Art's office back at the dental school.

The first program of "Dentistry Update," aired on September 2, 1990, after Art's term as ADA president had ended. The program was a success and continued on the air for four full seasons, ending in the summer of 1993. Topics were lively, well researched, and gave viewers a depth of knowledge about modern dentistry that had not been seen before or since.

A sample of reports and panel discussions included the following topics: Dentistry and Computer Imaging, Vital Teeth and Periodontal Treatment, Pain Control, Esthetic Dentistry, Maxillofacial Prosthodontics, Oral Cancers, Endodontics, Root Canals, Sports Dentistry, Cosmetic Dentistry, Geriatric Dentistry, and much more. (A listing of all topics and program original airdates is provided in Appendix A.)

Coming at a time when the infectious nature of AIDS was a national topic, several reports and panel discussions touched on the subject including new methods of infection control that have now become standard throughout the industry.

The program, and the public service messages succeeded in its two principle goals: addressing oral health awareness, and increasing visits to dentists' offices nationwide. Within weeks of the campaign's commencement, surveys revealed a noticeable upswing in dental office appointments and visits.

At a time when so many in his profession were questioning the prospects for growth in an industry that seemed to have stalled under the burden of recession and an untreatable and essentially unidentified infectious disease, Art Dugoni promised his colleagues that a better future was ahead. As the decade of the 1980s concluded, the results had proven this persistent voice for optimism and confidence to be correct.

* * * *

No review of Art's term in the leadership of the ADA would be complete without mentioning the gentleman who served as Art's executive director. "Tom Ginley," Art recalls fondly, "was a wonderful leader. Talented staff can make you look good, and Tom was a very gifted executive."

Equally important to Art was his old P&S classmate and his best friend, Bill Allen, who was associate executive director prior to Art's presidency and after. Dr. Allen was based in Washington, heading up the ADA's legislative office.

Under his purview came legislation that affected every aspect of the dental profession, from research, to education and practice.

Art explains, "During my years as the ADA's president-elect and president, Bill opened Washington's doors for me. He was the ultimate people person; Bill connected me with individuals of prominence in both houses of Congress. Both Bill and his wife Marky made a great team. They had wonderful social grace; they could communicate well with everyone from the handyman to US Senators. When they did events, they never let anything drop; they knew the better your personal relationship, the better your professional relationship."

Two others who played important administrative roles were Dr. Michael Perich, previously mentioned, and his wife, Paula Perich. Mike Perich, who Art coaxed back to volunteering as an instructor one day a week at Pacific's student clinic, loved the experience of helping to guide and cultivate a future generation of dentists. Inspired in part by Art's view that the profession of dentistry had a dynamic future, Mike left California in 1985 to take an administrative position in Chicago with the ADA. Paula, a communications expert, joined the ADA on the same day in 1985 as her husband did. She served as assistant executive director, membership & marketing services, and was instrumental in creating the media opportunities utilizing Art both in public service work, Lifetime Television, and a wide variety of other broadcast interviews.

"Like Kathleen O'Loughlin, today's Executive Director of the ADA, competent, highly talented administrators and staff," Art explains, "are the key ingredient in moving a professional organization forward. When combined with a committed and involved membership, there is no limit to what can be accomplished."

* * * * *

During these dramatic years in his leadership of dentistry, the opportunity to weave together his love of education and pride in his profession perhaps best presented itself in the work he did with Dr. Bill Harman on the previously mentioned, ADA's SELECT program.

Bill, as discussed in the previous chapter, earned his doctorate in education.

He was a brilliant young pianist growing up in Ohio who had the opportunity to study under the legendary Cleveland Orchestra conductor George Szell.
Harman's future in education started as a piano teacher at the age of thirteen.
This led him to his growing fascination with the process of how we learn. Eventually, Bill gained a doctorate in the field and was attracted into dentistry because the woman he met in college and later married knew from her youth on
that she wanted to become a dentist.

In 1986, Bill Harman came to Chicago to accept the challenge of reinvig-
orating interest in dentistry as a promising career choice. "We chose the name,
SELECT," Dr. Harman explains, "because we were determined to go after the
best and the brightest. Deans wanted to call it recruitment, but that was not our
goal. We viewed it as the encouragement of highly qualified individuals toward
a promising career."

That same year, two years prior to his selection for the ADA's presidency,
while serving on the ADA's executive board, Art Dugoni and Bill Harman
began working together.

Art quickly realized that Harman's ideas on how to re-engage students nationally in viewing dentistry as a promising career was lacking only a national spokesman. Armed with a strategy to reverse a downward trend in dental
school applications, Art spoke at key college career advisors' conferences on
how dentistry was not an obsolete profession, but one on the verge of a golden
era. Art picked up the baton and led the charge forward, and before long, dental
education and the profession itself would never be the same.

"At the time," Harman stresses, "our student enrollments were not in decline;
they were in a free fall. Art realized that dentists bore part of the responsibility
for this. When they saw the relatively small decline in their own practice, many
of them became convinced that the best times for dentistry were in the past."

As discussed in Art's own history, many promising young people have encountered a family dentist who encourages them to consider dentistry as a profession. During dentistry's challenging years, that was not happening, and its
impact on the field was apparent.

Harman's fondest recollection of Art in action came at a college counselors' conference in Snowbird, a year-round Utah mountain resort destination.

"I can remember that event to this day," Dr. Harman recalls fondly. "His presentation at Snowbird laid the foundation of where we needed to go. That presentation began the building of a consensus. The message was direct and powerful, and counselors left the conference with a clear message of why they should recommend dentistry as a wise career choice."

"I am very proud of what I did to change the view of the profession. And I'm proud of the work Bill Harman and I did together," Art says. This was perhaps the best example of the "great persuader," as evangelist for the vision of an increasingly dynamic profession. After Snowbird, Art made many more such presentations in his campaign to reinvigorate and re-imagine the future of dentistry.

* * * * *

The man who claimed that his DNA was missing the gene that allowed him to say, "No," finally did find that word when it came to the presidency of the Federation Dentaire International, (the World Dental Federation) FDI.

After Art had concluded his term as the ADA's president, it was clear that the FDI was out there.

"The organization had agreed that I would be their choice to be president, but it was a four year commitment, two years as president-elect and two years as president," Art explains.

"Art could and should have been the president of the FDI," says Dr. Clive Ross, a former FDI president who worked closely with Art during the years, 1992 to 1998, a time in which Art served as the organization's treasurer. "It was a sad day for the international community when Art decided not to pursue the presidency of the FDI. The office was definitely his for the taking."

It has never been an easy thing for Art to walk away from an opportunity in which he could effect change and help to create a brighter future for his beloved profession. But, looking back on the opportunity to lead the world dental community, Art says, "At the time, I was being pulled in several different directions. You should never take on a responsibility unless you can make a meaningful commitment. And with chapters scattered widely around the globe, travel on behalf of the FDI would have been particularly daunting."

Art strongly cautions against taking on a position because you would be honored to have the title. "If you can't add to what the organization is doing, don't do it. I was part of a huge movement along with Dr. Clive Ross of New Zealand, Dr. Per Ake Zillen of Sweden, and many others in making an important difference with the FDI, but the demands involved, if I was to do the job as president that I wanted to do, were simply too great. Not to mention that I would have had to give up my deanship at the dental school."

In taking on the role of treasurer, Art believed he could make a significant contribution toward creating financial stability for the federation, and thereby help to assure its future. "Far more important than the title was that, by working together, we were able to strengthen the FDI and make it a more effective organization in representing dentistry on the world stage."

As with so many other professional organizations, Art was quick to realize that the FDI was walking away from multiple opportunities to improve their financial standing. A case in point was annual conferences and regional meetings where, for example, if Singapore put on an event, they kept all the money for sponsorships, booth fees, advertising, and more. "By developing a model for sharing conference revenue and increasing membership dues," Art explains, "it wasn't long before an anemic balance sheet looked a lot healthier."

* * * * *

During his service with the FDI as its treasurer, and while continuing his deanship at Pacific, in 1994 and 1995, Art took on the added responsibility of serving as the president of the American Association of Dental Schools, AADS, later renamed the American Dental Education Association, ADEA.

When Art took over as the AADS president, there was an atmosphere of distrust in the ADA's rank and file, in which dental school deans were viewed as living in their ivory towers, oblivious to the realities of maintaining a successful dental practice. The leaders of the AADS, in turn, were intimated by the power and scope of the ADA. To help heal this rift, Art Dugoni was recruited by leaders on both sides of the divide.

"Each organization had a lot to offer each other," Art explains. "However, working together, they could reduce the cost of education, and they could be better positioned to push the National Institute of Health to bring more research dollars into education, which ultimately benefited the profession. The development of composite resins, the continuing improvement of high-speed handpieces, and much more, all came out of research." Through cooperation, everyone benefited: the academic institutions, the practitioners, and ultimately the patient.

In this role, Art followed his instinct to, once again, as expressed by Voltaire, "raise himself above the ideas of the times." Where others were still looking back at the significant challenges to dental schools and the dental profession during the 1980s, Art was preaching preparedness for the twenty-first century.

To Art's view, the decade of the 1990s was a logical bridge between two eras of dental education, and many of the changes he brought about at Pacific, he wanted to see institutionalized throughout dental education. That included the humanistic model of teaching, recruitment and retention of fulltime faculty, educators who had both feet in the world of academics, research, and practice... International programs, graduate programs, and continuing education in advanced dentistry. Beyond the focus on undergraduate studies, to Art's view, it was incumbent upon all schools to promote continuing education programs to keep practicing dental professionals current with developments in dentistry.

As we'll cover in the next chapter, in Art's view, the financial health and future of dental education could never rest solely on student tuitions and fees. Annual giving, endowments, endowed chairs, research underwriting and community supported oral health care programs would all have to be a part of the mix.

Art's mantra to his fellow educators and dental school administrators could be expressed as: "If it ain't broke, make it better anyway." As an activist dean, he cautioned others that the "most dangerous place is behind your desk."

Most importantly, in Art's role as president of the AADS, he had the platform to stress his philosophy of what school interaction with its student body should ideally look like.

First and foremost was to honor the dignity of each and every student and, in so doing, enhance his or her sense of self-worth. It was his unshakeable belief that a school with a family environment reduced stress and encouraged the sense that everyone mattered and supported each other's success.

An important part of the mix in making all this work is early intervention programs for students having a difficult time meeting academic expectations, and rewards for student performance in the areas of academic and clinical pursuits and professional manner.

One other innovation Art brought to student recognition at Pacific, introduced after his presidency of the AADS, an event that he wished to see standardized throughout dental education, was the "White Coat Ceremony." It was an idea that he borrowed from medical schools, in which students are honored as they make the transition between the strictly academic portion of their education and the clinical patient work that is a critical component in the last two years prior to receiving their doctorate.

The wearing of the white coat marks that transition in which patient responsibility becomes an important and memorable step into your professional future. It also, as Art explained, marks the point at which fellow students and educators extend to an undergraduate the salutation of "doctor."

Dr. Eddie Hayashida explains, "People thought it was another 'crazy idea from Art Dugoni when he suggested the white coat ceremony, but history again proved him to be right."

White coat ceremonies today are not only highly anticipated events in the student experience at Pacific, but have become traditional at dental schools throughout the country. Not surprisingly, Art Dugoni has been an honored guest and a featured speaker at many of these ceremonies.

In August of 2010 in Milwaukee, Wisconsin, Art spoke to the students at Marquette University's School of Dentistry and explained the symbolic importance of the event:

"The wearing of the white coat for the first time is a professional milestone. A student wearing the coat is taking on the responsibility of a health care professional. It signifies to patients that you will strive to regard them with: the utmost respect, treat their illnesses to the best of your ability, listen carefully, and preserve the dignity of each individual. It means, too, that you are expected to conduct yourself in a manner consistent with those in your chosen profession, not simply as a student practicing as you learn."

Art envisioned the ceremony as a moment when students and their families could come together and reflect on what it means to be a doctor. Art continued: "The respect which society assigns to the dentist is related to the professional values and responsibilities of this calling. The compassion, kindness, self-sacrifice, scientific expertise, ethics, humanity, and equanimity of future dentists require that these values be taught and modeled by all of us.

"Today's milestone in your life will remind you of the importance of these attributes as you begin this wondrous journey toward becoming a doctor. Your future roles in alleviating human pain and suffering must be firmly anchored in these values."

Most touchingly, in every one of his addresses across the nation, and in various spots around the globe, Art spoke to future dentists about the difference between doctors and "regular business people."

The Marquette speech, of course, touched on this all-important topic:

"Doctors are not like regular business people, and dentistry is not just another business. There are essential and fundamental differences that you need to grasp and embrace."

In the normal function of business, Art explained, both the seller and the buyer of goods and services tries to make their best deal. In normal business transactions, buyers must take care that what they are buying represents the value they anticipate and will meet their expectations.

In theme and words expressed by the dental school's resident ethicist and professor of dental practice, Dr. Bruce Peltier, and passed along by Art to Marquette's dental school students:

"Health care is different from regular business for two essential reasons: First, there is typically much more at stake in health care, and second, unlike the buyer-seller relationship, the doctor—patient relationship does not consist of an exchange between equals. In the first instance, there is much at stake for patients. What you young doctors do is often irreversible. You cannot take it back and exchange it or return the product and get your money back, when a tooth has been extracted, that is it. When a preparation has been cut, you cannot put the tooth structure back on. When you give a child a drug or anesthetic overdose, the consequences can be severe.

There are no real ways for patients to evaluate the situation other than to decide whether to trust you as their doctor. Your professional status is a wonderful privilege, but it comes at a price. You must be trustworthy to keep your privileged status."

Finally, Art gave these white coat recipients, as he has thousands of others, these guiding principles:

"You are there to serve your patients, not the other way around; your patients must be sacred to you, and their fear of the process can cause all kinds of inexplicable behavior; You will not succeed without developing a strong doctor-patient relationship, and finally, always tell the truth, even when it's embarrassing."

Art always reminded students that their professional competence was inextricably tied to the quality of their character. The future of dentistry is in the hands of each and every one of its practitioners.

* * * * *

In his years of leading dentistry, Art was relentless in his insistence that dental students have a prominent role in determining each professional organization's future course. To Art, entrusting the next generation with a deep sense of responsibility is a critical step in creating future leaders. Only in a profession that cultivated and shared responsibility with its youngest members would the promise of a bright future be fully recognized.

An essential part of Art's lasting legacy to the future of dentistry may well come in the form of legions of students that he inspired, not only as dean of the Pacific Dental School for twenty-eight years, but his decades of mentoring and inspiring dental students, both here at home, and abroad.

Professional leadership for Art is rooted in the decision to get involved. In explaining to students how his career as a professional leader evolved, he would explain, "If you don't get involved, someone else will make the decisions affecting your profession. I got involved early on because I wanted to influence change, and I wanted to make a difference."

Typical of so many of his generation he embraced that eternal truth President Reagan spoke of: "If not us, who? If not now, when?"

Peter DuBois, the executive director of the California Dental Association, expressed a wonderful recollection of working with Art in 2004, in anticipation of Pacific's School of Dentistry's naming celebration weekend as it was to be re-christened the Arthur A. Dugoni School of Dentistry.

"I will never forget my first encounter with Art Dugoni," DuBois began. "I doubt anyone ever forgets his or her first impression of Dr. Dugoni…I was still working in San Francisco, and several people had urged me to introduce myself to Dr. Dugoni. We first met in his office. We sat close to each other, near a corner of his desk. Art leaned toward me as we began to talk…During the next three and a half hours, we walked every floor of the Pacific School of Dentistry, had dinner, and never stopped talking. The experience was exhilarating.

"More than once during our time together that evening, I would look at Art, see the sparkle in his eye and the glee in his smile and experience the wonder and joy he exudes about his life, his family, and his work. His charisma emanates from the sense that you are with a person who engages life fully, is determined to make a difference for as many as possible, and has the capability necessary to do so. I will never forget my early morning encounter with Art on the second day of our House of Delegates last year. The day before, Art had given the keynote address and received the CDA's highest honor, the Dale F. Redig Award — both events concluded with rousing standing ovations. And yet, early the very next morning, there was Art, sitting at a table in the CDA staff office drafting a document. 'Hey Art,' I greeted him, 'what are you working on?' He looked up, his eyes sparkling, his smile full of boyish enthusiasm, 'Oh, I'm working on a resolution for the house, I want them to consider taking some bigger steps with licensure reform.' When most would still be savoring the acclaim of the previous day, Art Dugoni was already at work on encouraging another initiative for the profession.

"Art Dugoni's greatness, however, stems not from what he does, which has and continues to be of awesome significance, but rather from who he is. As with all great leaders, Art's extraordinary impact ultimately derives from his personal fundamentals: integrity, dedication to family, respect for others, humility, passion, positive outlook, energy, hard work, and commitment to excellence in service to others."

* * * * *

In November 2013, at the age of eighty-eight, Art addressed the delegates at a CDA conference and urged them to, as the poet Henry Wadsworth Longfellow suggested, "Leave behind us footprints on the sands of time."

Art told them of attending his first dental society meeting sixty-three years earlier and deciding then that he wanted to take part in creating the future of dentistry. He urged the gathering, each in their own way, to play a role in leading their industry forward. "Leadership is a world of passion — of vision... seizing what needs to be done — and having the courage to do it. Persist long enough and the whole world will share in your vision."

ADA Executive Director Tom Ginley, and ADA Legislative Director, and longtime friend, Bill Allen, stand behind Art at the ADA's Chicago headquarters.

The Oklahoma Dental Association named Art Chief Micco Lvputke Nukkoso. A Creek name meaning (believe it or not) Chief Straightening Bear.

Native Son Aspires Towards Presidential Bid

California Caucus

25¢   Thursday, October 23, 1986   ★★★★

AAD For ADA
13th District Decides On Dugoni

Doctor Arthur A. Dugoni
Portrait of a CDA President

By Beth MacLeod
REPRINTED WITH PERMISSION. CONTACT POINT, VOLUME 60, NO. 3, 1980

Arthur Dugoni has one consuming and overriding interest - the profession of dentistry and all its many components. He has practiced dentistry since 1948; he has mastered two specialties—prosthodontics and orthodontics; he began teaching, in UOP, in 1951; and at the same time he began his extraordinary work for the good, not of his practice alone, but of his en-

Investing Ourselves In The Future

By Arthur A. Dugoni, DDS, MSD President, California Dental Ass'n.
REPRINTED WITH PERMISSION, THE CDA JOURNAL, SEPTEMBER 1980

Last year, I was privileged to make 34 visits to component dental societies and boards of directors. If I came away with any impression after those visits, it would be that so many owe so much to so few. The dedication of those individuals who are concerned about their profession and its future is formidable.

Unfortunately, there also seems to be a great deal of lethargy and apathy amongst many dentists. I believe that

Art "moving up through the chairs," ultimately
runs for the ADA presidency unopposed.

Art at the podium urging his profession forward:
"Where there is little risk, there is little reward!"

Chapter Twenty

The Art of Giving

Little in Art's childhood would have led one to suspect that philanthropy would play a significant role in his life. When you grow up in a small home where your bedroom doubled as the family's dining room, and you hoped that a threadbare pair of pants would make it through another winter, the very idea of "giving your money away," would seem absurd.

Other than the coins dropped every week into the collection plate at church, every dollar that came into the Dugoni home went for shelter, food, clothing, and education. A few spare dollars in the rock bottom days of the Great Depression went for entertainment, but those dollars were few and far between.

"It was my mom, Lina, who got me to make the first big gift of my life," Art explains. "It was the year I came back to San Francisco from Seattle, and I was busy creating a new orthodontic practice."

John Tocchini had committed the school to building a new campus on Webster Street in Pacific Heights, after all, those "termites holding hands," preventing the total collapse of the old P&S building, could only do their job for so long.

Understandably, there was a lot of excitement and interest in the project. Tocchini knew that he had to do two things to turn the project into a reality. One was to secure a generous federal assistance grant, and the other was to rally alumni, faculty, and friends of the school, to donate in support of a badly needed new facility.

"I gave a gift of a thousand dollars, which in the early 1960s was a lot of money," Art explains. "Lina believed that so much of what happened in my life started with the day I walked into Ernie Sloman's office that making an investment in the school's future was the right thing to do. Looking back on it, I'm glad she encouraged me to make that gift. It was the first time in my life I gave serious thought to the collective power of philanthropy to both change institutions and change lives."

Fifteen years after taking his first major step into philanthropy, when Art assumed the deanship and started to develop his own list of future goals for the school, he knew that so many of the things he wanted for the future of the school depended on identifying the financial resources to turn dreams into realities.

"There were only three avenues of revenue to creating the school I knew we could be," Art explains, "tuition, clinic income, and donations."

John Tocchini started the filling of the month club, which back then in the 1950s and '60s meant having graduates set aside five, ten, or fifteen dollars from their monthly income and donating that money to the school. It was a great idea in its time, but not one that would meet the financial challenges that Art faced in the 1980s.

When Art became dean, the school had a two-person development staff and the $60,000 that the school's fundraising team brought in annually went principally to covering the staff's salaries and expenses.

Of course, what Art did not realize in the early days of his deanship, was that the stagnant economy of the late 1970s was about to get considerably worse and help trigger a steep decline in dental school enrollments and therefore tuition-generated income.

Minus significant philanthropy or tuition increases, improving the school's financial position meant enhancing clinic income as the school's only other source of revenue. But propelling the faculty forward into updating the efficiency of the clinic and therefore producing additional revenue through its operation was about as easy as moving that proverbial cemetery.

Art, never one to back away from a challenge, raised clinic income, but it grew slowly. Modest increases in the school's tuition ($65,000 being the cost for the entire three years, about one quarter of its current three-year cost) failed, of course, to change the school's financial picture.

It's also important to note that during the first five years Art served as dean, inflation was growing at an average rate of 10%. With the high rate of inflation challenging the US economy, what you could buy for a $1,000 in 1978 cost over $1,500 in 1983.

Art, bucking the headwinds of a challenging economy, saw beyond the present and put his faith in the future. In truth, that future took time and patience to reach. During that time, Art mastered the financial challenges of the CDA, the ADA, and later the FDI with greater ease than gathering the needed resources to enhance the dental school's ever-precarious financial standing.

Philanthropy was increasing but in small steps. Then, almost twenty years into his deanship, a miracle occurred. In 1997, the year after the dental school celebrated its centennial, another son of Italian immigrants, Arthur A. Molinari, who had been raised in North Beach and graduated from the school two years before Art Dugoni was born, gave a gift of five million dollars in memory of his wife Ruth and their only child, Joan. Molinari, the son of a deli shop owner, started his practice with the support of his North Beach family, their many friends, and the family's loyal customers. In fact, Art's grandparents were once patients of Dr. Molinari, who practiced in the same North Beach office for sixty-four years. Molinari had a deep love and respect for the school and fond memories of his favorite instructor, later the school's dean, Dr. Ernie Sloman.

That Molinari family gift was a game-changer. It redefined the nature of philanthropy at the school. It stirred Art's imagination as well. There was so much that could be accomplished in redefining the school's future if the needed financial support could be secured. Perhaps philanthropy, not fundraising, was the key.

To many, these two terms may seem interchangeable. But there is an important difference. Fundraising more often pertains to the needs of today. Specific projects that are underfunded, but nevertheless need to be done, such as renovating classrooms, upgrading technology capabilities, or repairing the damage caused by a flood or fire. Philanthropy takes a wider vision and attempts to peer forward into the hoped-for future of an institution. In Latin, the word "philanthropia," was taken from Greek and means, "love of humanity."

In that light, the shift that Art made in his final years as dean and in his final role as a leader of his profession, when he agreed to accept the presidency of the American Dental Association Foundation, was a natural extension of his work in the field of humanism…one generation gathering the financial resources to assure the educational success of the next generation.

It took several years after the Molinari gift was given for this new vision to come together. The story of how that occurred is fittingly dramatic. This was a time when, as Dr. David Chambers explains, "There was a shift of paradigm. The school went from lasagna dinners and pledge-gathering phone banks to having a professional development staff." Certainly, it was a sea change in how the school envisioned its future.

In 2000 and then again in 2002, Art requested that the development team and the school's foundation board have off-site planning sessions to form an effective plan of action. The first Sonoma meeting was billed as an open exchange of ideas, but when Art saw that the outside facilitator was not moving the process forward, "Art," as Chambers explains, "essentially took over the meeting."

"He took a piece of butcher block paper," Chambers recalls, "and asked what we would need to do to create a new pre-clinical patient simulation lab. Art then put up another piece of paper and asked, if we could equip a research facility, what it would include? Before long, there wasn't a part of wall space that wasn't covered with strips of butcher block paper."

The depression-era teenager who once wrapped sausage in butcher-block paper was now, nearly sixty years later, laying out a vision on that same paper for a school that would lead dental education well into the next century.

There were a lot of grand thoughts to which everyone present knew real numbers would have to be attached. But Art had worked his magic lifting a room, as he had so often done in the past, from focusing on the "Why and How?" to discussing the "Why not?"

"Art's confidence and enthusiasm took us from a mindset of accomplishing the next project to achieving a vision," Dave Chambers explains. "It's hard to tell a student that he or she needs to pay 10% more in fees and tuition to help pay for the school's future. But to ask graduates to contribute to the school that played an essential role in their success, that's reasonable."

Not long after, an additional truth occurred to Art: Endowments were truly at the heart of any great institution. Endowments could reduce the cost of education and help fund professorships and department chairs that would change the school's stature.

"We created endowments to secure the future of the dental school. Endowed professorships," Art explains, "and endowed department chairs. Both allow you to go after the very top people in their field. If salaries are paid out of endowments, it doesn't have to impact tuitions so substantially. Philanthropy forces you to think big, to stop and ask the question: What can we achieve, what future can we create?"

Art's passion for the power of philanthropy is something that clearly evolved with the passing years. That five million dollar gift soon led to bigger plans. Entering the final decade of his deanship, Art began working with the school's foundation board on a plan that caused dental school deans throughout North America to redefine what was possible in the area of philanthropic support for dental education. It was a dream that started with a foundation board retreat in Sonoma and took flight two years later in a cave built into the side of a mountain on the property of a Sonoma County winery.

The vintner was a retired dentist, a former associate dean, and one of Art's dearest friends, Dr. James Pride, the same man who had been there for Art Dugoni in the past. He and his wife, Carolyn, had purchased the Vineyard at Summit Ranch in 1990 and renamed the property Pride Mountain Vineyards.

Pride, who was there to offer a quick way home when Art and Kaye were desperate to reach their critically injured son, offered Art a place where he and the Pacific Dental Education Foundation board could meet, have dinner, share some of California's best wines, and dream bigger than they ever had before.

That night became legendary in the years to come as each attendee suggested different parts of a vision to transform Pacific into what Art described as the "Four Seasons" of dental schools.

Dreams and ideals that had been written down on butcher-block paper in brainstorming sessions suddenly began to feel obtainable. It had been the kind of open-ended, far-sighted conversation that Art had learned over the past two decades, produced the best results.

Eventually, a plan was developed to create a far-reaching campaign that would redefine the school's stature in dental education. They christened their effort the Commitment to Excellence Campaign and set a seven-year goal to raise $50 million. This was a fund-raising goal never before attempted by any dental school in the United States or Canada, and it was quickly dismissed by many as yet another classic case of "Dugoni's crazy ideas."

Months before the decisive meeting, Art had approached Dr. Craig Yarborough, who at the time was responsible for student admissions and asked him to consider taking up the role of associate dean for development.

Reluctant at first to leave a position he excelled at and greatly enjoyed, Yarborough took up the challenge. Once he had completed his search for the person to oversee the daily operation of the campaign and take charge of the school's in-house development staff, the campaign began to take shape. With a long history of fundraising, Dr. Berney Neufeld, a huge man with a gentle touch, welcomed a challenge. Neufeld had the years of experience to know that the campaign had set a very big goal.

The Sonoma planning retreat had been one of those times when a volunteer board attempts to will itself forward, but at the same time, individual board members could not help but wonder what everyone else is "really thinking?"

Pacific's campaign goal, in comparison to the billion dollar endowments of a Harvard, Stanford, Cornell, New York University, and other institutions, may indeed appear modest. But look a little closer. Today, approximately 550 students are enrolled in all of the dental school's various degree programs. In addition to the DDS program, students pursue degrees in international studies, orthodontics, oral maxillofacial surgery, and on the Stockton campus, fifty hygienists are educated and trained. When all these programs are combined, the school graduates 178 doctoral degree candidates and twenty-five hygienists each year. Harvard has approximately 7,200 undergraduates and 14,000 postgraduates enrolled at any one time. By any measure of student enrollment and potential alumni support, the school's $50 million campaign goal was audaciously ambitious.

Additionally, the amount might seem like a small number when compared to a hot tech stock's valuation, but when you're talking about individuals reaching into their pocket and making substantial gifts, it can represent a very long road to travel. Ironically, Art's first adventure in raising funds for the school, his gambit to pay off the school's printing bill by raffling off a 1948 Plymouth was now fifty years in the past. How small that badly needed $7,000 seemed now.

Neufeld expanded the horizons of the campaign with his persistent advice to "think big." And Yarborough, as an alum with a long affiliation with dental school, was not only a walking directory of the school's active alumni base, but as best described by Art's successor, Pat Ferrillo, "Craig Yarborough bleeds the university's colors of orange and black."

Along with these two key staff members, Art contributed one of the things he does far better than most, he rallied every viable constituency to the cause. Staff or faculty, students or parents, affiliate organizations and most importantly, his loyal alumni. All were called upon to help recognize this bold dream. The child in him that once searched desperately for the few spare coins his mother had handed him for the church's collection plate now embarked on a tireless effort to spread the gospel of a new age for his beloved dental school.

The campaign started with the discouraging news from a top outside development consulting firm that the goal of $50 million was simply too big to be accomplished. The donor base was too small to turn the goal into a reality. Art reviewed the study results with his development staff who gathered all the available information. He then made the decision to go full-speed ahead. Art persistently believed that the school's constituent audiences would rise to the occasion. It was no small gamble for a dean who had established a distinguished record. To reach $50 million Art knew he and many others would have to work tirelessly. Thirty million dollars could do a lot of good for the school, but missing the mark by nearly half would still have brought the sting of disappointment.

On the last evening of their retreat, the inspired but uncertain board members went to Pride winery; they toured the facility, which concluded on a beautiful terrace overlooking the property with a view of the rolling hills of Sonoma.

It was just as the sun was setting and the gentle chill of a perfect wine country October evening stirred its own special moment of inspiration.

"It was one of the more amazing days of my life," Yarborough recalls. "We had twenty-five foundation board members in attendance, their spouses, university staff and a few special guests. All totaled, it was a gathering of about sixty-five people. The setting could not have been more perfect. We entered the caverns where the wine aged, and our hosts, Jim and Carolyn Pride, had arranged for the dinner to be served right there."

At the end of the dinner, Jim Pride stood up and spoke about how much the dental school had meant to him and how deeply he valued the work that Art Dugoni had done in moving the school into the top tier of dental schools in the nation.

"Jim stunned the audience," Yarborough explains, "by announcing that he and Carolyn would make a two million dollar gift to the campaign. It was a defining moment for everyone who was there. This dream of raising $50 million seemed a lot more possible with the Prides pledging 4% of the total goal at the very start."

Convinced that this campaign was a worthwhile venture that would fundamentally change the future course of the dental school, Art spoke at dozens of dinners and other events, constantly encouraging partnership in the campaign as an essential step in securing the future, both for the school, and as an important way of moving the profession forward.

"Every fundraising leader dreams of having the perfect CEO; Art Dugoni was that in every sense," Berney Neufeld says. "In my business, that is a very rare thing. Art was the individual who made philanthropy one of the institutional values of Pacific. In fact, to Art, philanthropy is an essential humanistic value."

As Dr. Neufeld further explains, "The class of '66 is one of the best examples of how transformative a leader Art was. This was a class that vowed not to support the school after graduation in any manner. This was a fact that Art realized during the first years of his deanship. Some people who were angry with the school during the time of Tocchini's filling of the month club, took a removed patient's filling and sent it into the school as an expression of disdain for their alma mater, and to ridicule the very thought that they would think of committing even a token of their earnings to the school."

Dean Redig was the first to change those negative views, and later Art's charm offensive brought about all but a total reversal of any lingering animus toward the school.

The best testament to that reversal is that the Class of '66 was one of the school's top donor classes throughout the campaign. Art turned their attention from the disappointment that they had felt as students into the pride they shared in the fact that their dental school was now in the forefront of educating the next generation of their chosen profession's leaders."

Emblematic of that reversal, it's interesting to note that the campaign chair, and its single biggest donor, Dr. Ron Redmond, was also a member of the Class of '66.

"Art tapped into the DNA of this institution like no other individual and it showed whenever he gathered with the alumni," Neufeld explains. "His deep love for the school and what it meant in his life and his career was infectious. Art was the right man at the right time, and he was absolutely essential to the school's success."

Neufeld suggested that the oversized influence that Dugoni had on the success of the campaign was made obvious by the commitments made to it by various individuals. "We had thirteen donors at the seven-figure level and one hundred at the six-figure level. You have to have a charismatic leader to bring that kind of donor forward."

In the end, the multi-year effort, named the Commitment to Excellence, not only reached its stated goal of $50 million, but far exceeded that number, raising over $65 million. Along the way, Art Dugoni not only gave generously of his time, but he and Kaye gave of their treasure as well. In addition to donating a portion of his annual salary to the campaign, Art, who as previously stated, was a frequent guest speaker at various dental organizations and dental schools throughout the nation, requested that all of his honorariums be given to the school in support of the campaign.

For key donors and alumni groups throughout the Bay Area and ranging from Southern California to Arizona, Utah, Hawaii and elsewhere, Art attended countless functions and fundraisers throughout the years of the campaign, essentially making the same pitch that this school, "gave you and me the successful careers and the lives that we have enjoyed. Now is the time, our time, to give something back. To make a real and lasting difference."

Art's vision of the school's future was inspiring to potential donors. From a dental hygiene program on the Stockton campus to offering programs in international studies (IDS), oral maxillofacial surgery, advanced general dentistry, continuing education, orthodontics, and much more, Pacific's School of Dentistry evolved into one of the nation's premier schools, leading the nation toward a new century of clinical excellence. Test results for its students' post graduate licensing exams were consistently at or near the top, and the school sent more people into positions of responsibility in organized dentistry with more students and graduates taking part in the CDA, the ADA, and a variety of other organizations, than any other dental school in the nation. This was a point of particular pride for Art Dugoni; a testament to his insistence that dentists had to see beyond the cubicle that is their practice space and both engage and lead in professional organizations, as well as in their communities.

Pacific even had its own celebrity dentist, Dr. Bill Dorfman, Class of 1983, regularly featured on the hit ABC reality show, *Extreme Makeover*. Dorfman generously made his own "seven figure" contribution to the campaign.

* * * * *

In 2003, at age seventy-eight, with the success of his own school's campaign well underway, Art stepped back onto the national stage when he assumed the presidency of the American Dental Association Foundation. Barkley Payne served as the association's executive director and recalls fondly the first time he met Art Dugoni.

"I began working at the ADA in 1999. The day I met Art, he had been asked to serve on a special committee, and because he was delayed in transit, he arrived after the meeting began. When he did arrive, he dominated the room. He reminded me of those old EF Hutton commercials in the sense that, when he began to speak, everyone leaned in, concerned that they not miss a word. It's electric. He just had command of the room. Art had the ability to not only read the room, but elevate participants to a higher level than they thought to go."

Looking back on his years working with Art, Payne recalls his unique ability to make everyone feel respected and heard. "Whenever I had a difficult issue," Barkley recalls, "I would stop and ask myself: 'What would Art do?'

"Under Art's direction, the ADA Foundation planned and executed a national public relations campaign, *Dental Education: Our Legacy — Our Future*, involving nearly 150 dental schools, organizations, and specialty groups, to raise awareness and address the critical challenges facing dental education, including faculty shortages, student debt, aging facilities, lagging government support, escalating costs, and lack of diversity. Within two years of its launch, the effort achieved nearly 50% of its goal to raise more than $1.3 billion."

From his unique vantage point, Payne observed that Art, although nearing eighty, continued to be a force for innovation. "He was way ahead of his time in realizing the importance that different audiences, including students, were having and would continue to have on the profession. He was keenly aware that the role of women in the profession was taking on a dramatically new dimension. Art was a personal champion for me, he knew the voice of minorities, students, allied professionals, and educators all needed to be heard."

"Through his work in philanthropy," Payne continues, "Art wanted to get dentists to see themselves as philanthropic, as opposed to charitable. It was Art's goal to elevate them to the role of philanthropists investing in the future of dental education. He had unshakeable faith in the idea that today's student is tomorrow's donor. If they were inspired during their years at dental school, they will one day invest in the future of dentistry."

* * * * *

While not achieving a billion dollar educational endowment, the foundation's efforts were instrumental in the creation of improved facilities, expanded research, new scholarships, additional endowed chairs and other critical needs that, taken as a whole, significantly advanced dentistry and dental education.

Through his work with the foundation, Art had a national platform from which he could stress the essential role philanthropy plays in creating a better future. Philanthropy is rewarding to Art in deeply meaningful ways. It causes people to focus in on issues that define their profession and gives them the opportunity to make thoughtful gifts in support of excellence.

As for the cynics, there will always be a dozen reasons not to participate in philanthropy, but cynicism has never been a behavior Art embraced. "People are going to invest in the future or simply take a narrow view of what role they can play in helping to shape tomorrow. All your good intentions and efforts can be turned upside down if the funds are not available to allow you to accomplish your goals," Art further explains. "In the end, philanthropy is about relationships. Personal determination, professional fellowship, team spirit, is all those things that are not so easily calculated but in the final analysis make a huge difference."

Art standing beside an honor roll of donors, all whom invested in the future of the dental school.

Everyone points to Kaye, on the night of her winning Pacific's Medallion of Distinction.

Arthur Molinari shares with his alma mater the rewards of a lifetime of careful investment.

Dr. Bill Dorfman, once a student, returns to the school to announce his own seven-figure gift.

Chapter Twenty-One

Passing the Torch

Arguably, the concept of retirement and the nature of Art Dugoni don't fit well together. Not long after Steve Dugoni had entered his sixties, he shared with his father that he was beginning to think about retiring from the orthodontic practice in South San Francisco that his dad founded a half-century before. Art looked at him with surprise and said, "If you retire, what in the world are you going to do?"

In truth, there were several times Art considered laying down the responsibility of being dean of the dental school. But Art was simply unwilling to take that final step. There was always more to do and more he could contribute in pursuit of excellence.

But the very idea of stepping away from doing the job that he loved caused him an endless degree of personal anguish. Art foretold that in a February 1988 newspaper interview when, at age sixty-two, he said, "I still have a lot to do here. I can think of a hundred projects I'd like to see done. I don't plan on retiring, because this is what I love. It keeps me healthy, and it keeps me going."

Nevertheless, Art was always troubled by the idea that the deanship would simply become too demanding a burden for him to execute with the vigor that he knew, far better than most, the position required.

The first time Art gave serious consideration to retirement was as he approached age sixty-five. Having been appointed dean at age fifty-three, retirement at sixty-five would have come twelve years after assuming the deanship; certainly a time in office in line with the historic average of his predecessors. As Art recalls, "I was considering announcing my decision at the annual alumni conference in 1990, but at the last moment, I pulled back. There was still so much more I wanted to accomplish. In the end, I kept this first retirement date to myself and decided to keep moving forward with completing my goals for the school."

Ten years later, in 2000, approaching seventy-five, Art gave the idea serious thought once more. January of that year, the Commission on Dental Accreditation completed their once every seven-year review of the dental school, which is standard procedure for all accredited dental schools in the United States. The school came through the process with no recommendations and eighteen commendations for excellence. That is a very exceptional accomplishment for any school. As Art proudly said in a memo to faculty, staff, and students, "We knocked their socks off!"

The commission is an independent accrediting body recognized by the US Department of Education. In their report, many areas of the school's performance were singled out for praise:

"The school is commended for developing a research program that has become an integral part of the curriculum and the advancement of dental and basic science knowledge among its students."

Additionally, "The school is recognized for its institutional commitment to provide faculty development activities such as the formal degree programs; how well the facility has been maintained and renovated over the past thirty-three years with a high level of cleanliness throughout; for the well documented standards of care and a patient-centered clinical program; successful fundraising for capital improvements and endowments; and for developing a comprehensive self-study program."

Perhaps most affirming to Art's efforts over the past twenty-two years of his deanship was a "commendation for improvements in overall planning activities and specifically, the use of continual assessment to evaluate achievement of its institutional goals."

All of this played into Art's retirement thinking for two main reasons. First, the commission's report was so complimentary of virtually every aspect of the school's program that this was certainly a chance for him to go out on top. Second, when Art held back in 1990 from announcing his retirement at sixty-five, he placed a personal line in the sand telling himself and Kaye that he would not stay on as dean beyond the age of eighty, a milestone birthday he would reach in June 2005.

Art, however, also knew that there was one more goal still to be reached. In 2000, the "Commitment to Excellence Campaign" was just entering the public phase of its $50 million drive. The school's development team, as discussed in the previous chapter, had just begun to set and focus on its goals. The sterling accreditation report was a summit, but a campaign that could play such an important role in securing the school's future was a significantly higher peak.

There was great symmetry in considering that, during his earliest years as dean, the dental school faced its greatest financial challenge since 1923 when Dean Arthur McDowell took control of the institution. To enter his deanship at a time of great financial peril and leave an institution secure in its financial future proved to be too tempting a goal. The capital campaign did not have a set date for completion. But it was hoped that it could achieve its ambitious goals by 2005. If Art could reach this one last goal by age eighty, he could successfully complete nearly three decades of unprecedented progress for the dental school, and leave his successor with an institution that would be the envy of dental schools across North America.

What did Kaye Dugoni think of Art, once again, delaying a decision to retire? Apparently, she took it in stride. Having watched as Art worked long days and nights at his office, she often told friends, "The school is Art's mistress." This was an apt description, considering that Art would spare no effort to improve the operational quality or the stature of his beloved school.

As previously detailed, the campaign had many goals, but none loomed so large in Art's view as endowments. His mantra, an essential pillar of the foundation of his philanthropic philosophy, could be summed up in seven words: "Great institutions are supported by great endowments," he reminded all, particularly potential donors, with that singular purpose that is so characteristically Art. To have both a successful future and to be an institution of unmatched excellence, endowed chairs, professorships, and scholarships would have to be an essential part of the mix.

Funding the school's future, at least in part by endowed funds, goes back to a question Art considered in 1978 when he assumed the deanship: What makes great schools great? Endowments are a critical part of achieving greatness. They allow institutions to build upon the things that they do well. For example, funding the positions of top educators, while controlling the cost of education. Art's dream was to have every full professorship endowed at a million dollar plus level.

"When I entered the deanship," Art explains, "the school had one endowment. At the time I retired in 2006 we had 125, with over another seventy-five being funded." Included in that number is two endowments that the Dugoni family began: The Dr. Arthur A Dugoni Endowed Professorship in Orthodontics, and the Art & Kaye Dugoni Student Scholarship Endowment.

* * * * *

After the initial launch of the quiet phase of the Commitment to Excellence campaign, Art was invited to a dinner meeting at Harris Steakhouse on Van Ness Avenue in San Francisco. It was a small group, consisting of university president, Don DeRosa, the chair of the university's board of regents, Donald O'Connell, Craig Yarborough, and long-time serving Pacific Dugoni Foundation (then Pacific Dental Education Foundation) member, Gary Mitchell. When Art learned that both the university president and the top regent would be attending the dinner, he thought: "Maybe this was going to be a nice way of telling me it was time to leave; I was a bit nervous, wondering what was up. Certainly, it had to be significant."

There is still a look of surprise that comes over Art when he recalls the moment he learned the real purpose of that evening's gathering. It was to propose that, at the campaign's conclusion, the University would formally announce its intention to name the one hundred-plus-year-old dental school in his honor. "I was shocked when the president told me. My first response was 'I wish my parents were here; they would be so proud'." Then I reasoned we could get $50 million for naming rights to the entire school. Don DeRosa responded to my comment by saying, 'Art you gave us $50 million worth of leadership with your life.'"

Art smiled and looked at all the smiling faces looking back at him. Silent for a time, Art explains, "I wanted to freeze the moment, pull out my phone and call Kaye."

Rarely rendered speechless, Art gathered his thoughts and decided to lighten the moment. "Okay, put my name up with Velcro on the back of it," he told them. "If someone comes along with $50 million, we can certainly put it to good use."

Mitchell, who first floated the idea of renaming the school, and Yarborough recall that, to them, the most memorable moment of the dinner was, "Art wiping a tear away and telling us how he wished his parents had lived to hear this."

As detailed in the previous chapter, the campaign not only stayed on target, but exceeded its original $50 million. Once the decision was made to name the school for Art, the topic was seldom raised so that the focus could be kept on the campaign and what its success would mean to the future of the institution.

As is inevitably the case for busy people, the next few years passed quickly and before long, it was time to begin the formal planning for a gala weekend of events to celebrate the school's renaming. Beginning Friday, August 27, 2004 and concluding on Saturday, August 28, the event was masterfully coordinated by the school's longtime director of public relations, Kara Sanchez. For Sanchez and the members of her committee, it was a labor of love.

Less than a year before his eightieth birthday, the school that had been so much a part of Art's life for over six decades formally took his name. The School of Dentistry at the University of the Pacific was renamed University of the Pacific, Arthur A. Dugoni School of Dentistry.

The first event of the two-day celebration was the unveiling of the school's new name on a stage set up on the plaza adjacent to the school's formal entry lobby. Students wore black and orange T-shirts displaying the new name, while staff and faculty wore pins bearing the school's new logo. The new school flag was hoisted to the cheers of the crowd, and an oil painting portrait of Dr. Dugoni to hang in the lobby alongside a case celebrating his life in photographs and memorabilia was unveiled.

Organizers had planned for 500, and over 700 attended. Don DeRosa and others spoke warmly of Art. Following President DeRosa was Patrick Cavanaugh, the university's vice president for business and finance. Over their years of working together, Art and Pat had developed a deep mutual respect. "As the dean of a school, you're only as good as the people who help you turn visions into reality; Pat was essential in helping to make several of my 'crazy ideas' into reality."

As for Cavanaugh, upon leaving his post a decade later he wrote, "It was easy to work with Art…to contribute to his vision for excellence. In fact, it wasn't work at all; it was a privilege to do things for Art that others thought might be impossible. Art always knew they were possible, and I liked proving he was right."

Art came up to the stage looking grateful and overwhelmed. He thanked everyone for their love and support over his many years. He touched the attendees when he talked about all the special moments of his life, adding with great affection, "It was a special moment in 1943 when I met a special lady who stole my heart, Kaye Dugoni."

But the morning naming ceremony was highlighted by a wholly unanticipated and completely unscripted moment: Grandson Nic Rouleau, son of Art and Kaye's eldest daughter, Mary, and her husband Bert, took the stage and sang the hit song from the 1997 musical, *Jekyll and Hyde*, "This is the Moment." His voice rang out pitch-perfect as he sang the song's final memorable lyrics:

When I look back,

I will always recall,

Moment for moment,

This was the moment,

The greatest moment

Of them all!

Here was a high school senior singing a song in honor of his grandfather's special day. Generally, the audience thought it was lovely gesture, and they were prepared to listen politely. What no one knew that day was, eight years later, Nic would be on Broadway playing the lead, Elder Price, in the smash hit musical, *The Book of Mormon.*

The future Broadway star created an amazing moment. He commanded the stage with a masterful voice and a confident demeanor. Not something anyone expected, looking at this smiling adolescent still battling to overcome acne. When he finished, the audience, after a moment of stunned silence, cheered loudly.

Art, the proud grandfather, bounded back up on the stage, moved to tears, as were many others, he said, "This is what it's all about. It doesn't matter how many distinguished service awards you receive or how many plaques are on your wall, it's moments like this. It really comes down to family, family that forgives you when you're not around. I'm so proud of my grandson, and there are fourteen more just like him."

Off script, it was a moment of great joy. Here was the family man, distinguished educator, professional leader, and public figure reduced to a moment where seemingly the span of his life flashed before him. It was the essence of humanism in a setting of formal ritual.

Joyously, he shared the story of his grandpa Benedetto Bianco handing out parts to a Puccini opera after one of the family's legendary Sunday feasts back home on Glover Street. You could sense all those memories were with Art as he explained, to the delight of the audience, how Benedetto would take the lead and encourage everyone to join in, then he paused, looked at Nic, and with a sly smile that was uniquely Art, he said, "You see, it's all in the genes."

* * * * *

Later that day and continuing into the next, a national leadership symposium was held at the Fairmont Hotel located atop San Francisco's prestigious Nob Hill. As explained in Kara Sanchez's summary report of the weekend's events: "It was a national call to address significant issues in dental education, including the rising cost of dental education, student indebtedness, and faculty shortages." The hope was to bring together a group of four hundred. The event, however, drew a much larger group than the planners expected, with over 900 industry and educational leaders in attendance.

Every one of the speakers at the event, including the two keynote speakers, John Chambers, President and CEO of Cisco Systems, and Dr. Gordon Christensen, generously agreed to speak without an honorarium. Additionally, all speakers, including Dr. Clive Ross, of New Zealand, traveled to San Francisco at their own expense.

Dr. David Chambers began the event by asking the attendees, "Where will we get the next generation of Art Dugonis?" Each speaker returned to a similar theme, regardless of the challenges that dental education, clinical practice, or research faced in the coming years, Art's style of inclusive and positive leadership created a model worth studying and emulating if these challenges were to be successfully met.

All speakers, beginning with John Chambers, spoke of the importance of seizing the moment to offer yourself as an agent for change. John Chambers stressed that the ability to recognize change is an essential ingredient of effective leadership. In turn, it is key, as Art Dugoni consistently demonstrated, to be able to "articulate a vision, create a positive culture, and communicate effectively," if one hopes to move at the speed of a rapidly changing world.

Dr. Christensen said, "I know of no one who has had a greater impact on the field of dentistry than Art Dugoni." Christensen, who focused on an array of characteristics that create an atmosphere of effective leadership focused on the power of communication. "Leaders you respect have open lines of communication all the time. Their staff members know that they can talk to their leader on important matters rapidly and easily. As a result, constant interaction at all organizational levels is stimulated, and a team spirit is developed. Undermining and negative feelings of staff members are reduced or eliminated by good communication."

What Christensen was describing is reflected in many aspects of Dugoni's leadership style. Perhaps it is encapsulated in Art's practice of "management by walking about, MBWA." As discussed earlier, Art would schedule various times each week to walk through an area of the school unannounced and visit with

students, faculty, and staff. He firmly believed that, for an organization to function with a cohesive spirit of unity and purpose, its leader needed to be viewed
as accessible and approachable.

Dr. Tony Volpe, the vice president for clinical research at Colgate Palmolive
told conference attendees: "It may come as a surprise to some in the audience
that Art was not born as the 'Dean of Deans.' He earned that title…building
sustained relationships with a huge network of individuals, taking chances and
moving into important areas before others recognized or felt comfortable doing
so, and treating everyone with the greatest respect possible."

Dr. Clive Ross, past president of the World Dental Federation, FDI, spoke
of his experience working with Art during their time together serving on the
organization's executive board. "Art has that extraordinary ability to quickly understand people, to work with and nurture them and to get the best out of them
while giving great respect to the individual."

Finally, Dr. Harold Slavkin, then dean of the USC School of Dentistry and
former director of the National Institute of Dental and Craniofacial Development said that Art was one of the few voices that could offer an "unconvention-
al perspective with bracing authenticity." Slavkin shared his view that, like his
beloved California, "Art Dugoni is an undisputed original. He grew up within
a large Italian family in the shadow of the Depression and World War II, and
he experienced and was profoundly influenced by the remarkable events of the
second half of the twentieth century…Art's voice is one that should be heard by
all those who would aspire to lead thoughtfully and effectively in our own time."

* * * * *

The stunning Rotunda at San Francisco's City Hall was the setting for a lav-
ish cocktail and fundraising dinner on Saturday night August 28th. The original
plan anticipated 400 guests at $1,000 per person; nearly 700 attended, requiring
tables to be placed on both levels of this historic setting. Then mayor, Gavin
Newsom, who was joined by his predecessor, former mayor, Willie Brown, began the night's festivities saying, "Few people realize the enormity of the con-

tribution the Pacific School of Dentistry has made in the life of San Francisco and the extraordinary person who, for so many years, has been the steward of this institution." He then presented a proclamation declaring that this day was to be recognized in honor of "an extraordinary leader, Dr. Arthur A. Dugoni."

The weekend's most amazing event, however, was saved for last. The "Gala Naming Celebration," filled the city's dazzling Louise M. Davies Symphony Hall, diagonally across Van Ness Avenue from the front steps of City Hall. Once again, the planned attendance was vastly exceeded as 1,639 filled the orchestra and mezzanine of this grand home of the San Francisco Symphony. In a dazzling, Academy Award-style setting, video tributes came from California Senators, Diane Feinstein and Barbara Boxer followed by Governor Arnold Schwarzenegger's state proclamation in recognition of Art Dugoni, which was read by University President Don DeRosa. In addition to representatives from all of America's dental associations, over half of the nation's dental school deans were in attendance.

It was Art's moment to shine. And he did not disappoint the huge gathering as he spoke briefly and emotionally about his family, his profession, and his life at the dental school.

"There were three words that I used beginning in 1978 to launch the framework that would create our future: pride, passion, and performance. Pride that a three year program could be the best in the nation; passion in everything we did as faculty and staff; and a dedication to drive everyone to the highest level of performance."

Comedian Bill Cosby, wearing an orange and black T-shirt emblazoned with the new logo of the Arthur A. Dugoni School of Dentistry, took the stage for a one-hour performance.

Looking back several years later on the weekend's events, Art still smiles in amazement. "My favorite moment was when I had the entire Dugoni family on stage. That was quite a crowd. Lucky for us, symphony hall has a big stage. I don't know if anyone deserves that much love and attention, but it certainly was wonderful."

* * * * *

Two months after that remarkable weekend, Don DeRosa announced in a memo to staff, faculty, and students, that Art and he had agreed that this was "a good time for a leadership transition." The university president further explained that Art had agreed to remain as dean until 2006.

With Art's help, the university created a list of the top deans in the country. The search was open to candidates inside and outside of the school. President DeRosa, however, had never chosen to promote a candidate from inside one of the university's schools to be a new dean. In spite of having a number of strong internal candidates, it was likely that, in the case of the dental school's future dean, this same pattern would apply.

Several of the country's top dental school deans applied for the position, somewhat to the surprise of many of their colleagues. "Do you really want to be the dean that follows Dugoni? Those are certainly big shoes to fill," was the prevailing thought within the small-knit community of deans.

In that group of applicants was Dr. Patrick Ferrillo, the relatively new dean of the UNLV School of Dentistry, and dean previously of Southern Illinois University's School of Dental Medicine.

After a long process of interviews at the school and with the university, Ferrillo's selection was formally announced in 2005. On June 30, 2006, one day after Art celebrated his eighty-first birthday, Dr. Ferrillo took charge of the Dugoni School of Dentistry, the school's eighth dean in its 110-year history.

"Pat came at the right moment," Art says, "with a $65M campaign being completed, he came into what was now a thriving institution, and he has greatly enhanced it. He's made me proud. His direction in curriculum improvements, with the help of his executive associate dean, my one-time student, Nader Nadershahi, has been outstanding. His budget enhancements have been very positive. Starting a graduate program in endodontics, and so much more, like his expansion of our school internationally into China, South Korea, and Egypt, and educational exchanges with Saudi Arabia."

As Dr. Alan Gluskin, co-chairman of the dental school's endodontics program explains, "This school has been blessed to have the right dean step in at the right time. Dale Redig changed the school's entire academic system, a critical contribution to the school's ongoing success. Art Dugoni made the school a highly respected institution, not just on a national, but an international stage as well. Now Pat Ferrillo has ensured the school's continued success well into the twenty-first century. It's quite amazing when you view the sweep of events over the long arc of history."

Soon after the start of Dr. Ferrillo's deanship, he organized the start of a new strategic plan called "Advancing Greatness." Out of that plan's careful development the decision to leave the school's Webster Street campus evolved. In a rapidly changing profession, in spite of numerous updates, after a half-century of service, the facility was not well-suited to meet the changing needs of students, faculty, staff, and a changing patient population. Additionally, situated in what is now one of America's most affluent zip codes, the Pacific Heights neighborhood of San Francisco is far from an ideal location for generating patients for the school's public clinics.

After an exhaustive search both near the city's center and along its picturesque waterfront, the university settled on the purchase and refurbishment of an old office building on Fifth Street between Market and Mission. Located just one block from the Powell and Market transportation hub, where BART and MUNI light rail, street car, cable car, and several bus lines converge, greatly expands the accessibility of the school's new home to students, faculty, and staff. Most importantly, these new transportation options far better serve the school's lower-income patients.

Ironically, the school's address, 155 Fifth Street, is less than a five minute walk to the site of the school's first home at 818 Howard Street; a remarkable journey spanning 118 years from the school's past to its future. Particularly welcome news is the fact that with tech giants Yahoo, Twitter, and new office, retail, and residential projects begun or preparing to begin, such as the massive 5M project at Fifth and Mission, it's clear that the Dugoni School's new home is situated in an area of seemingly boundless potential. In fact, one of the largest public improvement projects ever undertaken in San Francisco, the new four billion dollar Transbay Terminal will make mass transit access to the area from all eight Bay Area counties more accessible than ever before.

The new campus, dedicated on March 7, 2014 and beginning full operation at the start of the 2014-2015 academic year, will likely be the crowning touch of the Ferrillo years, who with singular purpose set the goal of making Pacific Dugoni the "leading dental school in the world." It was a bold and daring move on the part of Ferrillo and the university's new president Pamela Eibeck, who replaced the retiring Don DeRosa in 2009. A walk through the new school reveals Ferrillo and Eibeck's shared vision for the school's new home. A stunning and ultra-modern facility in which it's clear that all who enter will find a welcoming environment for countless decades to come.

Proof of that was the decision made in early 2011 to buy a seven-story building in which the top two floors would be available for lease until an undetermined date in the future when the school might need still greater expansion space. In early 2014, the building's office space was leased to Eventbrite, a fast growing online ticketing service, which allows various event organizers to sell tickets and promote events using such platforms as Facebook and Twitter. This agreement will diminish the project's investment cost and enhance its financial viability. Meanwhile, in 2012, a deal was struck with Trumark Urban, a Bay Area residential condominium developer to convert the old school in Pacific Heights into seventy-seven luxury condo units, many with sweeping views of the Golden Gate Bridge, helped to assure the economic stability of the school going forward.

In every sense, all these changes capitalize on the dramatic changes that have occurred in San Francisco in the last decade...The rapid expansion of the South of Market real estate market, where construction cranes dot today's landscape; and the evolution of the Webster Street campus, as nearby Fillmore Street has transformed into one of the city's most desirable shopping areas; and the surrounding neighborhood has become home to some of America's wealthiest families. "In total, the Dugoni School under Dean Ferrillo," as Art proudly suggests, "has seized the moment and, by doing so, has helped to secure an awesome future."

* * * * *

During the last four years of Art's twenty-eight-year deanship, his long battle with prostate cancer began. No reason to stop when there was still so much to be done, Art explains that his faith led him to conclude that this "was just another turn on life's long road."

In 2002, with his PSA rising dramatically, a certain sign of trouble ahead, and a biopsy that revealed two cancerous lesions, Art's reaction was to study everything he could about the current state of treatment of the disease.

"I read five books, perhaps seventy-five articles, and I realized there was a wide range of options," Art explains. "At the advice of my internist, I went up to Seattle to meet with the doctor who created a new approach of using radioactive isotopes. He advised against proceeding. So I went back to San Francisco and, armed with what I learned in Seattle, I had radiation. My attitude was I could beat this…Forty-one days of radiation, five days a week. But the radiation, as it often does, did a lot of collateral damage."

Art recalls that each day he'd arrive for his procedure, he was greeted by a waiting room that hung heavy with what he describes as a sense of "gloom and doom." Art being Art had to change that.

"I started conversations with my fellow patients. One patient I remember to this day, who was having radiation to the throat, wrote me a lovely note saying that, if it hadn't been for me, she would have lost all hope. It's always wonderful to know that you helped someone at a time of great need."

Beyond the love and concern of Kaye and their large family, Art found abundant support for his own cancer battle from faculty, staff, alumni, and students whenever he sent out email updates to the full school. Art decided early-on that he did not want his condition to be the topic of rumors. It was far better to sacrifice a degree of privacy and share where he was in his treatment.

"Rumors thrive when people are kept in the dark," Art says. "The support I got back from so many members of our school family was terrific. It's an immeasurable lift to know that so many people are caring about you and cheering you on."

Two years later, Art's PSA suddenly began to rise again. This time it had spread to his spine. Art went back to the fight and started another full round of radiation.

Art, however, always the man to network and diligently search for new paths and new solutions, had a long-time acquaintance who had a client that led a team at Stanford University Medical Center that helped pioneer a procedure called "Cyberknife." The technique allowed the doctors to go after specific cancer spots on the lower spine without the collateral damage caused by Art's earlier rounds of radiation.

"I'm the absolute optimist," Art says. "I've had a variety of treatments. I was down when the cancer reappeared, and I was worried that I would not be here for Kaye. But I'm positive about the future. My faith in God, in Jesus, and the Blessed Mother have taken care of me all my life. I've been blessed and fortunate through a long life. Whether I deserved all that good fortune, I have no idea. I've always thanked God and continue to do so for all the wonderful things that have come my way, especially Kaye, my children, grandchildren, and great-grandchildren.

"You have to keep on keeping on! Taking a chance and calling Kaye when I graduated from dental school at twenty-three, I think I was guided. Making a decision at fifty-three to give up a private practice and take up the deanship…I might not have heard the angels sing, but that was the right choice for me. All the dreams that I've accomplished: creating endowments, the international dentistry program, starting an oral maxillofacial program, a dental hygiene program, the three plus three and the two plus three academic programs, other advanced degree programs, and strengthening a humanistic model that honored each and every student and making it one of our core institutional values. In 1978, I told my faculty and staff that USC School of Dentistry was the best in the nation, and I said that we would take their thunder away and we did.

"One of my goals was 100% success on state and national boards," Art continues. "A lot of school deans thought we were responsible only for education, not success on board exams; I never saw it that way. I was determined to make board passage a top priority. Every sports team spends far more time in practice than they do in playing the game. Often, students did not like taking mock state boards so that they would be ready for the game. Still, there were schools in California that had high failure rates, and I think that is indefensible. We sent everyone to the June boards and made it the rule that you had to pass the national board to graduate. You could not, in fact, take the state board without passing the national board. If we had students who could not do what we prepared them for, shouldn't we take some responsibility for that? It became part of the culture of our dental school, and today it is accepted procedure."

Life is often a bittersweet combination of individual will and circumstances well outside the realm of our control. Art's life has not been a short one. At the time of this book's publication, 2014, Art is eighty-nine and now engaged in the third round of his running battle with prostate cancer.

Sixty-five years after that cold snowy day in Spokane when they exchanged their vows, Kaye's health problems grow worse as well. But while her mind is not always clear, she still smiles brightly when Art enters the room, saying joyously one day to her caregiver, "That's my man!"

In the nearly 120 years since the founding of the dental school, it has had only eight deans. Three of those eight, McDowell, Sloman, and Inskipp, died in succession, while in office, and all were in the prime of life. That truth alone served as a reminder to Art of the blessings of longevity. His destiny has been to enjoy a much longer and more richly rewarding life.

In addition to a twenty-eight-year deanship, Art has experienced a long and active post-deanship as well. A blessing, yes, but for an individual as motivated as Art, he enjoys a constant challenge to stay relevant and involved. Undoubtedly, there are highly driven individuals who fade quietly into the sunset, but on life's stage, that was never a role Art played well. Rather, he has continued traveling, speaking, and remaining active in a variety of ways.

Each year, Art greets new students entering the Arthur A. Dugoni School of Dentistry. And he continues speaking to students at other dental schools, Midwestern, Marquette, and Arizona, to name just a few. He shakes hands with these future doctors with the same excited anticipation he has experienced for decades: "The honor," Art explains, "of touching tomorrow."

"With each of these students, I have renewed faith simply in knowing that I am standing on the threshold of my profession's future."

Art has traveled hundreds of thousands of miles carrying a message of unshakeable faith in the future of a profession he did so much to shape. In speaking to graduating classes, symposiums on professional ethics, dental education, envisioning the future, Art consistently brings a message of inspiration. He faithfully appealed to his listener's better angels, whether quoting Mahatma Gandhi or Yogi Berra.

Near the end of his life, Albert Einstein wrote in a letter to an old friend: "People like you and me never grow old. We never cease to stand like curious children before the great mystery into which we were born."

Art's own youthful curiosity has also been irrepressible. Regardless of his accomplishments, he has insistently believed that there is always more to learn and more to discover. "What has been done well one year can be made better the next," he insists. "Like the process of education itself, excellence is not a destination, it's a path."

For Art, that path is one he has pursued doggedly from his days at St. James High School through all he accomplished as both a dean and a leader of his profession. Those who thought Art would make a quiet exit from his profession did not understand the man. At eighty-nine, he is still agitating for change and improvement. He has never valued the undisturbed tranquility of maintaining the status quo over the challenge of reinvention and redefinition. He has never comfortably embraced silence over participation.

As the debate over allied health professionals in dentistry broadened, he encouraged others to join the conversation. "The profession should own the issue," he explains. "Their education, their scope of responsibility, and their supervision and direction. We the profession should decide these roles in our system of care, not the legislators."

On moving dentistry forward into a new century, he said, "As a learned profession based on science and inquiry, we should welcome and embrace continued evaluations, research, and studies, regardless of our current perceptions, experiences or biases.

"A learned profession can never close its mind or heart to new ideas. We must continue to evaluate, test and demonstrate all modalities that stretch the envelope of our knowledge. This may result in progress that benefits and improves our patients' health, wellbeing, and quality of life.

"The debates and discussions that ensue from the presentations of studies, research endeavors in clinical trials, modes of practice, and their eventual outcomes, are the benefits to a free society. They are the contributions of a learned profession to that society."

A part of Art has always seen the classroom as a pulpit:

"Education is a transformational process, getting to the end result of creating a doctor, a scientist, a clinician, an ethical practitioner; that's our job. This is why I have so often said we build people; along the way they become doctors. A professional person should example a higher level of responsibility. The patient trusts you, which means you should have the highest level of behavior. Do unto others, as you would have them do onto you. Not what is in the best interest of your pocketbook, but in the best interest of your patients. You did not fall in love with the idea of being a doctor because you wanted to be a seller of services; you wanted to care for people!"

At the 2014 graduation ceremony for the University of the Pacific's Arthur A. Dugoni School of Dentistry, two speakers addressed the impact Dean Dugoni had on their lives. One was Dr. Ron Redmond, who, as that commencement speaker attributed the success of his long career in dentistry to what Isaac Newton called, "standing on the shoulders of giants." He explained to the audience how he was inspired and encouraged to enter the specialty of orthodontics by Art Dugoni. "One caring and committed educator can make all the difference, if you understand that giants give you a boost to see what, for you, might be an uncertain future. Art Dugoni is the reason for my seeing into the future. He took the time to care and talk to me about my career options. He made a difference that enhanced my life and later the lives of my family."

The 2014 valedictorian, Kristy Rodgers, graduating forty-eight years after Dr. Redmond, currently a regent, told this story,

"I felt privileged to be accepted to the Pacific Dugoni family. As my first year started, I wanted to do the very best that I could, but was overwhelmed with the demands. While trying to survive, I attended a lecture by Dr. Dugoni where he shared the quote, "We build people, and along the way they become doctors." I was so touched by his words. More important than prepping the perfect 3MOD or a LAVA crown prep was the people that we would become. I have had the incredible privilege of seeing this transformation occur in my life and the life of my classmates, while attending the best dental school in the country. I am proud to be a part of a class of individuals filled with so much compassion, integrity, intelligence, amazing clinical skills, patience, and ingenuity."

On stage, clothed in the gown and hood that he had worn dozens of times before, Art quietly shed a few tears, gratefully recalling a lifetime of sharing with countless thousands of students, colleagues, cherished friends, and loved ones his fervent belief that, "One person with patience, persistence and passion, can create ripples of positive change that reach far out into the future." His life, his work, and his legacy, are living testaments to that ideal.

Art with San Francisco Mayor, Gavin
Newsom, at the City Hall Rotunda dinner
honoring his twenty-eight year deanship.

Retiring Dean Art Dugoni with
his successor, Dean Pat Ferrillo

Art, as Dean
Emeritus, at a
university function.
To his immediate
left is Provost Phil
Gilbertson, and
to his left,
Pacific Vice President,
Patrick Cavanaugh.

Three generations of Dugoni orthodontists. Grandsons
Brian Dugoni and Aaron Rouleau, with Art and Steve Dugoni.

At the Symphony Hall Dugoni Gala: Mary, Art Jr., Russell, Steve, Kaye,
Art, Diane, Michael, and James gather for a night to remember.

Epilogue

Over a lifetime of special moments, the Ellis Island ceremony was one that Art particularly cherished.

After the evening ended, in the middle of the harbor as the lights of Ellis Island began to recede, a deep boom shattered an otherwise-peaceful night.

A huge red starburst lit up the sky. Followed by another burst of white and a third one of blue. It was a farewell salute to that year's honorees before they returned home to their private lives, hopefully never to forget the generations that came upon these waters many years before.

Art thought of the Biancos and the Dugonis as a cool breeze rose from the dark waters that surrounded him. Once again, memories of his parents and grandparents rushed through his mind and touched his heart. He was quite certain that all their spirits had been with him the entire night. A century before, they had brought their meager possessions and priceless dreams to this very place. Over the span of a long life, Art has carried their dreams forward in his own remarkable journey.

His chosen profession had taken him to many more places than he could possibly remember. All those millions of miles crossing America and circling the globe had brought him back to the place where his family's American journey began.

When the fireworks ended, the night again was still. Art fixed his eyes on the distant lights of a great shore and knew with certainty that the quest for excellence would continue. In moments of triumph and tragedy, this was surely the work of generations.

Art in 2008 wearing the Ellis Island Medal of Honor.

Acknowledgements

There are many people to thank for the creation of this book. First and foremost is Dr. Ron Redmond, University of the Pacific Regent, a 1966 graduate of the dental school and a longtime member of the Pacific Dugoni Foundation. When I approached Dr. Redmond about supporting this project, I discovered he shared my view that this was an important undertaking, so that both Art's contemporaries and future generations could know more about the life work of this legendary figure in the fields of dentistry and education.

Additionally, I thank the entire board of the Pacific Dugoni Foundation, who also joined in support of this effort. I also thank Dr. Craig Yarborough, associate dean of the Dugoni School of Dentistry at the University of the Pacific, for his invaluable assistance in seeing that this book found the supporters that it needed to become a reality.

A special thank you to the University of the Pacific's retired provost, Dr. Phil Gilbertson, who, in addition to providing the foreword to this book, shared generously with me his time and insights into the Dugoni era at Pacific.

The single most daunting effort in creating this book was gaining a better understanding of Art Dugoni's earliest years. There was little in the way of written materials specifically related to the lives of family members and friends that impacted Art's formative years. And, as you may suspect, when studying the life of an individual who is now approaching age ninety, I was blessed to have a handful of his contemporaries to interview, individuals from the generation prior to Art's have, as you might expect, long since passed on. I am greatly indebted to members of Art's family, specifically, Evelyn Dugoni, Art's sister, Patricia Dugoni, the widow of Art's late brother William, Art's sons: Steven, James, Russell, Arthur and Michael; and his daughters, Mary and Diane, additionally, cousin Robert Bianco, son of Art's Uncle Leo, and cousin Jeanne Brunetti Ireland. All of whom, without exception, were generous with their time.

One family member went above and beyond in helping to bring the distant past back to life, Art's cousin Yolanda Statham, daughter of Maria Dugoni, Art's father's older sister.

In addition to her travels back to the Dugoni family's roots in Northern Italy, she kept papers, photos, and records of Vittorio, even several items from his shop on Stockton Street. Additionally, without the oral history that Yolanda and Art's sister Evelyn provided, Vittorio's story would have been greatly diminished by the hand of time.

I also thank all of the colleagues who generously shared their insights on the life and times of Art Dugoni. Those include, Dr. Irwin Marcus, Dr. Nader Nadershahi, Dr. Robert Boyd, Dr. Robert Christoffersen, Dr. Alan Gluskin, Dr. Eddie Hayashida, Dr. Cindy Lyon, Dr. Berney Neufeld, Dr. Michael Alfano, Dr. Tony Volpe, Dr. Burton Press, Dr. Kathleen O'Loughlin, Dr. Chuck Wilson, Dr. Michael Perich, Dr. Reginald Hession, Dr. Clive Ross, Helen Cherrett, Roy Bergstrom, Mike Sudzina, Barkley Payne, and Patrick Cavanaugh,

To two of Art's colleagues, Dr. David Nielsen, and Dr. David Chambers, I owe a special word of thanks. In addition to their unique perspectives regarding Dr. Dugoni's career, both of these individuals gave me research assistance in recreating those crucial moments in previous decades when Art cast a wide shadow across both dental education and the dental profession

A special thank you as well to the distinguished educator who took on the daunting task of filling Art Dugoni's oversized shoes, Pacific Dugoni's current dean, Patrick J. Ferrillo, for his kind and helpful support throughout this project.

At the Dugoni School, I wish to thank Joan Yokom, who gave generously of her time in helping to assemble a photographic history of Art's personal and professional life. Thanks as well to administrative staff members Karen Yamamoto, and Michelle Rosaschi, who were always happy to assist me whenever I went looking for a missing piece of the Dugoni story, and Art's former Executive Administrative Assistant, Tere Hanson.

An additional thanks to David Eastis, the executive director of the Dugoni

School's Alumni Association, for his faithful assistance whenever an extra set of hands and eyes were needed.

Finally, I am deeply indebted to Dr. Dorothy Dechant, the Dugoni School's archivist who lent invaluable assistance in gathering papers relevant to the near- ly seventy-year history of Art Dugoni as student, faculty member, department chair, and dean of the school of dentistry. It is individuals like Dr. Dechant who keep the flame of history burning brightly, so that we can better see the future by learning of the trials and the triumphs of the past.

Appendix A

Program Topics and Original Airdates of *Dentistry Update* Lifetime Medical Television 1990 – 1993.

1990

September 2, 9, 16, 23, 30 - Periodontal Diagnosis; Esthetic Dentistry; Vital Teeth; Dentistry and AIDS; Periodontal Treatment; Ergonomics of the Dental Office; Dentistry and OSHA.

October 7, 14, 21, 28; November 4, 11, 18, 25; December 2, 9, 16, 23, 30 - Periodontal Diagnosis; Esthetic Dentistry; Vital Teeth; Dentistry and AIDS; Periodontal Treatment; Ergonomics of the Dental Office; Dentistry and OSHA; Esthetic Procedures; Non-Vital Teeth; Adult Orthodontics; Dentistry and the Aging Population; Implants and Dentistry; Dentistry and the National Practitioner Data Bank.

1991

March 3, 10, 17, 24, 31 - Pain Control in Dentistry; Temporomandibular Disorders; Genetics in Dentistry; New Techniques for Root Canal.

May 5, 12, 19, 26 - Computers and Imaging in Dentistry; Dental Amalgam and Alternative Restorative Materials.

June 2, 9, 16, 23, 30 - Computers and Imaging in Dentistry; Dental Amalgam and Alternative Restorative Materials; Lasers and Dentistry; Esthetic Dentistry and Prosthodontics.

July 7, 14, 21, 28 - Pain Control in Dentistry; Temporomandibular Disorders; Esthetic Dentistry and Prosthodontics; Lasers and Dentistry; Genetics in Dentistry; New Techniques for Root Canal.

August 4, 11, 18, 25 - Computers and Imaging in Dentistry; Dental Amalgam and Alternative Restorative Materials; Esthetic Dentistry and Prosthodontics; Lasers and Dentistry.

September 1, 8, 15, 22, 29 - Esthetic Dentistry and Prosthodontics; Dental Amalgam and Alternative Restorative Materials; Computers and Imaging in Dentistry; Genetics in Dentistry; New Techniques for Root Canal.

October 6, 13, 20, 27 - Maxillofacial Prosthodontics and Oral Cancer; Lasers and Dentistry; Dental Forensics and Child Abuse.

November 3, 10, 17, 24 - Highlights of the ADA Annual Meeting in Seattle; Dental Forensics and Child Abuse; Maxillofacial Prosthodontics and Oral Cancer.

December 1, 8, 15, 22, 29 - Highlights of the ADA Annual Meeting in Seattle; Endodontic Surgery with Lasers; Sedation and Management of the Patient with a Disability in the Private Dental Office; Update in Fluoride and Antiplaque Therapies; Highlights of the ADA Meeting in Seattle; Part 2; Street Drugs our Patients Use and Abuse: What You Need to Do; Dental Computing-A Glimpse of the Future; Microsurgical Repair of the Temporomandibular Joint; Dental Forensics and Child Abuse; Maxillofacial Prosthodontics and Oral Cancer.

1992

January 5, 12, 19, 26 - Highlights of the ADA Annual Meeting in Seattle, Part 2; Street Drugs our Patients Use and Abuse: What You Need to Do; Dental Computing-A Glimpse of the Future; Microsurgical Repair of the Temporomandibular Joint; Dental Forensics and Child Abuse; Esthetic Dentistry and Prosthodontics; Maxillofacial Prosthodontics and Oral Cancer.

February 2, 9, 16, 23 - Periodontology; Dental Forensics and Child Abuse; Microsurgery and Arthroscopy of the Temporomandibular Joint; Dental Amalgam and Alternative Restorative Materials.

March 1, 8, 15, 22, 29 - Adult Orthodontics and New Technologies in Endodontics; Computers and Imaging in Dentistry; Esthetics in General Practice; Periodontology; Microsurgery and Arthroscopy of the

Temporomandibular Joint.

April 5, 12, 19, 26 - Adult Orthodontics and New Technologies in Endodontics; Esthetics in General Practice; Pediatric Dentistry; Periodontology.

May 3, 10, 17, 24, 31 - Access to Care; Periodontology; New Implant Techniques; Adult Orthodontics and New Technology in Endodontics.

June 7, 14, 21, 28 - New Implant Technologies; Esthetics in General Practice; Access to Care.

July 5, 12, 19, 26 - Management of Medically Compromised and Geriatric Patients; Microsurgery and Arthroscopy of the Temporomandibular Joint; Sports Dentistry; Microsurgery and Arthroscopy of the Temporomandibular Joint.

August 2, 9, 16, 23, 30 - Sports Dentistry; Management of Medically Compromised and Geriatric Patients; Tooth Whiteners and Public Health Dentistry and Prevention; Esthetics in General Practice; Management of Medically Compromised and Geriatric Patients.

September 6, 13, 20, 27 - Tooth Whiteners and Preventive Dentistry; Pediatric Dentistry; Sports Dentistry; Tooth Whiteners and Preventive Dentistry.

October 4, 11, 18, 25 - Access to Care; Adult Orthodontics and New Technologies in Endodontics; New Implant Technologies; Pediatric Dentistry.

November 1, 8, 15, 22, 29 - Management of Medically Compromised and Geriatric Patients; Convention Highlights, Part 1; Convention Highlights, Part 2; Convention Highlights, Part 1; Convention Highlights, Part 2.

December 6, 13, 20, 27 - New Implant Technologies; Sports Dentistry; Convention Highlights, Part 1; Convention Highlights, Part 2.

1993

January 3, 10, 24, 31 - Convention Highlights, Part 1; Convention Highlights, Part 2; Esthetics in General Practice; Adult Orthodontics and Technologies in Endodontics.

February 7, 14, 21, 28 - Infection Control-Office Procedures; Periodontology; Microsurgery and Arthroscopy of the Temporomandibular Joint.

<u>March 7, 14, 21, 28</u> - New Implant Technologies; Management of Medically Compromised and Geriatric Patients; Sports Dentistry; Lasers and Dentistry.

<u>April 4, 11, 18, 25</u> - Pain Control in Dentistry and TM Disorders; Computers and Imaging in Dentistry; Dental Forensics and Child Abuse; Esthetics in General Practice.

<u>May 2, 9, 16</u> - Adult Orthodontics; Technologies in Endodontics; Pediatric Dentistry; Periodontology.

<u>June 6, 13, 20, 27</u> - New Implant Technologies; Management of Medically Compromised and Geriatric Patients; Sports Dentistry; Lasers and Dentistry.

<u>July 4, 11, 18, 25</u> - Pain Control in Dentistry and TM Disorders; Computers and Imaging in Dentistry; Dental Forensics and Child Abuse; Esthetics in General Practice.

Appendix B
Dental Society Positions Held

SAN MATEO COUNTY DENTAL SOCIETY
President, 1960
Editor, Treasurer, President-Elect
Parliamentarian, 2 years
Board of Directors, 16 years
Trustee, 6 years

Chairman of the following San Mateo County Dental Society Committees:
Advisory Committee - Dental Assistants Training Program, College of San
Mateo, Chairman (2 years), Member (7 years)
Membership Committee
Ethics Committee, 2 years
Seminar Committee
Dentist, Patient Relations Committee
Nominating Committee

CALIFORNIA DENTAL ASSOCIATION
President, 1982
President-Elect, 1981
Vice President, 1979-1980
Secretary, 1972-1975
Board of Trustees, 16 years
House of Delegates, 1958-present

Joint Executive Council

Committees:
Postgraduate Instruction Committee, 7 years
Chairman, Dental Health Day, 2 years
Reference Committee - Chairman, 4 years, Secretary, 2 years
Ethics Committee, 3 years
Annual Meeting Committee, 3 years, and Chairman 1 year
Public Information Committee, 2 years
Council on Membership Services, Chairman
Finance Council
Scientific Consultant, California Dental Association Journal
Council on Dental Education, Chairman, 1975-1978
Council on Legislation
Chairman, Executive Search Committee for the Chief Executive Officer,
1978 and 1995
Chair, Dr. Lewis J. Turchi Committee for President-Elect of the
American Dental Association, 1998
Task Force on Licensure Reform, 2003, 2004

AMERICAN BOARD OF ORTHODONTICS
President, 1985
Vice President, 1984
Secretary-Treasurer, 1983
Director, 1979-1986

AMERICAN DENTAL ASSOCIATION
President, 1988-1989
President-Elect and Treasurer, 1987-1988
Trustee (13th District), 1984-1987
House of Delegates, 1965-present
Council on Dental Education, Consultant, 1973-1982

Chairman, Annual Session, Committee on Clinics and Motion Pictures, 1972
Reference Committee, 7 years
Council on Scientific Sessions, Consultant, 1973-1982
Ad Hoc Committee on Scientific Sessions, 1975-1976
Ad Hoc Committee on Expanded Functions, 1975-1976
Ad Hoc Committee on Continuing Education, 1977-1978
Ad Hoc Committee on Proprietary Schools, 1977-1978
Chairman of the Board, ADA Risk Purchasing Group, Inc., 1989
Consultant, American Dental Association, Board of Trustees, 1989-1990
Consultant, Council on Dental Education, 1992-1995
Council on Dental Education Committee on the Escalating Cost of
Dental Education and Student Indebtedness, 1992
Honorary Officer, 1998 American Dental Association 139th Annual Session,
San Francisco, California
Honorary Officer, 2003 American Dental Association 144th Annual Session,
San Francisco, California

AMERICAN DENTAL ASSOCIATION FOUNDATION
President, 2003-2010

FEDERATION DENTAIRE INTERNATIONALE
Treasurer, 1992-1998
Delegate, 1988-1998
Elected to the Council, 1991-1998
Chair, Finance Committee, 1991-1998
Constitution and Bylaws Committee, 1991, 1996, 1997
Executive Committee, 1992-1998

OMICRON KAPPA UPSILON (HONOR SOCIETY)
DELTA DELTA CHAPTER
President, 1970
President-Elect, 1969

Vice President, 1968

Chairman, Committee on Objectives, 1970-1983

Chairman, Nominating Committee for Honorary Members, 1979-present

AMERICAN FUND FOR DENTAL HEALTH

Trustee Advisor, 1988-1989, 1994-1996

Director, 1990-1993

Chairman, Nominating Committee, 1991-1992

AMERICAN ASSOCIATION OF DENTAL SCHOOLS

President, 1994-1995

President-Elect, 1993-1994

Member, Council of Deans, 1979-2006

Member, House of Delegates, 1978-2006

Council of Deans, Administrative Board, 1983-1984

Council of Deans, Secretary, Administrative Board, 1984

Council of Deans, Chairman-Elect, Administrative Board, 1985

Council of Deans, Chairman, Administrative Board, 1986

Executive Committee, 1993-1996

Member, President's Commission on the Cost of Dental Education, 1998-1999

Reference Committee on Association of Administrative Affairs, March 1999

AMERICAN DENTAL EDUCATION ASSOCIATION

(formerly AADS)

Member, Nominating Committee, Council of Deans, 2002

PACIFIC COAST SOCIETY OF ORTHODONTISTS, CENTRAL SECTION

President, 1972-1973

Program Chairman, President-Elect, 1971

Director, 9 years

Alternate Delegate, American Association of Orthodontists, 1976-1981

Delegate, American Association of Orthodontists, 1977-1980 and 1982

Senior Director, Pacific Coast Society of Orthodontists, 1977-1982

AMERICAN COLLEGE OF DENTISTS
(NORTHERN CALIFORNIA)

President, 1975

Vice President, Northern California Section, 1974

Past Chairman (Executive Committee), 1976

Advisory Committee, Northern California Section

Executive Committee, Northern California Section

Local Consultant

INTERNATIONAL COLLEGE OF DENTISTS

Counselor, 1974-1976

Deputy Regent, 1977-1981

Chairman, Screening Committee, 1981-1997

Counselor, 2000-2002

WESTERN CONFERENCE OF DENTAL EXAMINERS
AND DENTAL SCHOOLS

President, 1983-1984

President-Elect, 1982

Vice President, 1981

CALIFORNIA DENTAL SERVICE (DELTA DENTAL)

Board of Directors, 1976-1979

Treasurer, 1977-1979

Second Vice President, 1978

SANTA FE GROUP

Founding Member, 1994

Member, 1994-2011

OTHER

Clinician and Essayist - Presented over 700 lectures, papers, clinics, and essays
to professional groups and constituent and component dental societies
Board of Directors, California Dentists Guild, 1971-1972
Chairman, Orthodontic Memorial Lecture - University of the Pacific, 1970-
1985
Appointed to President Atchley's University of the Pacific Strategic Planning
Committee, 1991-1992
Appointed to the University of the Pacific's Promotion and Tenure Committee,
1991-1994
Advisory Council, Pacific Graduate School of Psychology, Palo Alto,
California, 1992-1995
Master of Ceremonies, 14th Annual Meeting of the International Association
of Pediatric Dentistry, Drake Hotel, Chicago, Illinois, October 1993
Honorary Officer, 134th American Dental Association Annual Session, San
Francisco, California, November 5-9, 1993
Appointed to University of the Pacific's President Search Committee, 1994-
1995
Appointed to University of the Pacific's Cabinet Committee, 1994-1995
Chair, Search Committee for Chief Executive Officer, California Dental
Association, 1995
Chair, Search Committee for Institutional Advancement Vice President,
University of the Pacific, 1995-1996
Appointed to the Executive Planning Committee for University of the
Pacific's Sesquicentennial Celebration, 1998-2002
Appointed to the Advisory Board of The Partnership For Tobacco Cessation,
an initiative of *Oral Health America*, 1998-2002
Appointed to the President's Expanded Cabinet of the University of the
Pacific, School of Dentistry, 1998-2002
Member, Harris Fund Advisory Committee, American Dental Association,

1998-2001

Appointed to the American Association of Orthodontists Task Force on Recruitment and Retention of Orthodontic Faculty, 1999, 2000, 2001

Panelist, Pediatric Forum on the Recruitment and Retention of Pediatric Faculty, American Association of Dental Schools, March 1999

Mayor's AIDS Leadership Forum, San Francisco, California, April 29, 1999

International College of Dentists Counselor, 2000

Consultant, Arizona School of Health Sciences on the feasibility of creating a needs-based school of dentistry in the State of Arizona, October 26-27, 2000

Member, Friends of the National Institute of Dental and Craniofacial Research Board of Directors, 1999-2002

Appendix C
Publication Articles and Interviews

"Valedictory Address," *Contact Point*, October 1948
"Some Symptoms of Nerve Disorders Noticeable to Dentists," *Contact Point*, December 1948
"Dentistry for Children-Our Responsibility," *Arizona State Journal*, June 1956
Contributor to Textbook, Operative Dentistry, 4th Edition, McGehee, True, Inskipp
"The Challenge of Operative Dentistry," *New Jersey Society of Dentistry of Children Bulletin*, April 1957
"The Philosophy Behind the Amalgam Special Clinic," *Contact Point*, January 1959
"The Philosophy of High Speed Teaching of Undergraduates," *Contact Point*, November 1959
"Dento-Craniofacial Survey of Children Three to Eight Years of Age," M.S.D. Thesis, May 1963
"Omicron Kappa Upsilon President's Address," *Contact Point*, 1970
"International Continuing Education in Dentistry," *Journal of the California Dental Association*, November 1974
"Current Status of Expanded Functions for Dental Auxiliaries," *Journal of the California Dental Association*, September 1975
"Undergraduate Dental Education in Perspective," *Journal of the California Dental Association*, February 1976
"Let's Hear it for the Dental Team," *Journal of the California Dental Association*, May 1980

"The Role of Orthodontics in the Predoctoral Education of a Dentist,"
American Journal of Orthodontists, May 1981

"Ask the Dean," *Contact Point*, vol. 59, no. 2, page 28, 1981

"Changing Dimensions in Dentistry and Dental Education," *Pacific Review*,
November 1981

"A Drop Out is a Cop Out," *San Mateo County Dental Society Bulletin*,
January 1982

"Ask the Dean," *Contact Point*, vol. 60, no. 1, page 6, 1982

"What Price Professionalism?" *Journal of the California Dental Association*,
April 1982

"Ask the Dean," *Contact Point*, vol. 60, no. 2, page 7, 1982

"Changing the Nature of Dental Care," *TIC Magazine*, vol. XLI, no. 9,
September 1982

"Investing Ourselves in the Future," *Journal of the California Dental Association*,
September 1982

"Ask the Dean," *Contact Point*, vol. 60, no. 3, page 7, 1982

"Ask the Dean," *Contact Point*, vol. 61, no. 1, page 7, 1983

"Managing a Dental School in the Context of a Slow Economy," *Journal of
Dental Education*, March 1983

"Ask the Dean," *Contact Point*, vol. 61, no. 2, page 7, 1983

"Future Challenges for Dentistry: Finding a Better Way," *Journal of the
California Dental Association*, April 1983

"Ask the Dean," *Contact Point*, vol. 61, no. 3, page 6, 1983

"President's Report-1983," *Journal of the California Dental Association*, July 1983

"Ask the Dean," *Contact Point*, vol. 61, no. 4, page 9, 1983

"Our Future is Fantastic," *XI PSI PHI Quarterly*, vol. 82, no. 3, Spring 1984

"Ask the Dean," *Contact Point*, vol. 62, no. 1, page 9, 1984

"Our Future is Fantastic," *Journal of the American College of Dentists*, vol. 51,
no. 1, Spring 1984

"Directions in Dental Education and Practice," *American Journal of Orthodontics*,
vol. 85, no. 5, May 1984

"Ask the Dean," *Contact Point*, vol. 62, no. 2, page 9, 1984

"Graduation Address," (presented at Loma Linda University, June 8, 1984),
guest editorial, *International Journal of Oral Facial Myology*, vol. 10, no. 3, 1984
"Dental Education and Accreditation" guest editorial, *American Dental
Association Newsletter*, October 8, 1984
"Ask the Dean," *Contact Point*, vol. 62, no. 3, page 30, 1984
"Policy Implications of the Rand Study," *American Dental Association Newsletter*,
Council on Dental Care Programs, January 1985
"Ask the Dean," *Contact Point*, vol. 63, no. 2, page 6, 1985
"Let's Sing Along with Dentistry," *Journal of the California Dental Association*,
July 1985
"Viewpoint, The Future of the Dental Profession," *The Advisor*, a publication of
the National Association of Advisors for the Health Professions, Inc., vol. 6,
no. 1, Fall 1985
"Ask the Dean," *Contact Point*, vol. 63, no. 3, page 7, 1985
"Our Profession - Let's Sing Along," *American Journal of Orthodontics*, vol. 88,
no. 4, October 1985
"The Future of the Dental Profession," *The Journal of Dental Education*, vol. 49,
no. 12, 1985
"Ask the Dean," *Contact Point*, vol. 63, no. 4, page 6, 1985
"The Future of the Dental Profession," *XI PSI PHI Quarterly*, vol. 84, no. 4,
1986
"Ask the Dean," *Contact Point*, vol. 64, no. 1, pages 8-9, 1986
"Future Demands for Dental Care," *American Journal of Orthodontics*, vol. 89,
no. 6, June 1986
"The Economics of Dentistry," *American Journal of Orthodontics and Dentofacial
Orthopedics*, vol. 90, no. 1, July 1986
"Ask the Dean," *Contact Point*, vol. 64, no. 2, 1986, page 31, 1986
"Report of the President of the American Board of Orthodontics to the
Directors of the American Board, March 2, 1986," *American Journal of
Orthodontics and Dentofacial Orthopedics*, vol. 90, no. 2, August 1986
"Ask the Dean," *Contact Point*, vol 64, no. 3, page 31, 1986
"Challenges Facing Private Dental Schools - UOP Ready for the Many

Challenges of the Future," *Journal of the California Dental Association*, vol. 14, no. 12, pages 82-87, December 1986

"Ask the Dean," *Contact Point*, vol. 65, no. 1, pages 30-31, 1987

"Ask the Dean," *Contact Point*, vol. 65, no. 2, page 4, 1987

"President-Elect Candidate Speaks Out," *American Dental Association Daily Bulletin*, October 12, 1987

"Ask the Dean," *Contact Point*, vol. 65, no. 3, page 7, 1987

"Ask the Dean," *Contact Point*, vol. 65, no. 4, page 7, 1987

Publications Review: "The Hillenbrand Era, Organized Dentistry Hillenbrand Glanzperiode," *Journal of the American Dental Association*, vol. 115, no. 5, November 1987

"The Future of our Profession," *The Orthodontic Education and Research Foundation Journal*, February 1988

"Ask the Dean," *Contact Point*, vol. 55, no. 1, page 5, 1988

"What Changes Do You See Occurring in Education Today That May Affect the Way Dentistry is Practiced in the Future," *San Francisco Dental Society Mercury* vol. 40, no. 2, April 1988

"Ask the Dean," *Contact Point*, vol. 66, no. 2, 1988, pages 29-30, 1988

"Ask the Dean," *Contact Point*, vol. 66, no. 3, page 2, 198

"The Future of our Profession - Will We Adapt," *Pennsylvania Dental Journal*, vol. 55, no. 5, pages 20-24, September/October 1988

"Ask the Dean," *Contact Point*, vol. 66, no. 4, page 2, 1988

"ADA's 1988/89 President Shares Goals and Concerns," *Dentistry 88, Journal of the American Student Dental Association*, vol. 8, no. 3, pages 4-9, October 1988

"Challenge, Change, Commitment - Did You Come to Play?" *Journal of the California Dental Association*, vol. 16, no. 12, pages 24-27, December 1988

"President's Address," *Journal of the American Dental Association*, vol. 117, no. 7, pages 818-819, December 1988

"The Specialty of Orthodontics," *American Journal of Orthodontics and Dentofacial Orthopedics*, vol. 95, no. 3, page 25A, March 1989

"Ask the Dean," *Contact Point*, vol. 67, no. 1, page 32, 1989

"Dugoni Inspires General Assembly With Inaugural Address," *Review of the*

Chicago Dental Society, vol. 82, no 2, pages 27-31, March 1989

"Ask the Dean," *Contact Point*, vol. 67, no. 2, pages 7-8, 1989

"Challenge, Change and Commitment," *Journal of the Philippine Dental Association*, vol. XLI, no. 4, pages 55, 11 and 26, March/May 1989

"Ask the Dean," *Contact Point*, vol. 67, no. 3, page 9, 1989

"The Changing Face of Dental Education," *Journal of the California Dental Association*, vol. 17, no. 10, pages 18-20, October 1989

"Our Profession's Future As We Head Toward the 21st Century," *Pacific Coast Society of Orthodontist Bulletin*, vol. 61, no. 4, pages 45-46, Winter 1989

"Ask the Dean," *Contact Point*, vol. 67, no. 4, page 9, 1989

"An Open Letter to Dr. David C. Hamilton," *The Great Lakes Association of Orthodontists News*, vol. 26, no. 1, pages 5, 11, and 13, Spring 1990

"Ask the Dean," *Contact Point*, vol. 68, no. 1, page 2, 1990

"UOP - The Uncommon Educational Experience," *Journal of the California Dental Association*, pages 35-37, December 1990

"Ask the Dean," *Contact Point*, vol. 68, no. 2, page 31, 1990

"To a Dental School Graduate," *Book-Legacy, the Dental Profession*, Pages 46-47, 1990

"Ask the Dean," *Contact Point*, vol. 68, no. 3, page 3

"The Use of Dental Amalgam," *The Journal of Practical Dentistry*, Quintessence International, vol. 22, no. 4, page 248, 1991

"Oranges and Peaches," convocation address, *Journal of the American College of Dentists*, vol. 58, no. 1, pages 31-35, Spring 1991

"Dentistry in the 21st Century: The Future Will Be Different - But Better!" *Dentistry in the 21st Century: A Global Perspective*, Chapter 5, by Arthur A. Dugoni, Pages 43-57, Richard J. Simonsen, Quintessence Publishing Company

"The Dental Amalgam Controversy," *The Journal of Practical Dentistry*, Quintessence International, vol. 22, page 335, May 1991

"Ask the Dean," *Contact Point*, vol. 69, page 28, Spring 1991

"Technological Changes in Dentistry," Interview with Christina Kent, *Medicine and Health*, September 5, 1991

"Licensure and Credentialing Position Paper," *Journal of Dental Education*, vol. 55, no. 12, pages 789-791, December 1991

Editorial, "Licensure by Examination - Is There a Better Way?" *Contact Point*, vol. 69, no. 4, page 2, 1991

"What Will the Future Bring?" *Journal of the American Dental Association*, vol. 123, pages 40-45, April 1992

"Licensure - Entry Level Examinations: Strategies for the Future," *Journal of Dental Education*, vol. 56, no. 4, 1992

"A Glimpse Into the 21st Century - What Will the Future Bring?" *Journal of the American Dental Association*, vol. 123, pages 59-64, May 1992

"Is Dental Education Too Far Removed From Reality?" editorial, *Contact Point*, vol. 71, no. 3, 1992

"An Era of Change in U.S. Dental Education," published proceedings of the 18th Annual Meeting of the Association for Dental Education in Europe, pages 16-17, July 19-24, 1992

"Ambition, Education, and a Desire to Serve," vignettes, *American Journal of Orthodontics and Dentofacial Orthopedics*, vol. 103, no. 1, pages 79-80, January 1993

"Dentistry in the Decade Ahead," *Journal of the California Dental Association*, vol. 21, no. 8, pages 38-40, August 1993

"Licensure - A House Divided," *Journal of Dental Education*, vol. 57, no. 10, pages 770-771, October 1993

La Odontologia en la Proxima Decada, Revista de la Federacion Odontologics Colombiana, vol. 47, no. 181, pages 19-24, September/December 1993

"Ask the Dean," *Contact Point*, vol. 73, no. 1, page 7, Spring 1994

"Education is a Path - Not a Destination," Proceedings of the Orthodontic Education Development Symposium, Orlando, Florida, pages 2-7, April 28-29, 1994

"The Cost of Higher Education and Its Implications for Dental Education," *Journal of Dental Education*, L.M. Hunt, A.A. Dugoni, H.I. Enarson, A.J. Formicola, J.R. Mingle, vol. 58, no. 6, pages 414-423, 1994

"President-Elect's Address," *Journal of Dental Education*, vol. 58, no. 7, pages 454-458, July 1994

"Feeding Each Other," *Key-International College of Dentists Publication,* pages 8-10, August/September 1994

"A Four-Part Model to Energize Ethical Conversations," Bruce Peltier, Ph.D., Arthur A. Dugoni, D.D.S., M.S.D., *Journal of the California Dental Association,* vol. 22, no. 10, pages 23-26, October 1994

"Spotlight on Today's Major Issues," *Journal of the California Dental Association,* First in a Series, vol. 125, pages 1321-1328, October 1994

"Spotlight on Today's Major Issues," *Journal of the American Dental Association,* Second in a Series, vol. 125, pages 1459-1465, November 1994

"Spotlight on Today's Major Issues," *Journal of the American Dental Association,* Third in a Series, vol. 125, pages 1591-1596, December 1994

"Survival of the Fittest," *Dentistry - Loma Linda University,* vol. 6, no. 2, pages 23-25, Fall 1994/Winter 1995

"A Changing America," *American Journal of Orthodontics and Dentofacial Orthopedics,* vol. 107, no. 5, pages 17-A and 18-A, May 1995

"The Policy for Dentistry's Future: The Pew Health Professions Commission, *Journal of the American College of Dentists,* vol. 62, no. 2, pages 35-38, Summer 1995

"Questions and Answers," The American College of Dentists Symposium, October 21, 1994, New Orleans, Louisiana, *Journal of the American College of Dentists,* vol. 62, no. 2, pages 44-48, Summer 1995

President's Annual Report 1994-95, *Journal of Dental Education,* vol. 59, no. 7, pages 687-690, July 1995

"Early Mixed Dentition Treatment: Post-Retention Evaluation of Stability and Relapse," Steven A. Dugoni, Jetson S. Lee, Jaime Varela, and Arthur A. Dugoni, *Angle Orthodontist,* vol. 65, no. 5, pages 311-320, 1995

"Critical Challenges: Revitalizing the Health Professions for the Twenty-First Century - The Third Report of the Pew Health Professions Commission," Richard E. Lamm, Edward H. O'Neil, Arthur A. Dugoni, pages 1-83, first release November 1995

"University of the Pacific Responds to a Changing Environment," *Journal of the*

California Dental Association, vol. 23, no. 12, page 58, December 1995

"Indebtedness and Dental Students: Letter to the Editor," *Journal of the American Dental Association*, vol. 27, page 298, March 1996

"Letter to the Editor," *Quintessence International*, vol. 27, no. 11, page 725, November 1996

"Survival of the Fittest," *Dental Alumni News*, University of Washington Dental Alumni Association, vol. 23, no. 4, Winter 1997

"Managed Health Care: Threat or Opportunity," *Journal of the Dental Association of South Africa*, Dr. Arthur A. Dugoni, Dr. David B. Nielsen, vol. 53, no. 3, pages 145-151, March 1998

"An Interview with 25 Distinguished Leaders in the Dental Industry and Profession," *Dental Manufacturers of America*, January 1999

"The Cost of Dental Education" report of the President's Commission, American Association of Dental Schools publication, Patrick Ferrillo, Arthur Dugoni, et al., February 20, 1999

"Alive and Kicking. American Student Dental Association Salutes 25 Dental Visionaries," *Journal of the American Student Dental Association*, vol. 19, no. 2, pages 17-18, Summer 1999

Extensively quoted in "Will Dentists be Overburdened in the Next Millennium?" Elisa Kronish, *Impact*, the News Magazine of the Academy of General Dentistry, vol. 27, no. 6, June 1999

"Survival of the Fittest," *Journal of the History of Dentistry*, vol. 47, no. 2, pages 89-93, July 1999

"Oral Health Care Professionals' Attitudes and Behaviors Regarding Domestic Violence: The Need for an Effective Response," contributing author. Paper presented at the American Association of Public Health Dentistry Annual Meeting, Honolulu, Hawaii, October 1999

"Dentistry's Future Based in Education," – Callahan Award, *Ohio Dentistry Focus*, vol. 73, no. 11, pages 5-6, November 1999

"The Decade Ahead: Finding A Better Way," *American Journal of Orthodontics and Dentofacial Orthopedics*, vol. 117, no. 5, pages 615-617, May 2000

"Education - Funding Woes - Private Dental Schools Face Tough Times,"

ADA News, vol. 32, no. 10, extensively quoted on pages 22, 23, and 26, May 21, 2001

"Allied Health Professionals," Letter to the Editor, *Journal of the American Dental Association*, vol. 132, pages 724-726, June 2001

"Let There be Light," *The Trident*, vol. IX, no. III, July 2002

"Letter to the Editor," *American Journal of Orthodontics and Dentofacial Orthopedics*, vol. 122, no. 2, pages 16A-18A, August 2002

"University of the Pacific, School of Dentistry: A Dental School That Serves the Practicing Profession - Our Environment is the World of the Private Practitioner," *Journal of the California Dental Association*, vol. 30, no. 10, pages 763-768, October 2002

"Let There be Light - Clinically Applied Research," *Dean's Report*, pages 5-7, Fall 2002

"Industry Perspective: An Interview with Dr. Arthur Dugoni, University of the Pacific," *Invisalign Clinical Update*, Volume 3, pages 3-7, Spring 2003

"A School is a Building with a Future in It," *Contact Point*, pages 12-14, August 2003

"Dean Dugoni Voices His Opinion About the Current California State Boards," *The Articulating Paper*, vol. 3, issue 1, pages 1 and 3, Summer 2003

"Protection of the Public," *California Dental Association Journal*, vol. 31, no. 11, pages 801-803, November 2001

"Commentary: Protection of the Public" (reprinted with permission from the *CDA Journal* Volume 31, number 11, November 2003), *American Dental Education Association Bulletin of Dental Education*, vol. 37, January 2004

"A Formula for Leadership Success," *Articulating Paper*, vol. 3, issue 2, pages 1, 2, 7, and 8, Winter 2004

"Protection of the Public," *California Dental Association Journal* "Feedback," vol. 32, no. 3, pages 213-214, March 2004

"The Case Against One-Shot Testing for Initial Dental Licensure," David W. Chambers, Arthur A. Dugoni, Ian Paisley, *California Dental Association Journal*, vol. 32, no. 3, pages 243-252, March 2004

"Four-Part Ask! What is This All About?" *The Trident*, vol. XI, no. 2, pages 8-9,

March 2004

"Four-Part Ask! What is This All About?" *Dean's Report*, page 30, Spring 2004

"Crisis Management - National Endowment for Dental Education," *Mouth*, vol. 24, no. 1, pages 8-9, Spring 2004

"Leadership in the Decade Ahead," *Dean's Report*, pages 5-7, Spring 2004

"Crisis Management - National Endowment for Dental Education," *ADA News*, vol. 35, no. 11, pages 4-5, June 2004

"Reviewing the Book on Teaching Practice Management in Universities," Interview questions and answers, *Dental Economics*, pages 30-34, October 2004

"If Not You, Then Who? Leadership Matters," selected excerpts from the Louis J. Grossman Memorial Lecture, speaker Dr. Arthur A. Dugoni, *Pinnacle*, vol. VIII, issue II, pages 5-7, Fall/Winter 2004

"Pursuing What's Best for Our Profession: Rising to the Challenges of Change, Commitment, and Competence," *Compendium of Continuing Education and Dentistry*, vol. 25, no. 12 (supplement), pages 18-19, December 2004

"Meeting the Challenges of Dental Education," guest editorial, *Journal of the American Dental Association*, vol. 136, page 16, January 2005

"New Age," *Delta-Sierra Dental Digest*, January-February 2005, vol. 32, no. 1, page 4

"In Memory of a Man Greatly Loved - Dr. Judson Klooster, Dean Emeritus, 1925-2004," *Loma Linda University Dentistry*, vol. 16, no. 1, pages 8-9, Winter/Spring

"Dental Education - Challenges and Opportunities," *Mouth*, Journal of the American Student Dental Association, vol. 25, number 1, page 16, Spring 2005

"What is Past is Prologue" - Editorial, *Contact Point*, pages 2-3, June 2005

"My Administrative Team, Chapter II," *Contact Point*, pages 20-24, June 2005

Portrait on the cover of the *Seattle Study Club Journal*, vol. 9, no. 3, including a tribute on page 15, 2005

"Occlusal Equilibration - The Major Part of Dentistry You May Be Neglecting," response to the editorial by Dr. Gordon Christensen, *Journal of the American Dental Association*, pages 850-854, July 2005

"A Giant Step Forward," letter to the editor, *American Journal of Orthodontics and Dentofacial Orthopedics*, vol. 128, no. 1, page 4, July 2005

"Licensure Reform in California," opinion paper, *Dean's Report*, pages 5-8, Summer 2005

"My View - The Price of Engagement," *ADA News*, vol. 36, no. 19, pages 8-9, October 17, 2005"Licensure Reform in California" editorial, *Contact Point*, pages 5-6, December 2005

"Securing the Future of the Dental Profession," *Dental Abstracts*, vol. 51, no. 2, pages 68-69, March/April 2006

"Seeing the Big Picture: Dr. Art Dugoni Discusses His Vision for a National Effort to Support Dental Education," *Global Health Nexus*, publication of the New York University, College of Dentistry, vol. 8, no. 1, pages 8-11, Spring/Summer 2006

"Making a Difference - Our Legacy - Our Future," *ADA News*, vol. 37, no. 13, pages 9-12, July 10, 2006

"Blurring the Lines Between General Dentistry and Dental Specialties," *AGD Impact*, pages 52-58, July 2006

"A Few Minutes with Dr. Arthur Dugoni. Questions offered by selected members of the AADE," *Editors' Newsletter*, American Association of Dental Editors, vol. 38, no. 1, pages 4-5, Spring 2007

"Quo Vadis Pacific?" *The Trident*, vol. 14, no. 3, page 10

"An Initiative Between GlaxoSmithKline and the American Dental Association, Oral Longevity A Caring Collaboration," A Message from the ADA President, ADA Foundation President, *Journal of the American Dental Association*, Special Supplement, page 2, September 2007

"Live a Life that Matters," International College of Dentists Convocation, MGM Grand Hotel, Las Vegas, Nevada, *Key 2007*, USA Section Journal of Events, pages 22-26, October 16, 2006

"Will You Make a Difference?" American Student Dental Association Ethics Day Keynote Address Excerpt, *The Articulating Paper*, vol. 7, issue 2, pages 1, 6, 8, December 2007

"Dr. F. Gene Dixon. Leader Extraordinaire," "In Memoriam" column, *The Mouthpiece*, San Mateo County Dental Society, pages 1-2, January/February 2008

"Viewpoint: My View - Dental Education Needs Our Help," *ADA News*, vol. 39, no. 3, pages 4-5, February 4, 2008

"Academic Dentistry," Answer to question on dental education, *ADA News*, vol. 39, no. 5, pages 4-5, March 30, 2008

"The Rot is Creeping Upward and Time is Running Out," (reprinted from the *ADA News*, February 4, 2008), Message from the Dean Emeritus, *The Trident*, vol. XV, no. 2, March 2008

"Making a Difference: Our Legacy – *Our Future*," *Xi Psi Phi Fraternity Quarterly*, vol. 103, issue 2, pages 12-13, Summer/Winter 2008

"ADA Foundation Helps Prepare Profession for Increased Use of Sedation, Anesthesia," *ADA News*, vol. 39, no. 8, page 28, April 21, 2008

"Paffenberger Research Center Marks 80 Years of Leadership" (commentary by Dr. Arthur A. Dugoni, ADA Foundation president), *ADA News*, vol. 39, no. 11, page 12, June 7, 2008

"Paffenberger Research Center Marks Eighty Years of Leadership" *ADA News*, vol. 39, no.11, page 12, June 7, 2008

"Dr. John Joseph Tocchini, 1912-2008," *Contact Point*, vol. 88, no. 2, page 7, Summer 2008

"My View, Stepping Up to the Plate in Hard Times." *ADA News*, vol. 40, no.19, pages 4-5, October 9, 2009

"Q&A: ADAF President Arthur A. Dugoni Addresses KPMG Report," *ADA News*, vol. 41, no. 14, page 8, August 2, 2010

"School of Thought," *AGD Impact* vol. 38, no. 10, page 6, October 2010

"A Conversation with Dr. Arthur A. Dugoni," *Inside Dentistry*, pages 32-36, February 2011

"Philanthropy and Dental Education: It Is Not Necessary to Change, Survival Is Not Mandatory," *Journal of Dental Education*, vol. 76, no. 3, pages 275-278, March, 2012

"Building Our Future, Embracing Our Legacy – Future New Campus

Positions at Pacific for Continued Greatness in Dental Education," *Trident*, vol. 17, no. 1 pages 7-8 August   2012

"Remembering A Lion of a Man: Dr. J. David Gaynor, TDIC Founder," *CDA Update*, page 15, February 2013

"It Is Not Necessary to Change, Survival Is Not Mandatory," *Contact Point*, vol. 3, no.1, pages 28-30, Spring 2013

"Road Signs on the Road of Life," *Journal of the CDA*, vol. 41, no. 7, pages 529-531, July 2013

Appendix D

A Career of Service

MAJOR POSITIONS HELD IN ORGANIZED DENTISTRY
* President, California Dental Association (1982)
* Trustee, American Dental Association (1984-1987)
* President, American Board of Orthodontics (1985)
* Treasurer, American Dental Association (1987-1988)
* President, American Dental Association (1988-1989)
* Treasurer (1992-1998) and Executive Council Member (1989-1998), World Dental Federation (FDI)
* President, American Association of Dental Schools (1994-1995)
* President, American Dental Association Foundation (2003-2010)
* House of Delegates, American Dental Association (1965-)
* House of Delegates, California Dental Association (1958-)
* House of Delegates, American Dental Education Association (American Association of Dental Schools) (1978-2006)
* Honorary Chair, ADA Foundation campaign, "Our Legacy – Our Future"

MAJOR POSITIONS IN EDUCATION
* Assistant Professor, Operative dentistry
* Assistant Professor, Pediatric dentistry
* Associate Professor, Pediatric dentistry
* Associate Professor, Orthodontics
* Professor, Orthodontics
* Chairperson, Department of Orthodontics

- Dean (1978-2006)
- Dean Emeritus (2006-)
- Senior Executive for Development (2006-)

INNOVATIONS/PROGRAMS DEVELOPED DURING DEANSHIP
- Enhanced humanistic education model
- Advanced Education in General Dentistry residency programs
- International Dental Studies program
- Oral and Maxillofacial Surgery program
- MSD orthodontic graduate program
- Increased the number of orthodontic and AEGD residents
- Established the Pacific Dental Education Foundation
- Graduate Medical Education support for residency programs
- Frontiers in Dentistry lecture series
- Clinical research presence
- Community outreach presence
- Thresholds and competencies to evaluate clinical performance
- 2+3, 3+3, and 4+3 honors programs
- "Ritz Carlton" state of the art facilities
- Creator of the first White Coat Ceremony for dental schools
- Creator of Pacific Pride Day
- BS/DDS program
- MBA and MA programs for faculty and staff
- A revitalized Alumni Association
- Dental Hygiene program
- Group Practice Mentor model
- Research and Clinical Excellence Day programs
- Doctoral program in Professional Education and Leadership for faculty and staff
- Leading the American Dental Association in a campaign to raise $1.3 billion for dental education as president of the Foundation
- One of the major leaders in promoting licensure reform in California

This included achieving the Western Regional Examining Board as an alternative to Dental Board of California examination; recognition of PGY 1 as an alternative to licensure; working diligently with the Dental Board of California to eliminate patients in the clinical examination in favor of a portfolio examination and evaluation of candidates for licensure

ENDOWMENTS CREATED DURING DEANSHIP
- 108 endowments
- 78 additional in process of being funded
- Three endowed chairs
- Nine endowed professorships
- Created Dr. Arthur and Katherine Dugoni Student Scholarship Endowment
- Created Dr. Arthur A. Dugoni Endowed Professorship in Orthodontics

HONORS AND AWARDS
- Valedictorian, St. James High School (1943)
- Valedictorian, College of Physicians and Surgeons (1948)
- Tau Kappa Omega Honor Society (1947)
- Omicron Kappa Upsilon Honor Society
- Presidential Citation, American Dental Association (1994, 1999)
- Phi Kappa Phi Honor Society (1999)
- Person of the Year, South San Francisco (1960)
- Bronze Medallion, National Academies of Practice (1987)
- Hinman Medallion for Leadership (1989)
- Medallion of Distinction, University of the Pacific (1989)
- Distinguished Alumni Merit Award, Gonzaga University (1992)
- Gold Medal, Orthodontic Education and Research Foundation (1993)
- Chairman's Award, American Dental Trade Association (1994)
- Pierre Fauchard Gold Medal (1996)
- Dr. Irving Gruber Award for Excellence in the Advancement of Dental Education (1997)
- Elected to American Men of Science

• List of Honour, World Dental Federation (FDI) (1998) – One of only 30 worldwide to hold this honor

• Participated over nine years in restructuring and revitalizing the World Dental Federation, especially creation of five for-profit subsidiaries and the development of major programs to enhance oral health and dental education in under developed and developing countries

• Selected as 1 of 25 distinguished leaders in the dental industry and profession by the Dental Manufacturers of America (1999)

• Selected as 1 of 25 leaders and visionaries by the American Student Dental Association (1999)

• International Callahan Memorial Award for Outstanding Contributions to the Dental Profession (1999)

• William J. Gies Award, American College of Dentists (2001)

• Award of Excellence in Dentistry, 13th District's International College of Dentists (2002)

• Willard C. Fleming Meritorious Service Award, Northern California Section of the American College of Dentists (2003)

• Dental school renamed University of the Pacific, Arthur A. Dugoni School of Dentistry (2004)

• William Thomas Green Morton 2005 Laureate Award, Academy of General Dentistry (2005)

• International Dentist of the Year Award, Academy of Dentistry International (2005)

• Order of Pacific, University of the Pacific (2006)

• Arthur A. Dugoni Lifetime Achievement Award, Alumni Association, University of the Pacific, Arthur A. Dugoni School of Dentistry (2006)

• Medallion of Excellence, University of the Pacific, Alumni Association (2006)

• 2007 Shils Award, Dr. Edward B. Shils Entrepreneurial Education Fund (2007)

• Jarvie Burkhart Award, New York State Dental Association (2007)

• Ellis Island Medal of Honor (one of 2,006 to hold this honor) (2008)

• William J. Gies Award, for Outstanding Achievement as a dental educator, American Dental Education Association (2009)
• Paragon Award, American Student Dental Association (2011)
• Roseman University of Health Sciences Award, Roseman University of Health Sciences, College of Dental Medicine (2011)

ORTHODONTIC AWARDS / HONORS
• Diplomate, American Board of Orthodontics (1970)
• Award of Merit, Pacific Coast Society of Orthodontists (1976, 2001)
• John Valentine Mershon Memorial Award Lecturer (1983)
• Jacob A. Salzmann Award and Lecturer (1987)
• Gold Medal, Orthodontic Education and Research Foundation (1993)
• Albert H. Ketcham Memorial Award (highest award by the American Board of Orthodontics) (1994)
• American Association of Orthodontists Foundation Award (1999)
• Lifetime Achievement Award, Pacific Coast Society of Orthodontists (2007)

DISTINGUISHED SERVICE AWARDS
• San Mateo Dental Society (1971, 1990)
• Pacific Coast Society of Orthodontics (1976)
• California Dental Association (1978)
• Pierre Fauchard Academy (1982)
• American Dental Association (1995)
• American Association of Dental Schools (2000)
• California Association of Orthodontists (2002)
• Dale F. Redig Distinguished Service Award, California Dental Association (2003)

HONORARY DEGREES
• Doctor of Humane Letters, Honoris Causa, University of Detroit, Mercy (1997)
• Doctor of Humane Letters, Honoris Causa, University of Louisville (2006)

- Doctorate of Dental Surgery Degree, Honoris Causa, Louisiana State University (2007)

PUBLICATIONS AND PRESENTATIONS
- Over 1,000 professional presentations
- Over 175 publications
- Presented 31 commencement addresses at U.S. dental schools
- Presented All University Convocation Address, University of the Pacific

FELLOWSHIPS
- American College of Dentists (1960)
- International College of Dentists
- Academy of Dentistry International (1980)
- American Academy of Pediatric Dentistry
- Diplomate of the American Board of Orthodontics
- National Academies of Practice
- Pierre Fauchard Academy
- Academy of General Dentistry (1992)
- American Academy of Oral Medicine

MILITARY SERVICE
- World War II – US Navy
- Korean conflict – US Marine Corp

ALUMNUS OF THE YEAR
- University of the Pacific, School of Dentistry (1983)
- University of Washington, School of Dentistry (1984)
- University of San Francisco (1988)
- Gonzaga University (1992)

WHO'S WHO
- Who's Who in America

- Who's Who in American Education
- Who's Who Among Students in American Colleges and Universities
- Who's Who in California
- Who's Who in Dentistry
- Who's Who in Medicine and Healthcare
- Who's Who in Science and Engineering
- Who's Who in the West
- American Academy of Science

Appendix E

Honors and Awards

Valedictorian - St. James High School, 1943 Editor-in-Chief, Gonzaga
University Bulletin, 1944
Who's Who Among American Students in American Universities and Colleges,
Gonzaga University
Tau Kappa Omega Dental Honor Society President of the Student Body,
College of Physicians and Surgeons Omicron Kappa Upsilon National
Dental Honor Society Valedictorian - College of Physicians and Surgeons,
1948 Fellow, American College of Dentists, 1960 Fellow, International
College of Dentists Biography listed in Who's Who in the West Biography
listed in Who's Who in Medicine and Healthcare Biography listed in Who's
Who in America Biography listed in International Who's Who Biography
listed in Who's Who in California Biography listed in Who's Who in
Dentistry Biography listed in American Academy of Science Who's Who
Biography listed in Who's Who in American Education Biography listed in
Who's Who in Science and Engineering Biography listed in Who's Who in
the World Person of the Year, South San Francisco, 1960 Diplomate, American
Board of Orthodontics, 1970
Distinguished Service Award - San Mateo County Dental Society, 1971 Elected
to American Men of Science Distinguished Service Award of Merit - Pacific
Coast Society of Orthodontists, 1976 Board of Directors Award - San Mateo
County Dental Society, 1977
California Dental Association - Appreciation Award - Chairman Council on
Dental Education, 1978

College of Diplomates of the American Board of Orthodontics, Charter
Member, 1979 Fellowship, Academy of Dentistry International, 1980 Honorary
Membership, San Francisco Dental Society, 1980 Elected to Pierre Fauchard
Academy

Director - American Board of Orthodontics, 1979-1986

American Board of Orthodontics, Secretary-Treasurer, 1983

American Board of Orthodontics, Vice President, 1984

American Board of Orthodontics, President, 1985

Honorary Membership, Academy of General Dentistry, 1982

Distinguished Service Award - Pierre Fauchard Academy (Northern California
Chapter), 1982

Alumnus of the Year - University of the Pacific, School of Dentistry, 1983

Elected to American Association of Dental Insultants, 1982

Alumnus of the Year - University of Washington, Orthodontic Alumni
Association, 1983

John Valentine Mershon Memorial Award and Lecture, American Association
of Orthodontists, May 1983

Alumnus of the Year - University of Washington, School of Dentistry, 1984

Honorary Officer, American Dental Association 1983 Annual Session,
Anaheim, California

National Academies of Practice, Founder, 1984

Honorary Officer, American Dental Association 1985 Annual Session, San
Francisco, California

Official Representative of the American Dental Association to American
Medical Association House of Delegates, 1985-1987

1986 California Dental Association Scientific Session - Dedicatee

Jacob A. Salzmann Award and lecture, American Association of Orthodontists,
May 1987

Elected to the National Academies of Practice as a distinguished practitioner,
received the National Academies of Practice Bronze Medallion, National Press
Club, Washington, D.C., September 12, 1987

Alumnus of the Year Award by the University of San Francisco, Health

Professions Society, May 19, 1988, Presidio Officer's Club, San Francisco, California

University of the Pacific, School of Dentistry, Alumni Association's Medallion of Distinction, presented at the 90th Annual Alumni Association Meeting at the Hilton Square Hotel, San Francisco, January 27, 1989

The Hinman Medallion for Leadership in Dental Progress, Atlanta, Georgia, March 18, 1989

The Pacific Coast Society of Orthodontists Annual Session (dedicated to Dr. Arthur A. Dugoni) Reno, Nevada, 1989

Honorary membership, Dental Manufacturers of America, 1989

Distinguished Career Citation, presented at the American Dental Association Meeting by the American Association of Orthodontists, Honolulu, Hawaii, November 5, 1989

Citation for Distinguished Service, presented at the American Dental Association Meeting by the San Mateo County Dental Society, Honolulu, Hawaii, November 5, 1990

Citation for Dedicated and Distinguished Leadership, presented at the Meeting of the American Association of Dental Schools by the American Association of Dental Schools, Cincinnati, Ohio, March 6, 1990

Appointed to the ad hoc committee of the Hall of Fame, Pierre Fauchard Academy, 1991, 1992, 1993, 1994

Honorary Fellowship Award, Academy of General Dentistry, 1992

Distinguished Alumni Merit Award, Gonzaga University, 1992

Chairman of the External Review Committee for the Clinical Core Centers for Preventive and Operative Dentistry, University of Washington

Merit Award and Medallion, Orthodontic Education and Research Foundation, February 1993

Executive Committee, American Association of Dental Schools, 1993-1996

President-Elect, American Association of Dental Schools, 1993-1994

President, American Association of Dental Schools, March 1994-1995

Immediate Past President, American Association of Dental Schools, 1995-1996

Honorary Officer, American Dental Association 134th Annual Session, San

Francisco, California, November 10, 1993

Pew Health Professions Commission, 1993-1996

Albert H. Ketcham Memorial Award, American Board of Orthodontics (highest award), 1994

American Dental Association's President's Citation, 1994

Selected for a video series, "Leaders in Dentistry," by the International College of Dentists, August 1994

American Dental Trade Association's Chairman's Award, November 1994

American Dental Trade Association Honorary Life Membership, awarded 1994

American Dental Association's Distinguished Service Award, October 1995

American Academy of Oral Medicine Honorary Membership, May 4, 1996, San Diego, California

Pierre Fauchard Gold Medal, "for outstanding contributions to the progress and standing of the dental profession," (the highest United States award of the Pierre Fauchard Academy), September 28, 1996, Pierre Fauchard Academy Meeting, Orlando, Florida

Doctor of Humane Letters, Honoris Causa, University of Detroit Mercy, Dearborn Michigan, May 17, 1997

Delegation Leader, Citizens Ambassador Program, People to People International, American Dental Association Delegation to the Republic of South Africa, August 9-23, 1997

Dr. Irving E. Gruber Award for excellence in the advancement of dental education, December 1, 1997, Greater New York Dental Meeting, New York, New York

Honored by American Dental Association Reception at the U.S. Consul General's Office, October 7, 1998, Barcelona, Spain

List of Honour, FDI World Dental Federation, October 8, 1998, World Dental Parliament, FDI World Dental Federation. The List of Honour is the highest award of the World Dental Federation and is limited to thirty living individuals who have made distinguished contributions to the World Dental Federation and its mission.

Honorary Officer, American Dental Association 139th Annual Session, San

Francisco, California, October 24-28, 1998

Selected as one of twenty-five distinguished leaders in the dental industry and profession, Dental Manufacturers of America, January 1999

Celebrated 50 years of marriage and renewed vows off the coast of Venice aboard the Grand Princess, February 5, 1999

Phi Kappa Phi Honor Society, University of the Pacific, April 16, 1999

Creation by the American College of Dentists of the Arthur A. Dugoni Fund of the Endowment of the American College of Dentists Foundation, April 1999

American Association of Orthodontists Foundation Award, May 1999 Selected as one of twenty-five leaders and visionaries by the Journal of the American Student Dental Association, Vol. 19, No. 2, Summer 1999 International Callahan Memorial Award for outstanding contributions to the dental profession, Ohio Dental Association, Columbus, Ohio, September 24, 1999

Presidential Citation, American Dental Association, Honolulu, Hawaii, October 9, 1999

FDI List of Honour, FDI World Dental Federation, presented in Mexico City. Selected from 500,000 dentists worldwide-only 30 individuals can hold this distinction at any one time, October 28, 1999

Black Tie Recognition Dinner, Grand Hyatt Hotel, Washington, D.C. Hosted by University of the Pacific and Dentsply International - Crystal Tiger Award from University of the Pacific and plaques from fellow deans at University of the Pacific, April 1, 2000

Distinguished Service Award, American Association of Dental Schools, Washington, D.C., April 2, 2000

Featured in article, "The Italian Connection," L'talo Americano, June 22, 2000

Honor Roll, Volume 72, Number 3. Fall 2000. Pacific Coast Society of Orthodontists Bulletin - The Honor Roll of the Pacific Coast Society of Orthodontists listed Dr. Dugoni in four specific areas on the Honor Roll: as dean of the University of the Pacific, 1978- present; as CDA president, 1982; as ADA president, 1988; and as the Ketcham Award winner, 1994.

Pacific Coast Society of Orthodontists 2001 Award of Merit, September 30, 2001, Hilton Hawaiian Village, Honolulu, Hawaii

William J. Gies Award, American College of Dentists, October 12, 2001,
Kansas City, Missouri

Award of Excellence in Dentistry, 13th District's International College of
Dentists, Anaheim Hilton Hotel, Anaheim, California, April 5, 2002

Distinguished Service Award 2002, California Association of Orthodontists,
Doubletree Hotel, Monterey, California, October 7, 2002

Elected to the American Dental Association House of Delegates, 2003-present

Willard C. Fleming Meritorious Service Award, Northern California Section
of the American College of Dentists, Westin St. Francis at the San Francisco
Airport, California, May 31, 2003

Dale F. Redig Distinguished Service Award 2003, California Dental
Association, Hyatt Regency Hotel, Sacramento, California, November 8, 2003

Rotary International Paul Harris Fellow Award for outstanding leadership and
public service, June 11, 2004

School of Dentistry renamed the Arthur A. Dugoni School of Dentistry, August
28, 2004.

Mexican Association of Public Health Award, in recognition for significant
contributions to world dentistry, August 28, 2004

Pierre Fauchard International Special Award - Pierre Fauchard Academy Silver
Medal, dated August 27, 2004, California Dental Association meeting, Marriott
Hotel, San Francisco, California, September 11, 2004

Elected to honorary membership in the Associazione Piemontese nel Mondo of
Northern California, January 2005

William Thomas Green Morton 2005 Laureate Award, for the advancement of
general dentistry, Academy of General Dentistry, March 2005

Meeting co-honoree, Angle Society of Orthodontists 36th Biennial Meeting,
Hyatt Regency, Incline Village, Nevada, August 21, 2005

Meeting dedicatee, along with other four California dental school deans,
California Dental Association Scientific Sessions, Moscone Convention Center,
San Francisco, California, September 9-11, 2005

International Dentist of the Year Award, Academy of Dentistry International,
Hyatt Regency, Penn's Landing, Pennsylvania, October 5, 2005

Arthur A. Dugoni Lifetime Achievement Award, Alumni Association, University of the Pacific, Arthur A. Dugoni School of Dentistry, Ritz Carlton Hotel, San Francisco, California, March 3, 2006

Doctor of Humane Letters, honoris causa, University of Louisville, Louisville, Kentucky, May 13, 2006

Order of Pacific, University of the Pacific's highest honor, for 55 years of service, presented at the All University Commencement, University of the Pacific, Stockton, California, May 20, 2006, and Arthur A. Dugoni School of Dentistry Graduation, Masonic Auditorium, San Francisco, California, June 11, 2006

Medallion of Excellence, 2006 Distinguished Alumni Awards, University of the Pacific, Alumni Association, Stockton, California, June 24, 2006

Honorary Doctorate of Dental Surgery Degree, Louisiana State University, 133rd Commencement Ceremony, Louisiana State University's Health Sciences Center, New Orleans, Louisiana, May 19, 2007

2007 Shils Award, Dr. Edward B. Shils Entrepreneurial Education Fund, Union League of Philadelphia, Philadelphia, Pennsylvania, June 7, 2007

College of Diplomates of the American Board of Orthodontics, 29th annual meeting dedicated to Dr. Arthur A. Dugoni, Ritz Carlton, Half Moon Bay, California, July 15-19, 2007

Jarvie Burkhart Award, New York State Dental Association, presented at the Foundation of Excellence Awards Luncheon, St. Regis Hotel, New York, October 12, 2007

Lifetime Achievement Award , Pacific Coast Society of Orthodontists, Monterey Conference Center, Monterey, California, October 15, 2007

2006 President's Award, San Mateo County Dental Society, Peninsula Golf and Country Club, San Mateo, California, December 7, 2007

Honorary Lifetime Membership, Marin County Dental Society, April 15, 2008

Ellis Island Medal of Honor, Ellis Island, New York, May 10, 2008

Alan J. Davis/SCADA Achievement Award, International Association of Student Clinicians, America Dental Association meeting, San Antonio, Texas, October 18, 2008.

Alpha Omega Achievement Medal, Alpha Omega International Dental

Fraternity Annual Meeting, Honors Night Program, Westin Kierland Resort and Spa, Scottsdale, Arizona, December 29, 2008.

Presidential Citation, American Dental Association, 2008.

2009 William J. Gies Award, presented by the ADEA Gies Foundation, for Outstanding Achievement – General Educator, in support of global oral health and oral health education, ADEA Annual Session, Sheraton Downtown Hotel, Phoenix, Arizona, March 14, 2009.

Elected to Honorary Membership, American Association of Dental Insultants, March 2009.

Presidential Citation, American Dental Association, 2009.

Lifetime Achievement Award, International College of Dentists/American College of Dentists, Spring Gala, Anaheim Hilton, Anaheim, California, May 15, 2010.

Lifetime Achievement Award, Northern California Section of the American College of Dentists, Annual Awards Banquet, Medallion Restaurant, Burlingame, California, May 22, 2010.

2010 Lifetime Achievement, American College of Dentists, ACD Convocation, in celebration of his 50 years of membership in ACD, Rosen Centre Hotel, Orlando, Florida, October 8, 2010.

Presidential Citation, American Dental Association, Orlando, Florida, October 9, 2010.

Heritage Society and Scholarship Luncheon, Gallery of Benefactor Portraits presentation to Dr. Arthur A. and Kaye Dugoni, University of the Pacific, Stockton, California, October 14, 2010.

Outstanding Family Award, Pacific Alumni Association, 52nd Annual Distinguished Alumni Awards Dinner and Ceremony, University of the Pacific, Stockton, California, November 6, 2010.

Paragon Award, inaugural recipient, American Student Dental Association, Disneyland Hotel and Resort, Anaheim, California, March 3, 2011.

Roseman University of Health Sciences Award, Inaugural DMD class, White Coat Ceremony, Roseman University of Health Sciences, College of Dental Medicine, August 19, 2011.

Reception honoring 60 years of service as a faculty member at the University of the Pacific, Arthur A. Dugoni School of Dentistry, San Francisco, California, September 1, 2011.

Inducted into 1851 Society as a lifetime member with Katherine A. Dugoni, University of the Pacific, Stockton, California, October 3, 2012.

Recognition Award, Consolalo Generale d'Italia, Italian Educators Dinner, Colosseo Restaurant, San Francisco, California, October 28, 2014

Joseph J. Schwarz Distinguished Alumni Award, Supreme Chapter, Xi Psi Phi Fraternity, McCormick and Kuletos Restaurant, San Francisco, California.

CPSIA information can be obtained at www.ICGtesting.com
Printed in the USA
LVOW10*1323230615

443220LV00002B/2/P